teach yourself...
WordPerfect® 6.0

by Kris Jamsa

**A Subsidiary of
Henry Holt and Co., Inc.**

First printing.

ISBN 1-55828-249-1

Printed in the United States of America

10 9 8 7 6 5 4 3 2 1

MIS:Press books are available at special discounts for bulk purchases for sales, promotions, premiums, fundraising, or educational use. Special editions or book excerpts can also be created to specification.

For details contact: Special Sales Director
MIS:Press
a subsidiary of Henry Holt and Company, Inc.
115 West 18th Street
New York, New York 10011

TRADEMARKS:
WordPerfect®
WordPerfect is a registered trademark of WordPerfect Corporation.
WordPerfect v.6.0 for DOS, © 1989, 1993 WordPerfect Corporation. All rights reserved. Reprinted with permission from WordPerfect Corporation.

Throughout this book, trademarked names are used. Rather than put a trademark symbol after every occurence of a trademarked name, we used the names in an editorial fashion only. Where such designations appear in this book, they have been printed with initial caps.

Development Editor: Margot Pagan
Editor: Dawn Erdos
Layout: Dawn Erdos

Dedication

To Kellie and Stephanie,

in my world of hectic schedules, deadlines, beta software, faxes phone calls, and Fed Ex . . . I can always count on you two! Thank you for understanding.

Acknowledgements

Writing a book using various releases of beta software is a challenging and often frustrating task. To begin, the software developers often fix errors and send new releases of the software almost faster than you can install them. When the developers add new capabilities, change the steps you must follow to perform a task, or even change a screen layout, everyone from the author, to the editors, to the page layout team wants to scream and give up. Everyone involved with the project holds their breath when a new beta release arrives, hoping that it only contains bug fixes. With these thoughts in mind, Steve Berkowitz, the Publisher at MIS Press, did what other publishers would not do—he waited until the final beta release before we finished and completed this book. MIS Press was committed to insuring that the information you received was correct and the most up to date.

Once again, I owe tremendous thanks to Phil Schmander, this book's technical editor. Phil personally edits each of my books—from WordPerfect to programming languages. Phil is very easily one of the most knowledgeable individuals in the computer industry. I also owe thanks to Kevin Hutchinson who spent many late nights helping design, revise, and work with the forms contained on this book's companion disk. As you put these forms to use, I'm sure that you will appreciate Kevin's efforts too.

Every book has one individual that has to pull together all the manuscript, illustrations, messages, and faxes. In the case of this book, that person was Margot Pagan. It was Margot's responsibility to call and tell me a new Beta was arriving and that screen shots may need to be redone. Likewise, Margot was the one who received my middle of the night faxes about chapters that weren't shipping because the beta was less than operational. Margot's efforts and patience are appreciated. Lastly, by delaying our manuscript until the last possible minute, a great amount of work and pressure was placed on Dawn Erdos at Solstice Communications, Inc. Dawn worked very quickly to typeset this book in time for printing. Her efforts are appreciated.

Table of Contents

Chapter 25:
Using Document Formatting Techniques 273

Introduction

With millions of users upgrading to WordPerfect 6.0, we wanted to make sure that we put together the best possible book on the market. As you read through the pages of this book and put the book's companion disk to use, I think you will agree that we have done just that. *Teach yourself . . . WordPerfect 6.0* covers just about every aspect of WordPerfect. The chapters are short and easy to read. You will find many screen illustrations that show you step-by-step what you will see on your own screen. By performing the exercises as you read, your learning is hands-on. Within minutes after starting a chapter, you won't just be reading about a topic, you will be applying and understanding it. There is no better or faster way to learn WordPerfect 6.0.

What's on the Disk?

My goals in writing this book are to teach you WordPerfect 6.0 using techniques that maximize your learning, make efficient use of your time, and let you have fun along the way. WordPerfect 6.0 is a very powerful product—but if you don't enjoy using it, you will never maximize its potential. Everyone wants to put WordPerfect 6.0 to use right off the bat. To help you do just that, the disk that accompanies this book contains twenty ready-to-use forms that range from a travel check list, to a weekly planner, fax cover sheets, custom letterhead, and much, much more.

As you finish lessons throughout the book, a chapter presents a different form that you can print, customize, and use time and again. To make this book the best buy for your money, we have included the forms on the companion disk. The following pages list the companion disk forms and the chapters in which you will find the form's presentation. Take time to examine these forms. I am sure you can find several that you will want to use right away at home and many that are perfect for your office.

Installing the Companion Disk Forms

The companion disk that accompanies this book contains twenty ready-to-use forms you can immediately put to use in WordPerfect. The pages that follow provide illustrations of each form. After you have successfully installed WordPerfect 6.0 (Appendix A of this book tells you how), you can install the forms on to your hard disk. The forms require 560 Kb of disk space.

The WordPerfect 6.0 installation creates the directory WPDOCS on your hard disk, in which it stores the document files that you create. Using the CHDIR command, select WPDOCS as the current dirrectory. Assuming that you installed WordPerfect 6.0 on drive C, issue the following command:

```
C:\>CD\WPDOCS <ENTER>
C:WPDOCS>
```

Your system prompt should change to C:\WPDOCS as shown. Next, place this book's companion disk in drive A or B. Depending on the drive in which you placed the disk, issue either the command:

```
C:\WPDOCS>A:WPFORMS <ENTER>
```

or

```
C:\WPDOCS>B:WPFORMS <ENTER>
```

The WPFORMS command uncompresses the files (they were compressed to fit on the floppy) placing them into the WPDOCS directory on your hard disk.

As you read through the book's chapters, different chapters discuss the steps you must perform to use a specific form. If WordPerfect displays an error message stating that it cannot find a document file, specify a complete path name to the document file—such as C:\WPDOCS\FAX-LOG.DOC or C:\WPDOCS\ACCOUNT.DOC.

FAX COVER SHEET

Company Name
Company Slogan

To:
Company:
Fax:
Phone:

From:
Pages:
Fax: (999) 999-9999
Phone: (999) 999-9999

Comments:

Chapter 9

MEN'S TRAVEL CHECKLIST

CLOTHING

❑	Coats	❑	Shoes
❑	Jackets	❑	Socks
❑	Neckties	❑	Suits
❑	Pants	❑	Sweaters
❑	Shirts	❑	Underwear

ACCESSORIES

❑	Belts	❑	Handkerchiefs
❑	Gloves	❑	Jewelry

TOILETRIES

❑	Aftershave/cologne	❑	Shampoo/conditioner
❑	Brush/comb	❑	Shaving razor
❑	Deodorant	❑	Shaving cream
❑	Hairspray/styling lotion	❑	Toothbrush
❑	Mouthwash	❑	Toothpaste

LEISURE & RECREATION

❑	Book	❑	Running suit
❑	Casual shoes	❑	Shorts
❑	Pajamas	❑	Suntan lotion
❑	Robe	❑	Swimsuit

MISCELLANEOUS

❑	Business cards	❑	Road maps
❑	Credit cards	❑	Travel tickets
❑	Flashlight	❑	Travelers checks
❑	Notebook & pen	❑	Umbrella

Chapter 10

WOMEN'S TRAVEL CHECKLIST

CLOTHING

❑	Blouses	❑	Skirts
❑	Coats	❑	Slacks
❑	Hosiery	❑	Suits
❑	Jackets	❑	Sweaters
❑	Shoes	❑	Underwear

ACCESSORIES

❑	Belts	❑	Hats
❑	Gloves	❑	Jewelry
❑	Handkerchiefs	❑	Scarfs

TOILETRIES

❑	Brush/comb	❑	Mouthwash
❑	Curlers	❑	Perfume/cologne
❑	Curling iron	❑	Razor
❑	Deodorant	❑	Shampoo/conditioner
❑	Hairdryer	❑	Skin care products
❑	Hairspray/styling lotion	❑	Toothbrush
❑	Makeup	❑	Toothpaste

LEISURE & RECREATION

❑	Book	❑	Running suit
❑	Casual shoes	❑	Shorts
❑	Pajamas	❑	Suntan lotion
❑	Robe	❑	Swimsuit

MISCELLANEOUS

❑	Business cards	❑	Road maps
❑	Credit cards	❑	Travel tickets
❑	Flashlight	❑	Travelers checks
❑	Notebook & pen	❑	Umbrella

Chapter 10

Weekly Time Planner

Week ending: / /

Monday
8
9
10
11
12
1
2
3
4
5

Tuesday
8
9
10
11
12
1
2
3
4
5

Wednesday
8
9
10
11
12
1
2
3
4
5

Thursday
8
9
10
11
12
1
2
3
4
5

Friday
8
9
10
11
12
1
2
3
4
5

Saturday

Sunday

Chapter 16

WHILE YOU WERE OUT

To:
Mr. Ms. Mrs.:
Of:
Phone:
☐ Called ☐ Please call
☐ Called back ☐ Wants to see you
☐ Came by ☐ URGENT
Message:

Date/time: By:

WHILE YOU WERE OUT

To:
Mr. Ms. Mrs.:
Of:
Phone:
☐ Called ☐ Please call
☐ Called back ☐ Wants to see you
☐ Came by ☐ URGENT
Message:

Date/time: By:

WHILE YOU WERE OUT

To:
Mr. Ms. Mrs.:
Of:
Phone:
☐ Called ☐ Please call
☐ Called back ☐ Wants to see you
☐ Came by ☐ URGENT
Message:

Date/time: By:

WHILE YOU WERE OUT

To:
Mr. Ms. Mrs.:
Of:
Phone:
☐ Called ☐ Please call
☐ Called back ☐ Wants to see you
☐ Came by ☐ URGENT
Message:

Date/time: By:

Chapter 22

PACKING LIST

Company Name
Company Slogan
9999 North Main Street
Anytown, USA 98765-4321
(702) 555-1212
(702) 555-1212 (Fax)

Ship To: Bill To:

P. O. Number	Order Number	Shipping Date	Ship Via	Shipping Weight	Number of Boxes	Packed By

Quantity Ordered	Quantity Shipped	Description

Chapter 24

FAX LOG

Company Name
Company Slogan
9999 North Main Street
Anytown, USA 98765-4321
(702) 555-1212
(702) 555-1212 (Fax)

< Fill out for each fax sent.

Date	Time	Fax Number Called	Business/Person Called	Pages	Caller

Chapter 26

PERSONAL INFORMATION

IDENTIFICATION

Name:		Date of Birth:		
SSN:		Place of Birth:		
Home Phone:		Business Phone:		
Home Address:		Business Address:		

EMERGENCY CONTACTS

Contact	Name	Relationship	Work Phone	Home Phone
Spouse				
Parent				
Parent				
Friend				
Bus. Associate				
Other				

EMERGENCY INSTRUCTIONS

MEDICAL INFORMATION AND INSTRUCTIONS

ADDITIONAL INFORMATION

Type	Company	Address	Phone
Health Insurance			
Location of Will			
Life Insurance Policy			
Safety Deposit Box			
Other			

Chapter 28

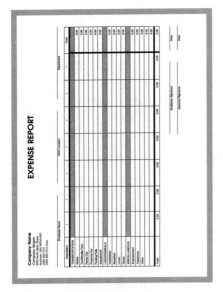

Chapter 29

Chapter 30

Chapter 31

Chapter 32

Chapter 33

Chapter 34

Chapter 35

Chapter 36

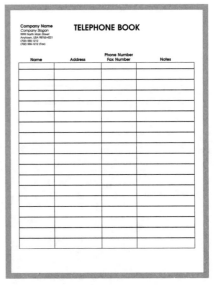

VEHICLE USE REPORT

Chapter 37

TELEPHONE BOOK

Chapter 38

MONTHLY BUDGET CHECKLIST

Chapter 39

ACCOUNT INFORMATION CHECKLIST

Chapter 40

Company Name
Company Slogan
9999 North Main Street
Anytown, USA 98765-4321
(702) 555-1212
(702) 555-1212 (Fax)

PURCHASE ORDER

Purchased from: Ship to:

P. O. Number	Purchase Date	Delivery Date	Order Taken By	Terms	FOB	Ship Via

Item	Quan	Units	Description	Price	Total
					0.00
					0.00
					0.00
					0.00
					0.00
					0.00
					0.00
					0.00
					0.00
					0.00
					0.00
					0.00
					0.00
					0.00
					0.00
					0.00
					0.00
					0.00
					0.00
					0.00

Sub-Total		0.00
Sales Tax (7%)		0.00
Shipping & Handling		
Total Order		0.00

Authorized Buyer   Date

Chapter 41

Getting Started

In this chapter you:

- ◆ Start WordPerfect 6.0
- ◆ Switch between WordPerfect's text and graphics screens
- ◆ Understand and use pull-down menus
- ◆ Use a mouse in WordPerfect
- ◆ Enable the button bar to maximize your ease of use
- ◆ Enable and use scroll bars to move through your document

Starting WordPerfect

If you have not yet installed WordPerfect 6.0, turn to Appendix A and follow the steps now. After WordPerfect is installed, use the DOS change directory command (CD) to select the WP60 directory as shown here:

```
C:\> CD \WP60
```

Then press **Enter**. Your DOS prompt should change as shown here:

```
C:\WP60>
```

If your system prompt does not change and DOS displays the message *Invalid directory*, you have not yet installed WordPerfect on your disk. Turn to Appendix A and install WordPerfect now.

Selecting the WordPerfect directory using the DOS CD (change directory) command is similar to opening the filing cabinet drawer that contains your WordPerfect files. By working in the WordPerfect directory, you can better organize your document files, ensuring that they are stored only in one location on your disk. When you later need to print or edit a document's contents, you can quickly find the document.

To start WordPerfect, type the letters **WP** at the DOS prompt and press **Enter**.

```
c:\WP60> WP <ENTER>
```

WordPerfect starts, displaying either its text- or graphics-based screen, as shown in Figures 1.1 and 1.2.

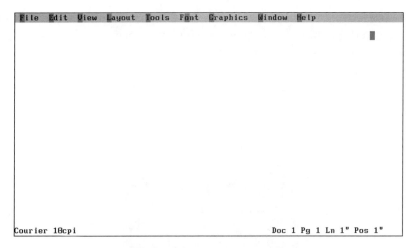

Figure 1.1 *The text-based screen.*

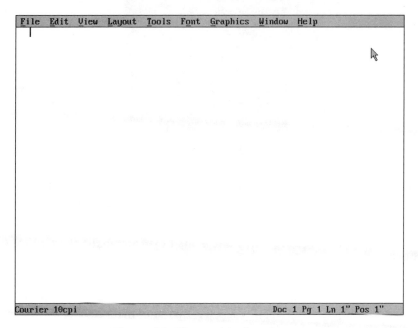

Figure 1.2 *The graphics-based screen.*

One of WordPerfect 6.0's most powerful features is its graphical work environment. Users often describe a graphical environment as WYSIWYG—what you see, is what you get. When you work in a WYSIWYG environment, a document's text and graphics that on your screen are displayed (what you see) are printed in the exact format (what you get). Because most users prefer to work in the WYSIWYG environment, all of the screens presented in this book use WordPerfect's graphics-based screens. If your screen displays WordPerfect in text mode, press the **Alt-V** keyboard combination by holding down your keyboard key labeled **Alt** and then press the **V** key (while the **Alt** key is held down). WordPerfect displays its View menu as shown in Figure 1.3.

Figure 1.3 *The View menu.*

Using your keyboard's **Down Arrow** key, highlight the **Graphics Mode** option and press **Enter**. WordPerfect displays the graphical interface shown in Figure 1.2.

NOTE **Understanding Ctrl-, Alt-, and Shift Key-Combinations.** To help you quickly perform common operations such as printing, spell checking, and saving a document, WordPerfect provides several predefined key combinations. **Ctrl**-key combinations are so named because you perform them by holding down the keyboard key labeled **Ctrl** and then pressing a specific key (while **Ctrl** is still depressed). For example, the **Ctrl-F3** keyboard combination directs WordPerfect to display a dialog box that lets you change from text to graphics mode and vice versa. In addition to **Ctrl**-key combinations, WordPerfect predefines several **Shift**-key and **Alt**-key combinations. These keyboard combinations work in the same way, except that you hold down either the **Shift** or **Alt** key while pressing the specified character. By remembering your commonly used **Ctrl**, **Shift**, and **Alt** key combinations, you can quickly perform operations without having to remove your fingers from the keyboard (to use a mouse for example).

Working in WordPerfect's WYSIWYG Mode. WordPerfect supports a text- and graphics-based screen display. The graphics-based display is often called WYSIWYG, meaning the information you print appears just as it is shown on the screen. Because WordPerfect's WYSIWYG mode is very easy to use, you will probably want to use the graphics mode all the time. To switch between text and graphics mode, press **Alt-V** keyboard to select WordPerfect's View menu then choose the desired mode.

Working with Pull-Down Menus

WordPerfect is a very powerful word processor that provides hundreds of different capabilities. Many of these capabilities are available by pressing various keyboard combinations. If you had to remember all of these keyboard combinations, however, you would quickly turn off your computer and you would begin hand writing your letters, memos, and reports. Luckily, WordPerfect makes its capabilities available to you through easy-to-use menu options. If you examine the top of your screen, you should find a menu bar as shown in Figure 1.4.

File Edit View Layout Tools Font Graphics Window Help

Figure 1.4 *The menu bar.*

The menu bar contains the names of WordPerfect's different menus. To use a specific menu, press **Alt** and the highlighted letter that appears in the desired menu name. For example, to select the File menu, shown in Figure 1.5, press **Alt-F**. To select the Edit menu press **Alt-E**. To access the Font menu, for example, press **Alt-O**. Note that the highlighted letter is not always the first letter of the menu name. If you are working with a mouse, you can quickly select a menu by aiming your mouse pointer at the menu name and clicking the mouse button.

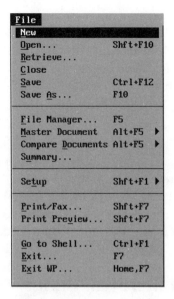

Figure 1.5 *The File menu.*

Selecting a Menu Option

A menu contains one or more options you can select using your keyboard or mouse. If you look closely at the menu, you will find that one option is highlighted. To select an option using your keyboard, press your keyboard's **Up Arrow** and **Down Arrow** keys to move the menu highlight to the desired option. Once the option is highlighted, press **Enter** to select the option. Also note that each menu option has one highlighted letter. If you type the highlighted letter, WordPerfect quickly selects the option. In the case of the File menu, for example, type the letter **S** to select the **Save** option. If you are working with a mouse, you can quickly select a menu option by aiming the mouse pointer at the option and clicking the mouse select button.

Canceling a Menu Selection

When you select a menu, there may be times when, after the menu is displayed, you decide you don't want to perform the desired operation, or that you realize that you have selected the wrong menu. To cancel a menu operation, directing WordPerfect to remove the menu from your screen, press the **Esc** key. If you are working with a mouse, cancel a menu's selection by aiming the mouse pointer at any location outside of the menu and clicking the mouse button. WordPerfect closes the menu, leaving the cursor in the menu bar. Using your keyboard's **Right Arrow** and **Left Arrow** keys, you can move the menu bar highlight from one menu name to another. To display the highlighted menu, press **Enter**.

```
File  Edit  View  Layout  Tools  Font  Graphics  Window  Help
```

Figure 1.6 A highlighted menu name.

If you are working with a mouse, you can quickly place the cursor in the menu bar by pressing the right mouse button.

Working with the Menu Bar

As you have learned, WordPerfect normally displays a menu bar of options at the top of your screen. WordPerfect considers the menu bar and your document text as two different screen regions. When you are editing your document, for example, you cannot use your Arrow keys to move the cursor into the menu bar. If you want to work in the menu bar you must press the **Alt**-key combination for a specific menu, or click the right mouse button as just discussed.

After you select and display a menu, WordPerfect lets you quickly display the menu to the right or left of the current menu selection by pressing your keyboard's **Right Arrow** and **Left Arrow** keys. For example, if the Edit menu is displayed, pressing the **Right Arrow** directs WordPerfect to display the View menu. Likewise, pressing the **Left Arrow** directs WordPerfect to display the File menu.

To return to your document from the menu bar, press the **Esc** key, or aim your mouse pointer into the document and click.

Understanding Menu Option Types

As you select different WordPerfect menus, you will find that some options have a right facing triangle after their name (▶), while some have three dots (*ellipses...*), and some have neither. Figure 1.7 illustrates WordPerfect's Graphics (*ellipses...*), and some have neither. Figure 1.7 illustrates WordPerfect's Graphics menu.

Figure 1.7 *The Graphics menu.*

The first option in the Graphics menu, **Retrieve Image** is followed by ellipses that tell you that when you select this option, WordPerfect displays a dialog box asking you for additional information.

Figure 1.8 *An ellipsis in a menu.*

If you select **Retrieve Image**, for example, WordPerfect displays the Retrieve Image File dialog box, as shown in Figure 1.9.

Figure 1.9 *The Retrieve Image File dialog box.*

WordPerfect uses dialog boxes when it needs more information about an operation. In the case of the Retrieve Image File dialog box, WordPerfect wants you to type in the name of the file containing the desired graphic. If the Retrieve

Image File dialog box is currently displayed on your screen, press the **Esc** key to cancel the operation, directing WordPerfect to remove the dialog box. If you are using a mouse, aim your mouse pointer at the dialog box **Cancel** button and click, or simply click your mouse's right button.

If you examine the Graphics menu **Graphics Boxes** option, it has a right-facing triangle. When you have an option followed by a triangle, WordPerfect cascades a second menu.

Graphics Boxes Alt+F9 ▶

Figure 1.10 *Right-facing triangle to cascade a menu.*

If you select **Graphics Boxes**, for example, WordPerfect cascades a second level of menus, as shown in Figure 1.11.

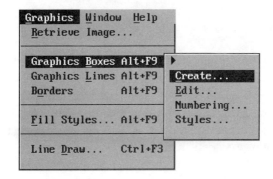

Figure 1.11 *Cascading a second level of menu options.*

Using your keyboard or mouse, you can select the desired menu option. If you press **Esc** or click the mouse outside the cascaded menu, WordPerfect cancels the current menu level.

If a menu option is not followed by ellipsis or a right-facing triangle, selecting the option directs WordPerfect to perform the desired operation, without the display of a dialog box or additional menu levels.

Working with Selected Menu Options

In many cases, a WordPerfect menu option works somewhat like an on-off switch. For example, consider the View menu shown in Figure 1.12.

Figure 1.12 *The View menu.*

Several of the View menu options are preceded by check marks (✔). The check mark indicates that the corresponding option is currently in use. For example, in the case of the View menu shown in Figure 1.12, the check marks tell you WordPerfect is using its Graphics Mode, which displays and supports pull-down menus. Depending on the menu, the operations WordPerfect performs when you select an option preceded by a check mark differ. In the case of the View menu, if you select **Text Mode**, WordPerfect removes the check mark from the Graphics Mode and places it in front of Text Mode. If you select **Pull-Down Menus**, WordPerfect removes the check mark from in front the option, without placing a check mark any where else. If you later select the option a second time (turning the option back on), WordPerfect places the check mark back in front of the option. In any case, if a menu option is preceded by a check mark, the option is currently enabled.

Turning the Menu Bar Back On. If you inadvertently remove the pull-down menu display, aim your mouse pointer at the status bar on the bottom of your screen and click the right mouse button. WordPerfect displays a menu bar from which you can select the View menu and turn the menu bar display back on.

Working with WordPerfect Menus. To make operations much easier for you to perform, WordPerfect provides menus that contain options you can quickly select using your keyboard or mouse. Every operation you need to perform is available as a menu option. To select a WordPerfect menu, hold down the **Alt** key and type the highlighted letter that is displayed in the menu's name. If you are using a mouse, aim the mouse pointer at the desired menu name and click.

To select a menu option, type the highlighted letter that appears in the option name or use your keyboard Arrow keys to highlight the option and press **Enter**. If you are using a mouse, aim the mouse pointer at the desired menu option and click.

To cancel a menu, press **Esc**, or aim your mouse pointer outside of the menu and click.

Understanding Shortcut Keys

As you perform different operations on a regular basis, you can take advantage of WordPerfect's predefined shortcut keys to quickly perform common operations without having to move your fingers from the keyboard to work with a mouse, and without having to traverse WordPerfect's menus. Most WordPerfect shortcut keys use the function keys (**F1** through **F12**) or function key combinations (such **Shift-F1** or **Shift-F7**). For example, WordPerfect uses the shortcut key **Shift-F7** to print your document. As you examine WordPerfect menus, you will find that many menu options list shortcut keys.

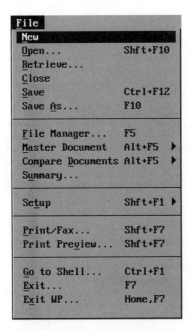

Figure 1.13 *Shortcut keys displayed on the right side of a menu.*

If you press one of the shortcut keys listed, WordPerfect immediately performs the corresponding operation.

Don't let shortcut keys intimidate you. In the past, one of the biggest user complaints against WordPerfect was that they had to memorize too many shortcut keys. WordPerfect 6.0 also provides you with a collection of buttons that are displayed immediately beneath the menu bar from which you can select to quickly perform commonly used operations. Whether you choose to remember shortcut keys or to use the button bar buttons, WordPerfect makes common operations very easy to perform.

Using the Esc Key

As you perform different operations in WordPerfect, you will work with menus and dialog boxes. If you should begin an operation that you decided you don't want to complete, you can normally end the operation by pressing the **Esc** key. If WordPerfect is displaying a menu or dialog box and you want to end the operation, just press **Esc**. WordPerfect normally removes the menu or dialog box from your screen, leaving your document unchanged.

Using Your Mouse

When you work in WordPerfect's graphics mode, it is very convenient to use a mouse. If you install a mouse driver (the software that lets your computer use the mouse) in your AUTOEXEC.BAT or CONFIG.SYS, WordPerfect should recognize the mouse driver and display your mouse pointer. If you have a mouse and WordPerfect does not display a mouse pointer, you need to tell WordPerfect which mouse driver to use. To begin, press **Alt-F** to select WordPerfect's File menu. Next, type **T** to select the **Setup** option. WordPerfect cascades the Setup menu, shown in Figure 1.14.

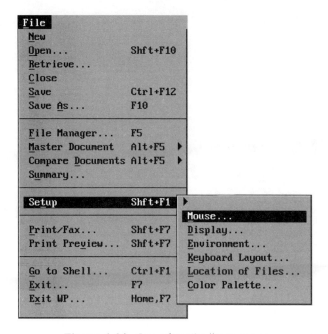

Figure 1.14 *Cascading the Setup menu.*

Type **M** to select the **Mouse** option. WordPerfect displays the Mouse dialog box, shown in Figure 1.15.

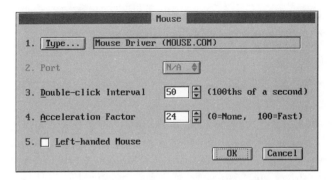

Figure 1.15 The Mouse dialog box.

Type **T** to select the **Type** button. WordPerfect displays a list of available mouse drivers within the Setup Mouse Type dialog box, shown in Figure 1.16.

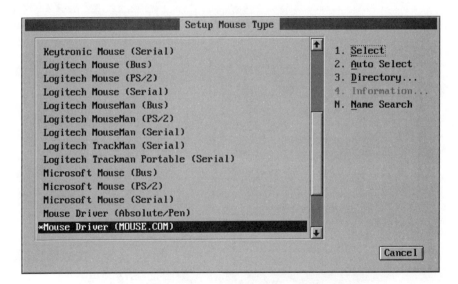

Figure 1.16 The Setup Mouse Type dialog box.

Using your Arrow keys, highlight your mouse type. Type **1** to select the mouse driver. WordPerfect redisplays the Mouse dialog box. Press **Enter** to select the **OK** option.

When you work with a mouse, the operations you perform are called *point-and-click* operations. To begin, move your mouse across your desk to aim (or point) the mouse pointer (on your screen) at a specific screen object, such as a menu. Next, press the mouse select button (normally the left mouse button). Pressing and releasing the mouse select button is called *clicking* the mouse.

Getting WordPerfect Ready for Use

If you have not yet selected WordPerfect's graphic interface:

1. Press **Alt-V** to open the View menu.
2. Select the **Graphics Mode** option.

Using the Button Bar

To make commonly used operations easy to perform, WordPerfect provides a button bar. The button bar contains graphic representations, called *icons* for each operation. Using the button bar, you can quickly click your mouse on the specific buttons to perform the corresponding operation. To turn on the display of WordPerfect's button bar, perform these steps:

1. Press **Alt-V** to open the View menu.
2. Select the **Button Bar** option.

The button bar contains icons four common operations. As shown in Figure 1.17, WordPerfect displays the button bar immediately beneath the menu bar.

Figure 1.17 *The button bar.*

Unless you tell WordPerfect to do otherwise, it places the button bar at the top your screen. In addition, WordPerfect uses a graphic symbol in each button that corresponds to the operation, as well as, placing the buttons textual name beneath the symbol. To help you better understand the function of each button, Table 1.1 lists the purpose of each.

Table 1.1 *WordPerfect's button bar button functions.*

File Mgr	Displays the File Manager.
Save As	Displays the Save As dialog box to store your file on disk.
Print	Prints your document.
Preview	Displays on screen a page that shows how your document will appear on paper.
Font	Displays the Font dialog box from which you can select the desired fonts.
GrphMode	Selects the WYSIWYG graphics mode.
TextMode	Selects the text mode.
Envelope	Displays the Envelope dialog box to address and print an envelope.
Speller	Checks your documents spelling.
GramaTik	Checks your document's grammar.
QuikFndr	Displays the QuickFinder File Indexer dialog box to help you locate a specific file on disk.
Tbl Edit	Begins a table edit operation.
Search	Displays the Search dialog box to search your document for specific text.
BBar Sel	Displays the Select Button Bar dialog box to choose a different button bar.
BBar Opt	Displays the ButtonBar Options dialog box to select how and where on your screen WordPerfect displays the button bar.

If you take a close look at your screen, you will find that some of the buttons listed in Table 1.1 are not displayed. Since WordPerfect only has a fixed amount of space on your screen to display buttons, not all of the buttons can be displayed at one time. Note the up and down facing triangles (some people call them arrows) at the start of your button bar. If you click your mouse on these arrows, WordPerfect displays the next (the down arrow) or previous (the up arrow) set of buttons.

Using Horizontal and Vertical Scroll Bars

As the size of your documents increase, WordPerfect provides scroll bars that let you quickly move through your document. In addition, scroll bars tell you your relative position within the document. WordPerfect provides two scroll bars. As shown in Figure 1.18, the vertical scroll bar appears along the right edge of your screen, while the horizontal scroll bar appears near the bottom of your screen.

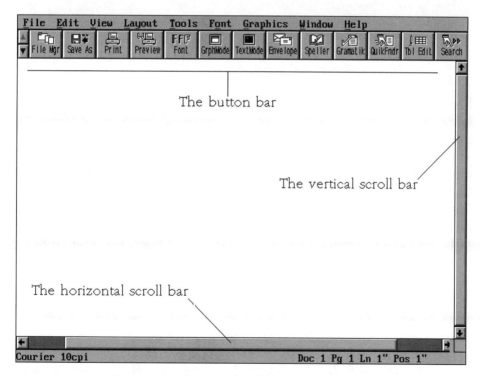

Figure 1.18 *The vertical and horizontal scroll bars.*

Within each scroll bar, is a *scroll block*. WordPerfect uses it to indicate the size of your document and the cursor's relative position in the document. When your documents are small, the scroll block appears quite large. As your document size increases, the size of the scroll block decreases. When the scroll block is displayed near the top of the scroll bar, the cursor is relatively close to the start of the document. When the block is near the middle of the scroll bar, the cursor is relatively close to the middle of the document. Likewise, when the block appears near the bottom of the scroll bar, the cursor is close to the end of your document. As you work with large documents, use the scroll block to determine your approximate position in the document.

To turn on the display of the vertical scroll bar:

1. Press **Alt-V** to select WordPerfect's View menu.
2. Select the **Vertical Scroll Bar** option.

To turn on the horizontal scroll bar:

1. Press **Alt-V** to open the View menu.
2. Select the **Horizontal Scroll Bar** option.

Using the scroll bars, you can quickly move to specific locations in your document. Each time your click your mouse on the scroll bar above or below the scroll block, WordPerfect performs a page up or page down operation just as if you pressed the **PgUp** or **PgDn** key. Likewise, if you aim the mouse pointer at the scroll block and hold down the mouse select button while move the block (called a *mouse drag* operation) WordPerfect moves the cursor to the location that corresponds to final block position. If you click your mouse on the arrows that appear at each of the scroll bar, you can quickly move the scroll block (and hence your cursor position within the document) in the direction of the arrow.

Summary

In this chapter you got WordPerfect started, selected WordPerfect's graphics mode, and turned on the button bar and scroll bars to make you more productive as you work with your documents. In addition, you learned how to work with WordPerfect menus, shortcut keys, and button bar buttons.

New Terms

◆ **Button bar.** One or more icons that WordPerfect displays on your screen on which you can click with your mouse to perform a common operation.

◆ **Clicking the mouse.** The process of pressing and releasing the mouse select button.

◆ **Dialog box.** A message box that WordPerfect displays when it needs more information before it can perform a command. For example, WordPerfect may use a dialog box to ask you for the name a file you want to edit.

◆ **Document.** Any memo, letter, report, form, and so on that you create in WordPerfect.

◆ **Shortcut key.** A key or keyboard combination, is predefined by WordPerfect, that you can press to perform a common operation, such as printing your document.

Chapter 2

Creating Your First Document

In this chapter you:

◆ Use WordPerfect to create a letter

◆ Position the cursor throughout your document using your mouse and keyboard

◆ Save your document to disk

Starting a Document

If you examine the top upper left corner of your screen, you should see the flashing cursor where the text you type appears. If the cursor is not in the upper-left corner of your screen (the *home* position), use your keyboard's Arrow keys to move the cursor there now. In this chapter, you use WordPerfect to create a letter similar to the one shown in Figure 2.1.

```
Mr. Mike Parish
Airline Gizmos, Inc.
1234 Main St.
Phoenix, AZ 85000

Dear Mike,

Thank you for your phone call this morning. Early Bird
Airlines is very interested in meeting with you to
discuss your newest gizmos for pilotless airplanes. We
agree that our airline can save a great amount of
money if we don't have to employ pilots.

I will be traveling to Phoenix next week to meet with
Davis Discount Airline Parts. Would it be possible for
us to get together for lunch? Please call me or send
me a FAX (702) 555-1212 at your earliest convenience.
I look forward to hearing from you.

Sincerely,



Ed Conroy
President, Early Bird Airlines
```

Figure 2.1 *A letter created using WordPerfect.*

To begin, type the following address, then pressing **Enter** at the end of each line:

```
Mr. Mike Parish
Airline Gizmos, Inc.
1234 Main St.
Phoenix, AZ 85000
```

Your keyboard works very much like a typewriter. To type the uppercase characters, hold down one of the **Shift** keys. If you mistype a letter, don't worry, you can quickly erase the letter using the **Backspace** key. Each time you press **Backspace**, WordPerfect erases the letter that appears immediately to the left of the cursor. After the letter is erased, you can type correct letter.

Your screen should look like Figure 2.2.

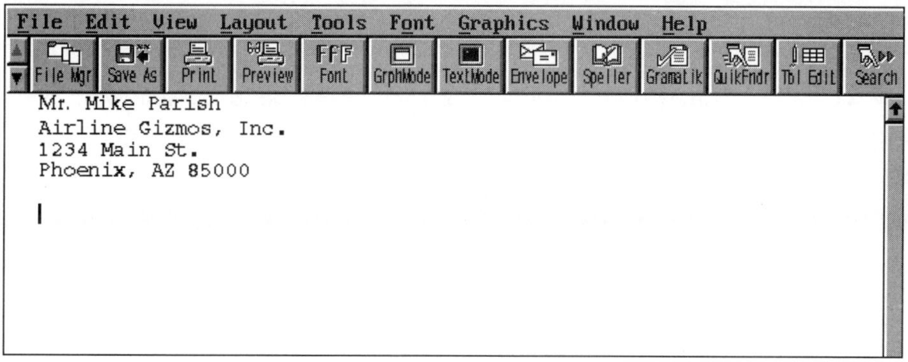

Figure 2.2 Addressing a letter in WordPerfect.

Press **Enter** to leave a blank line after your address. At the start of the new line, type the following greeting.

```
Dear Mike,
```

Press **Enter** twice–one time to advance the cursor to the line that follows your greeting and a second time to place a blank line between the greeting and the first line of your letter.

You have pressed the key at the end of each line of text. When you create a document using WordPerfect, press **Enter** following one–line entries, such as each line of address, the date, a greeting, and between paragraphs. When you type a paragraph's text, however, do not press **Enter** at the end of each line. Continue to type. When your text reaches the end of the line, WordPerfect automatically wraps the text to the start of the next line for you.

Correcting Typing Errors. WordPerfect makes it very easy for you to correct typing errors. If you mistype a letter, use the **Backspace** key to erase the mistake. Each time you press **Backspace** key, WordPerfect erases the character immediately to the left of the cursor. If you need to erase a character that is not immediately to the cursor's left, use the keyboard Arrow keys to move the cursor to the correct location, press **Backspace**.

When you need to erase more than one character, press **Backspace** key one time for each letter. If you hold down **Backspace**, WordPerfect quickly repeats the keystroke, possibly erasing a word, line, or even several lines if you are not paying attention.

Without pressing **Enter** at the end of each line, type in the following paragraph:

```
Thank you for your phone call this morning. Early
Bird Airlines is very interested in meeting with you
to discuss your newest gizmos for pilotless air-
planes. We agree that our airline can save a great
amount of money if we don't have to employ pilots.
```

As you can see, WordPerfect automatically wraps text from one line to the next. Press **Enter** to mark the end of your paragraph. Your screen should look like Figure 2.3.

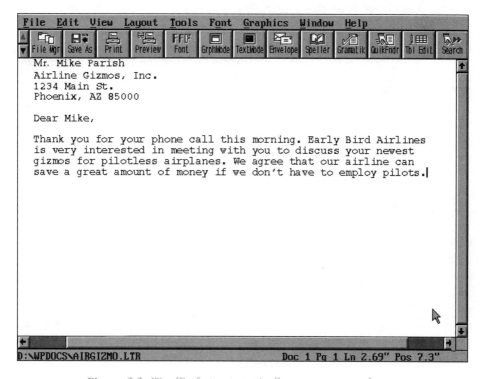

File Edit View Layout Tools Font Graphics Window Help

| File Mgr | Save As | Print | Preview | Font | GrphMode | TextMode | Envelope | Speller | GramaLik | QuikFndr | Tbl Edit | Search |

Mr. Mike Parish
Airline Gizmos, Inc.
1234 Main St.
Phoenix, AZ 85000

Dear Mike,

Thank you for your phone call this morning. Early Bird Airlines
is very interested in meeting with you to discuss your newest
gizmos for pilotless airplanes. We agree that our airline can
save a great amount of money if we don't have to employ pilots.

D:\WPDOCS\AIRGIZMO.LTR   Doc 1 Pg 1 Ln 2.69" Pos 7.3"

Figure 2.3 *WordPerfect automatically wraps paragraph text.*

Many users place a blank line between paragraphs, which makes each paragraph more distinct on the page. Press **Enter** to place a blank line after the last paragraph and type the following text:

I will be traveling to Phoenix next week to meet with
Davis Discount Airline Parts. Would it be possible
for us to get together for lunch? Please call me or
send a FAX to me (702) 555-1212 at your earliest con-
venience. I look forward to hearing from you.

Press **Enter** twice–the first time to mark the end of the paragraph, and the second time to create a blank line. Type the word Sincerely, and press **Enter** four times. Type the in the name and title as shown here:

Ed Conroy
President, Early Bird Airlines

Your letter should look like Figure 2.4.

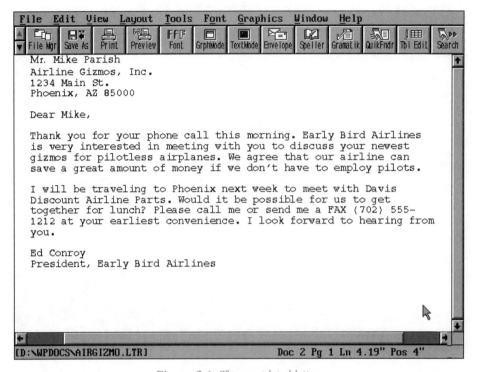

Figure 2.4 *The completed letter.*

Saving Your Document to a File on Disk

As you create documents using WordPerfect, you need to save the document's contents to a file on disk. If you don't save the document, the contents are lost when you exit WordPerfect, or if you computer is turned off. In this case, the letter only resides on your computer's electronic memory. If you were to turn off your computer, the letter would be lost.

Using Meaningful Filenames

When you assign a name to a file, you can use up to eight characters for the base name. The name that you use should describe the document's contents. By using a meaningful name, you can quickly recall a file's contents by looking at only the name. In addition to the eight-character name, you should use the three-character extension to describe the file's type. For example, files that contain letters might use the extension LTR. Files containing memos might use the extension MEM, while files containing a document might use the extension DOC. When you specify a filename, you separate the base name and extension using a period, such as BASENAME.EXT. Table 2.1 lists several different meaningful filenames and the corresponding file contents. Note how you can begin to guess a file's contents using only the basename and extension.

Table 2.1 *Meaningful filenames and document contents.*

Filename	Document contents
BUDGET93.RPT	A report describing the 1993 company budget
SALESMTG.DOC	A document describing the last sales meeting
IRSTAX93.LTR	A letter to the IRS regarding 1993 taxes
AIRGIZMO.LTR	A letter to Airline Gizmos, Inc.

Saving Your WordPerfect Document

To save the letter to Airline Gizmos, Inc. to the file AIRGIZMO.LTR, press **Alt-F** or click on the File menu using your mouse.

Select **Save As** and WordPerfect display the Save Document dialog box, as shown in Figure 2.5.

Figure 2.5 *The Save Document dialog box.*

WordPerfect automatically places the cursor within the dialog box's Filename option. Type in the filename **AIRGIZMO.LTR** and press **Enter** or click on the **OK** button using your mouse. Use either upper or lowercase letters within the filename. When WordPerfect stores the file on disk, It uses all uppercase letters. After you save the document to a file, WordPerfect removes the dialog box from your screen.

Fast Save As Operations. When you store your documents on disk, you must specify the name of the file within which you want to place the document. Save As specifies the desired filename. In addition to using Save As, you can click your mouse on the **Save As** button, or press **F10**.

After you assign a filename to a document, the status bar changes to include the filename.

Saving a Named Document

After assigning a filename to your document, quickly save it using the **Save** option. When you select **Save**, WordPerfect stores your latest changes. It already knows the document's filename, so it does not prompt you for one. The more often you save your document's contents, the less work you stand to lose in the event of a system error or power loss. For example, if you save your document to disk every five minutes, the most work you can lose is the change you made during the last five minutes. To quickly save your document's contents to disk, without using the **Save** option, press **Crtl-F12**.

Closing a Document

When you are done editing a document, and have saved your changes to disk, you can close the document, removing it from your screen. To close the current document, select close from the File menu. If you have saved the document changes to a file on disk, the document closes. If the document contains unsaved changes, WordPerfect displays a dialog box, shown in Figure 2.6, that asks you if you want to save the changes to disk.

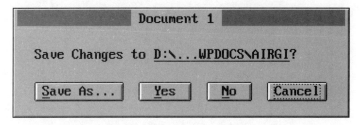

Figure 2.6 *The Save Changes dialog box.*

If the document has not yet been assigned a filename, select the **Save As** option to specify a filename. If the document has a filename, save the changes to the file by selecting **Yes** . If you decide you don't want to close the file (so you can continue editing), select **Cancel.**

In some cases, you will edit a file and make changes, only to later decide that you don't really want the changes after all. By selecting **Close** without saving the changes, you can discard your changes by selecting the **No** option in the Save Changes dialog box. Once you select the **No** , WordPerfect discards all unsaved changes you have made to the file.

Exiting WordPerfect

When you are done using WordPerfect, exit the program. As a rule, never turn off your computer while WordPerfect (or any program other than DOS is running). If you turn off your computer while WordPerfect has one or more document files open, you risk losing the file's contents. To end your WordPerfect session, return to DOS, select **Exit WP** from the File menu. WordPerfect displays the Exit WordPerfect dialog box asking you to save or discard the changes to open documents. If you have only been working with one open document at a time, the Exit WordPerfect dialog box looks like Figure 2.7.

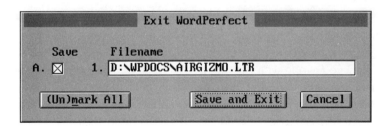

Figure 2.7 *The Exit dialog box.*

If you leave the X in the box labeled A, WordPerfect saves the changes to the file specified. If you remove the X, WordPerfect discards the changes. To set or clear the X, type an X in the box (which in this case is A), or click your mouse on the box. After you set or clear the X as desired, choose the **Save** and **Exit** option.

You can now turn off your computer or run other programs.

Understanding the File Menu Exit Option

If you examine WordPerfect's File menu, you will find options that are titled **Exit** and **Exit WordPerfect**.

Exit WordPerfect directs WordPerfect to end the current session, returning control to DOS. **Exit**, on the other hand, directs WordPerfect to exit the current document (optionally saving the document–but closing the document window). If you select **Exit**, WordPerfect displays a dialog box asking you if you want to save or discard the document changes. WordPerfect displays this dialog box even if you have previously saved your changes to disk. If you have other documents open, WordPerfect displays a dialog box asking you if you want to exit the next document as well. To avoid confusion, save or discard your files one at a time using **Save** and **Close**. When you are ready to end your WordPerfect session, use **Exit WP**.

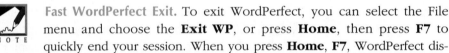 **Fast WordPerfect Exit.** To exit WordPerfect, you can select the File menu and choose the **Exit WP**, or press **Home**, then press **F7** to quickly end your session. When you press **Home**, **F7**, WordPerfect displays the Exit WordPerfect dialog box.

Summary

In this chapter you learned how to create your first WordPerfect document. You also learned how to save the document and the importance of using meaningful filenames. As you work with WordPerfect, remember that the more often you save your documents, the less work you will lose in the event of a system error or power loss. Lastly, remember that you should not turn off your computer while WordPerfect is active. Instead, use the File menu **Exit WP** option to end your WordPerfect session, returning to the DOS prompt. Once the prompt is displayed, you can turn off your computer.

New Terms

◆ **Closing a document.** The process of ending a document's editing session. When you close a document, you can save or discard your changes. WordPerfect then removes the document from your screen.

◆ **Document file.** A file on disk that contains a WordPerfect document.

◆ **Home position.** The upper-left corner of your screen display.

◆ **Named document.** A document whose contents has been saved to a file on disk.

◆ **Unsaved changes.** Editing changes you have made to a document that you have not yet saved to disk.

Editing Your Documents

In this chapter you:

- ◆ Start WordPerfect with a document name
- ◆ Make changes to a document and save the changes to disk
- ◆ Start a new document
- ◆ Open an existing document
- ◆ Insert, delete and change text within a sentence
- ◆ Learn shortcut techniques for moving through a document
- ◆ Learn shortcut editing keystrokes

Making Document Changes

One of the most powerful features a word processor offers you is the ability to quickly and easily make changes to your documents. WordPerfect is no exception. As you create documents, get into the mind set that you may have to make two or three revisions to the document before the document is correct. As such, you may create your document, print it, add or delete words or even sentences, print another copy, repeating these steps several times. Because WordPerfect makes it so easy for you make changes to your document you can revise a document several times in a matter of minutes.

The process of revising your document is *editing*. To many users, the term editing brings to mind the horrors of English-class term papers that were often returned with lots of red ink and grammar corrections. As you will learn, editing in WordPerfect is not threatening at all. In fact, in later chapters you learn how to quickly check your document's spelling and grammar using tools built into WordPerfect! By taking advantage of these tools and by spending a few extra minutes editing your documents, you can quickly produce documents that would make your English teacher proud. By the time you finish this chapter, you are going to be very comfortable working with WordPerfect document files, using shortcut keys, and making and saving changes to your document.

Starting WordPerfect with an Existing File

As you learned in Chapter 2, you must store your documents in files on disk. When you want to work with a specific document, you must open the corresponding document file. If it is not currently running and you want to open it, you can specify the filename when you invoke WordPerfect. For example, the following command starts WordPerfect and loads the file AIRGIZMO.LTR:

```
C:\> WP AIRGIZMO.LTR  <ENTER>
```

Starting WordPerfect with a Specific Document

If you need to start WordPerfect to edit a specific document file, you can specify the document's filename in your WordPerfect command line:

```
C:\WP60> WP FILENAME.DOC  <ENTER>
```

Opening a Document File

If WordPerfect is running, you can open a document file:

1. Open the File menu and select the **Open** option. The Open Document dialog box, as in Figure 3.1.

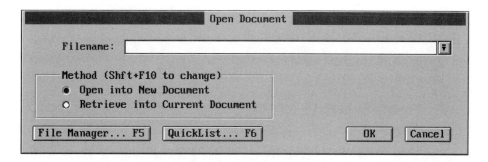

Figure 3.1 *The Open Document dialog box.*

2. To open a document, type in the document file's name and press **Enter**.

For example, to open the letter to Airline Gizmos, Inc., which you created in Chapter 1, type **AIRGIZMO.LTR** and press **Enter**. The file is opened displaying its contents. If you misspell a filename, WordPerfect displays a dialog box that states the file was not found, as in Figure 3.2

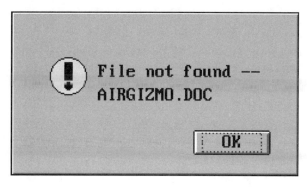

Figure 3.2 *The File Not Found dialog box.*

If it cannot locate your file, double check the spelling of the filename. In the case of the error message in Figure 3.2, the user typed the extension DOC instead of LTR. If this error message appears, select **OK**. The Open Document dialog box is redisplayed. Type in the correct document filename. By now you recognize the importance of using meaningful filenames. If you don't use meaningful names, you are likely to have trouble remember the names of your document files.

Opening a Document File

To open an existing document file for editing or printing:

1. Press **Alt-F** to open the File menu.
2. Choose **Open**.
3. In the Open Document dialog box, type in the document filename and press **Enter**.

Opening a Recently Used Document File

If you are using WordPerfect to open a document file that you have recently used, you can take advantage of the fact that it keeps track of the last four files you have opened. To open a recently used file:

1. Select the File menu **Open** option.
2. When the Open Document dialog box is displayed, click on the **Down Arrow** located at the far right of the filename box.
3. A pull-down list that contains the names of the last four files you have edited is displayed in Figure 3.3.

```
D:\WPDOCS\DAVIS.LTR
D:\WPDOCS\AIRGIZMO.LTR
D:\WPDOCS\SALES.RPT
D:\WPDOCS\BUDGET.RPT
```

Figure 3.3 The pull-down list of recently used document files.

4. To select one of the recently used files for editing, highlight the file and press **Enter**.

Getting Around Your Document

Open a document to edit:

1. Open the document file **AIRGIZMO.LTR**.

2. Using the Arrow keys, move the cursor from the top of your document to the bottom.

3. Hold down the Left Arrow key while the cursor moves back to the top of your document. (When you edit a document, you make extensive use of the Up, Down, Right, and Left Arrow keys to position the cursor.)

4. Use **PgDn** and **PgUp** to move the cursor to the end of your document and back again.

When you press the Arrow or PgUp or PgDn key and your cursor does not move, but rather, a number is written to your document, you have pressed the NumLock key. The *NumLock* key works like a toggle switch. If the NumLock light is lit, the keyboard uses the Arrow keys to move your cursor. The next time you press the key's corresponding digit it types. Normally, when your keyboard types the digits, it illuminates a small light, called the NumLock indicator. If this light is lit, press **NumLock** so you can use these keys to position your cursor.

Keeping Track of the Cursor Position

As you move the cursor throughout your document, you can use the scroll block that appears in the vertical scroll bar. This determines your relative position between the start and end of your document. If the block is near the top of the scroll bar, you are near the top of your top document. Likewise, if the block is near the middle or bottom of the bar, you are near the middle or bottom of your document. When you need more accurate cursor position information, you can use the status bar that appears at the bottom of your screen.

The status bar tells you the current page number, line, and column position. Using the Arrow keys, move the cursor throughout your document. As the cursor moves, note how WordPerfect updates its status bar position information.

When you need to start a document at a specific location, such as 1 1/2 inches from the top of the page, you can use the status bar's positioning information. Many users print letters on custom stationary by ensuring their letters start at a specific location.

Moving Around Using Your Mouse

If you are using a mouse, you can quickly move the cursor to a specific location by simply clicking the mouse pointer on the location. If the desired location is not in view, you can scroll it into view by clicking on the vertical scroll bar, or by dragging the scroll bar block. As you position the cursor using your mouse, note that WordPerfect updates the status bar positioning information.

Some Shortcuts for Moving Quickly through Your Document

As you have learned, using the Arrow, PgUp, and PgDn keys, you can move the cursor throughout your document. To help you quickly traverse your document, WordPerfect predefines several keystrokes you can use to quickly move throughout your document. Following is a description of the most common cursor positioning keystrokes:

- ◆ **Left Arrow** moves the cursor to the previous character.
- ◆ **Right Arrow** moves the cursor to the next character.
- ◆ **Ctrl-Left Arrow** moves the cursor to the previous word.
- ◆ **Ctrl-Right Arrow** moves the cursor to the next word.
- ◆ **Down Arrow** moves the cursor down one line.
- ◆ **Up Arrow** moves the cursor up one line.
- ◆ **PgDn** moves the cursor down one page.
- ◆ **PgUp** moves the cursor up one page.

- ◆ **Home, Up Arrow** moves the cursor to top of the screen.

- ◆ **Home, Down Arrow** moves the cursor to the bottom of the screen.

As you become more comfortable traversing WordPerfect document, turn to Appendix B that lists other key combinations.

Insert versus Typeover Mode

When you type in your document, WordPerfect inserts the characters you type in front of existing text, or it can typeover the existing characters, replacing a character with each keystroke. It calls these two modes of typing *insert* or *typeover mode*. To switch from one mode to the other, simply press **Ins** key. A status bar message is displayed telling you what mode you are in.

If you start typing and WordPerfect overwrites your existing text, you are in typeover mode. Press **Ins** to return to insert mode.

Deleting Document Text

As you type or when you revise (edit) your document, you may eventually need to delete text. You might just delete a character to correct a misspelling, or you may need to delete a word, line, sentence or even a paragraph. For a simple character delete, position the cursor in front of the character you want to delete and then press **Del**

You can also use the Backspace key to delete a character. When you press the **Backspace** key, it deletes the character that appears to the left of the cursor.

Each time you press the **Del** or **Backspace** key, it deletes one character. If you hold down one of these keys, WordPerfect rapidly deletes characters, possibly much faster than expected and more characters than you wanted. If you only want to delete a few characters, press **Del** or **Backspace** once for each character.

Deleting a Word, Line, or More

If you need to delete more than a character, WordPerfect predefines several keyboard combinations that let you quickly delete a word, line, or even a page. Following is a list of these predefined keystrokes:

◆ **Ctrl-Del** deletes the word that appears to the right of the cursor–if the cursor is in a word, it deletes the current word

◆ **Ctrl-Backspace** deletes the word that appears to the left of the cursor–if the cursor is in a word, it deletes the current word.

◆ **Ctrl-End** deletes text to the right of the cursor through the end of the line.

◆ **Ctrl-PgDn** deletes text from the right of the cursor through the end of the page.

An Editing Session

1. Open the File menu and choose **New**. An editing window opens.

2. Type the following text, including the errors (that appear in italics):

```
To put the world in right in order, we must first put
the nation in order; to put the nation in order, we
must first put the family in order; to put the family
in order, we must first cultivate our personal life;
we must we must set our hearts right.

                                    Confucius, 551 B.C.
```

3. Select the **Save As** option and save the document to your disk as FAMILY.DOC.

4. Using the Arrow keys, place the cursor in line one, in front of the first occurrence of the word *in*.

5. Press the **Del** key twice to delete the word and one more time to delete the space that followed.

6. Move the cursor to the second occurrence of the word *first*.

7. Press **Ctrl-Del** to delete the word.

8. Move the cursor to the second occurrence of the words *we must*.

9. Press **Ctrl-Del** twice to delete both words.

After you make changes to a document, you must save the changes to the document file. Select the File menu and choose **Save**. The difference between the

Save and Save As option is that Save writes the document's contents to the open document file, whereas Save As lets you specify a different file. After you save the document's contents, use the File menu **Close** option to close the document.

Retrieving a Document File

When you create documents, there may be times when you want to include the contents of an existing document in your current one. For example:

1. Open the File menu and select **New** .

2. Type the following text:

```
To: All Employees
From: Pat S.
Subject: Beer, burgers, and sheep herding
Don't forget the party this weekend. It starts at
10:30. Bring your bikes!
Pat
P.S. Today's thought is:
```

3. Include the quote from Confucius that you just stored in the file FAMILY.DOC, at the bottom of the memo.

4. Press **Enter** once or twice to advance the cursor one or two lines.

5. Open the File menu and choose **Retrieve**. The Retrieve Document dialog box is displayed in Figure 3.4.

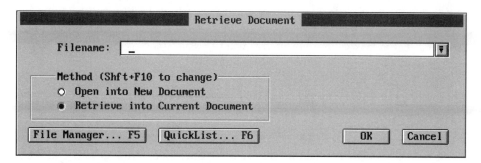

Figure 3.4 *The Retrieve Document dialog box.*

6. Type in the filename **FAMILY.DOC** and press **Enter**. WordPerfect inserts the document, as in Figure 3.5.

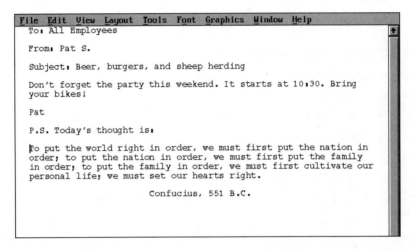

File Edit View Layout Tools Font Graphics Window Help

To: All Employees

From: Pat S.

Subject: Beer, burgers, and sheep herding

Don't forget the party this weekend. It starts at 10:30. Bring your bikes!

Pat

P.S. Today's thought is:

To put the world right in order, we must first put the nation in order; to put the nation in order, we must first put the family in order; to put the family in order, we must first cultivate our personal life; we must set our hearts right.

Confucius, 551 B.C.

Figure 3.5 *Inserting contents from one document to another.*

If you are working on a large document with other people in your office, you may assign different parts of the document to specific people. Later, using the File menu Retrieve option, you can build the document by retrieving all of the smaller pieces.

Discarding Changes to a Document

There may be times, when after editing a document you decide that you don't want to save your changes. In such cases, do not use the File menu Save option to save your changes. Instead, select the File menu **Close** option. WordPerfect displays a dialog box asking you if you want to save your changes. Select **No**. It discards the changes, closing your document.

Summary

Editing is the process of making changes to your document. As you edit, you may add, replace, or delete text. Whenever you change your document's contents, you must save your changes to the document's file on disk. To help you quickly edit your document, WordPerfect predefines keyboard combinations. Several of the commonly used combinations were presented in this chapter. Appendix B discusses all of WordPerfect's keyboard combinations.

New Terms

◆ **Editing.** The process of making changes to your document.

◆ **Retrieving a document.** The process of inserting a second document's contents into the current document.

Printing Your Document

In this chapter you:

- ◆ Select a printer
- ◆ Print one or more copies of your document
- ◆ Preview your printed output
- ◆ Learn to print the current document page
- ◆ Learn to print a range of pages
- ◆ Learn to control your print out quality
- ◆ Learn to control your printer and print jobs

Getting Ready to Print

As you create documents within WordPerfect, you will eventually want to print them. WordPerfect makes printer operations very easy while giving you control over a large number of options, such as the number of copies you want to print, the specific page numbers, or the print quality. To begin, load the document file AIRGIZMO.LTR that you created in Chapter 2.

Select **Print/Fax** from the File menu. WordPerfect displays the Print\Fax dialog box, shown in Figure 4.1.

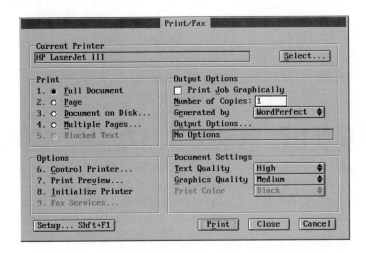

Figure 4.1 The Print/Fax dialog box.

Before WordPerfect prints a document, you must tell it the type of printer you are using. Look at the Current Printer option. If the box contains the text NO PRINTER SELECTED, select a printer. If the Print/Fax dialog box has a selected printer, skip the next section and continue reading. You only have to select a printer one time. WordPerfect remembers your printer type from one session to the next.

Selecting a Printer

If the Print/Fax dialog box contains the text NO PRINTER SELECTED in the Current Printer box, you must tell WordPerfect your printer type. To begin, with the Print/Fax dialog box active, press **S** to choose the **Select** button, or click on the button using your mouse. WordPerfect displays the Select Printer dialog box shown in Figure 4.2.

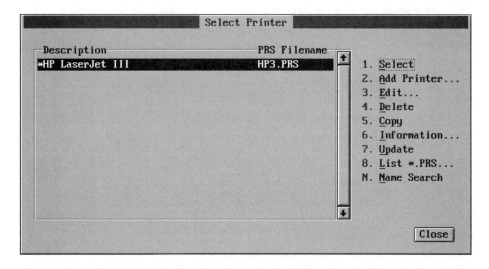

Figure 4.2 *The Select Printer dialog box.*

Press **A** or click your mouse on the **Add Printer** option. WordPerfect displays the Add Printer dialog box, which contains a list of supported printers, as shown in Figure 4.3.

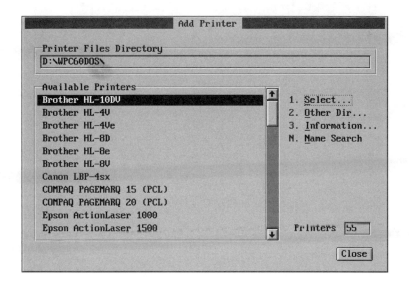

Figure 4.3 *The Add Printer dialog box.*

Using your keyboard's Up Arrow and Down Arrow, highlight your printer name. Type **S** or click on **Select**. The Printer Filename dialog box is displayed, as shown in Figure 4.4.

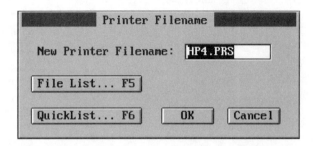

Figure 4.4 *The Printer Filename dialog box.*

Press **Enter** to select **OK**. Depending on your printer type, WordPerfect may display an additional dialog box. Press **Enter** to accept the dialog box defaults. WordPerfect displays the Edit Printer Setup dialog box, shown in Figure 4.5.

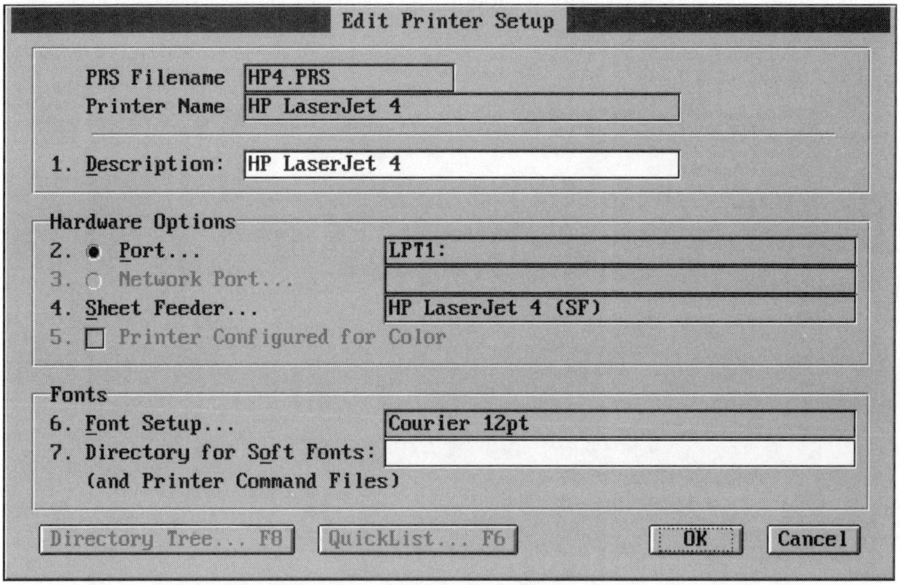

Figure 4.5 *The Edit Printer Setup dialog box.*

Make sure the printer port is correctly selected in the dialog box. If your printer is connected to a port other than LPT1, or if you are using a network printer, select the correct port settings by typing the number that precedes the option, or by clicking on the option. If you need to change port or network settings, WordPerfect displays a dialog box that lets you make the selections you need. When your printer settings are correct, select the **OK**. WordPerfect displays the Select Printer dialog box once again.

Working with Multiple Printers

If your computer has multiple printers, either attached directly to the computer or available on a network, you can add the printers to WordPerfect's printer list. To use a specific printer:

1. Select the **Print/Fax** option.
2. In the Print/Fax dialog box, choose **Select**.
3. Highlight the printer you want to use and choose **Select**.
4. Close the Select Printer dialog box.

Printing Your Document

The Print/Fax dialog box contains several options. If you use the default settings, WordPerfect prints your entire document. To print your document, type **R** or click on the **Print** button. WordPerfect will begin printing your document, removing the Print/Fax dialog box from your screen.

You may also press **Shift-F7** or select the **Print** button to open the Print/Fax dialog box.

When WordPerfect displays the Print/Fax dialog box, type **R** or click your mouse on the **Print** button.

Trouble-Shooting Your Printer

If your printer does not print, check the following:

◆   Is the printer turned on and on-line?
◆   Are the printer cables properly connected?

◆ Does the correct printer name appear in the Current Printer field?

◆ Is WordPerfect printing to the correct port? Choose **Select** from the Print/Fax dialog box, highlight the printer, and choose **Edit**. Make sure the port setting is correct.

If you cannot determine the cause of a printer error, make sure you can use the printer from outside of WordPerfect. Issue the following PRINT command to see if DOS can use your printer:

```
C:\WP60> PRINT  \CONFIG.SYS  <ENTER>
```

If your printer prints from outside of WordPerfect, but you cannot successfully print from within WordPerfect, contact WordPerfect's technical support. Make sure you know your printer type and port (such as LPT1 or COM1) before you call.

Previewing Your Document

Before you print a document, you may want to take a look at how the document will appear on a printed page. For example, if you are creating a letter, you might want to increase or decrease the top margin, depending on the letter's size. WordPerfect provides a print preview option that lets you view your printed document before you print it. To preview a document, open the File menu and choose **Print Preview**. WordPerfect changes the screen display, showing your document's first page, just as the document will appear on paper, as shown in Figure 4.6.

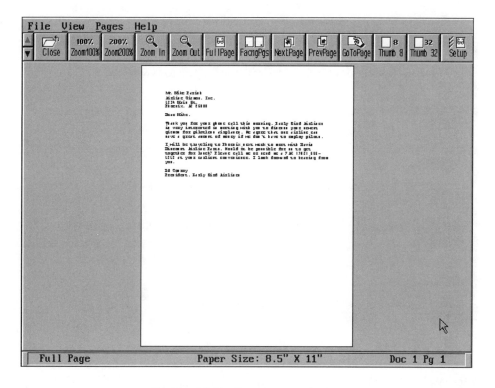

Figure 4.6 *The Print Preview display.*

The buttons in the Print Preview screen, are different. Table 4.1 contains a brief description of each button's purpose.

Table 4.1 *The Print Preview buttons.*

Close	Closes the Print Preview, displays the previous screen..
100% Zoom100%	Zooms in on the document, magnifying the image by 100 percent.
200% Zoom200%	Zooms in on the document, magnifying the image contents by 200 percent.
Zoom In	Increases the magnification of the document displayed.
Zoom Out	Decreases the magnification of the document displayed.
FullPage	Displays the full document page.
NextPage	Displays the following document page.
PrevPage	Displays the previous document page.
GoToPage	Prompts you for the desired page number.
8 Thumb 8	Displays eight miniature document page representations.
32 Thumb 32	Display thirty-two miniature document page representations.
SetUp	Configures Print Preview options.
BBar Edit	Customizes the Print Preview buttons.
BBar Opt	Customizes how WordPerfect displays the Print Preview bar.

Controlling Your Printout

As you have seen, WordPerfect's Print/Fax dialog box contains many different options. As your documents become larger, there may be times when you only want to print the current page, a range of pages, or you may want to reduce the quality of your output (for a draft copy) so that your document prints faster. Using the Print/Fax dialog box, you can quickly perform these operations.

Selecting the Number of Copies

By default, WordPerfect only prints one copy of your document at a time. To print more than one copy:

1.   Select **Print/Fax.**
2.   Type **N** or click your mouse in the **Number of Copies** box.
3.   Type in the number of copies you desire.
4.   Select **Print**.

Depending on your printer type, you may be able to have your printer (as opposed to WordPerfect) oversee printing each copy, which may improve your performance. To do this, type **E** to select the **Generated By** option and select **Printer**.

Selecting the Pages to Print

WordPerfect prints every page in your document unless you tell it to do otherwise. To print a specific document page:

1.   Move the cursor into the page you want to print.
2.   Select **Print/Fax.**
3.   Type **P** or click you mouse on the **Page** option.
4.   Select **Print**.

To print a range of pages, such as from 5 through 20:

1. Select **Print/Fax**.

2. Type **M** or click your mouse on **Multiple Pages**. WordPerfect displays the Print Multiple Pages dialog box, as shown in Figure 4.7.

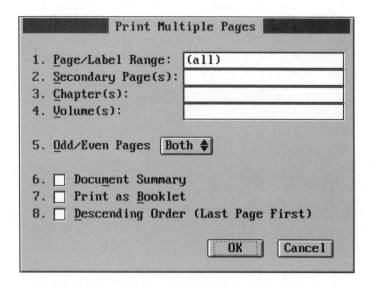

Figure 4.7 *The Print Multiple Pages dialog box.*

3. Select **Page/Label Range** and type in the desired pages such as 5-20 or 1,2,5.

4. Select **OK**.

5. Select **Print**.

Controlling Your Printout Quality

When you are working with a draft document copy, you may prefer to trade-off print quality for printer speed. By reducing the quality of your printout (especially printed graphics), you can substantially increase the speed at which your documents print. To control the quality of your printouts:

1. Select **Print/Fax**.

2. Type **T** to set the quality of your text output or click on the **Text Quality** box. Select **High**, **Medium**, **Draft**, or **Do Not Print**.

3. Type **G** to set the quality of your graphics output or click on the **Graphics Quality** box . Select **High, Medium, Draft** or **Do Not Print**.

4. Select **Print**.

By selecting **Do Not Print** , you can direct WordPerfect not to print either your document's text or graphics. If you don't print graphics, your document prints much faster. WordPerfect leaves the graphic location blank in the printed document.

Controlling Your Printer and Print Jobs

As the number and size of the documents you print increases, there may be times when you want to cancel one document's printing (a printing document is called a *job*), so that another document can print. You may want to determine what percentage of your document has printed and so on. To control your printer output, select **Print/Fax.** WordPerfect displays the Print/Fax dialog box. In the Print/Fax dialog box, type **C** or click on **Control Printer**. WordPerfect displays the Control Printer dialog box, shown in Figure 4.8.

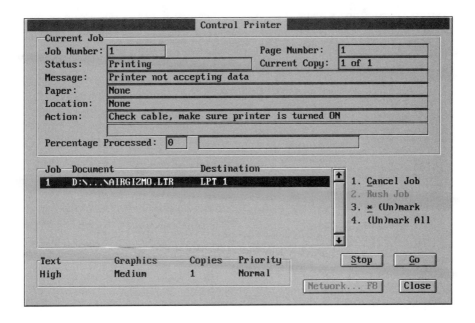

Figure 4.8 *The Control Printer dialog box.*

As you can see, this dialog box lists the names of all of the files you have directed WordPerfect to print (the current print jobs). In addition, the dialog box provides information that describes the current job status, such as the percent printed, current page number, current copy, and so on.

Rushing a Print Job

Using the Control Printer dialog box, you can highlight a print job and select **Rush Job.** This moves the job to the start of list, interrupting the printing of the current job. When the rushed job's printing is complete, WordPerfect begins printing the interrupted job from its beginning. To rush a print job:

1. Type **C** or click on **Control Printer**.
2. Highlight the desired job.
3. Type **R** or click on the **Rush Job**.

Canceling One or More Jobs

Using the Control Printer dialog box, you can cancel the printing of one or more jobs, including the job that is currently printing. When you cancel a print job, the document name is removed from the job list. To cancel a job:

1. Type **C** or click on **Control Printer**.
2. Highlight the desired job.
3. Type **C** or click on **Cancel Job**.

To cancel multiple jobs, you must first mark the desired jobs:

1. Highlight the desired job and press the asterisk key (*) or click on the **(Un)mark** option.
2. Repeat Step 1 for each job you want to remove.
3. Type **C** or click on **Cancel Job**.

Temporarily Suspending a Print Job

When you print large documents, there may be times when you want to temporarily suspend printing. To suspend your printer output:

1. Type **C** or click on **Control Printer**.
2. Type **S** or click on the **Stop** button.

To later resume printer operations:

1. Type **C** or click on **Control Printer**.
2. Type **G** or click on the **Go** button.

Summary

In this chapter you learned how to quickly print your document by selecting the Print/Fax option from the File menu. You also learned that WordPerfect makes it very easy for you print multiple copies, print specific document changes, or to control the quality of your printouts. Using Print Preview, you are able to see how your document looks on the page before you print it. Lastly, using WordPerfect's Control Printer dialog box, you learned how to view the status of your print jobs, how to stop and start print operations, how to cancel one or more print jobs, and how to rush a high- priority printout.

New Terms

*   ◆ **Draft copy.** A working copy of your document, not the final copy.
*   ◆ **Print job.** A document that is printing or waiting to be printed.
*   ◆ **Print preview.** An on-screen look at how your document will appear on printed pages.
*   ◆ **Selected printer.** The printer to which WordPerfect sends its output. If your computer has multiple printers attached, you must select one that will serve as the current printer.

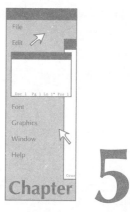

Chapter 5

Spell Checking Your Document

In this chapter you:

- ◆ Use WordPerfect's spell checker to correct misspellings
- ◆ Look up the spelling for a specific word
- ◆ Understand supplemental dictionaries
- ◆ Learn what a spell checker can and cannot do

59

Spell Checking Your Document

To check a document's spelling, open the **File** menu, select **New**, and then type the following text, typing all words as they appear, even if they are misspelled:

```
Dear Bill,

I wantd to thank you and Hillery again for haveing us
over for dinner last night. I'm still confused by
your idea of an automated helth care tax. Why would
you want to tax PCs? If my computr has a virus, I
should be able to use any viurs-checking softwear I
want. More importently, the software should be
affordible.

Sincerly,

Geroge
```

Select **Writing Tools** from the Tools menu. WordPerfect displays the Writing Tools dialog box, shown in Figure 5.1.

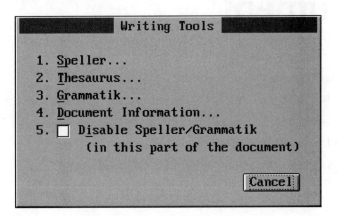

Figure 5.1 *The Writing Tools dialog box.*

Type **1** or click on **Speller**. WordPerfect displays the Speller dialog box, shown in Figure 5.2.

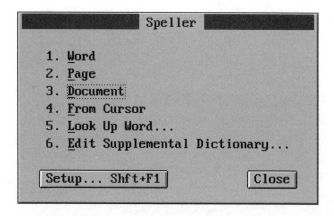

Figure 5.2 *The Speller dialog box.*

The Speller dialog box lets you select the portion of the document you want to spell check. In most cases, you spell check your entire document. You can look up the spelling for a specific word, or add a word to your own custom dictionary. Type **3** or click on **Document**. WordPerfect begins spell checking from the start of your document. Each time it encounters a word that is not in its dictionaries, WordPerfect displays the Word Not Found dialog box, shown in Figure 5.3.

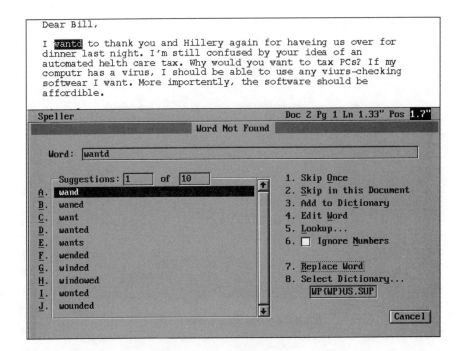

Figure 5.3 *The Word Not Found dialog box.*

When WordPerfect identifies a misspelled word, it highlights the word in your document, then displays a list of possible correct spellings. To select a suggested word, type the letter preceding the suggestion or click on the desired word. Replace the misspelled word *wantd* with *wanted*. For the name *Hillery*, WordPerfect displays the correct spelling, *Hillary*. When you correct the misspelling, WordPerfect continues checking your spelling. Using this technique, replace the following words:

◆ Hillery becomes Hillary

◆ haveing becomes having

◆ helth becomes health

Because WordPerfect does not have the word *PCs* in its dictionary, it displays the word as a possible misspelling. Because the word is correct, you can skip the word, skip the word in the current document, or add the word to the dictionary. In this case, type **3** or click on **Add to Dictionary**. Let WordPerfect correct the following words:

- ◆ computr becomes computer
- ◆ viurs- becomes virus-
- ◆ softwear becomes software
- ◆ importently becomes importantly
- ◆ affordiblebecomes affordable
- ◆ Sincerly becomes Sincerely
- ◆ Geroge becomes George

WordPerfect lets you know when the spell check is complete. As you can see, WordPerfect's spell checker is very easy to use, and it only takes a few minutes. You should spell check every document you create.

Checking the Spelling of a Specific Word

As you create documents, there will be times when you aren't sure of a word's correct spelling. If you have a dictionary handy, you can look the word up. If you don't, relax, you can quickly look up words using the spell checker. To look up a word's spelling, open the Tools menu, select **Writing Tools**, and select **Speller**. Type **5** or click on **Look Up Word**. WordPerfect displays the Look Up Word dialog box, shown in Figure 5.4.

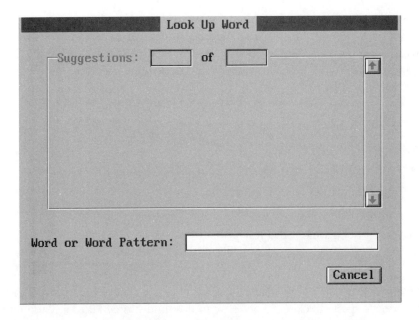

Figure 5.4 *The Look Up Word dialog box.*

Type in as much of the word as you know and then type the asterisk wildcard character (*). For example, if you want to know how to spell the word *Sincerely*, type **Sincer***. WordPerect displays the correct spelling, as shown in Figure 5.5.

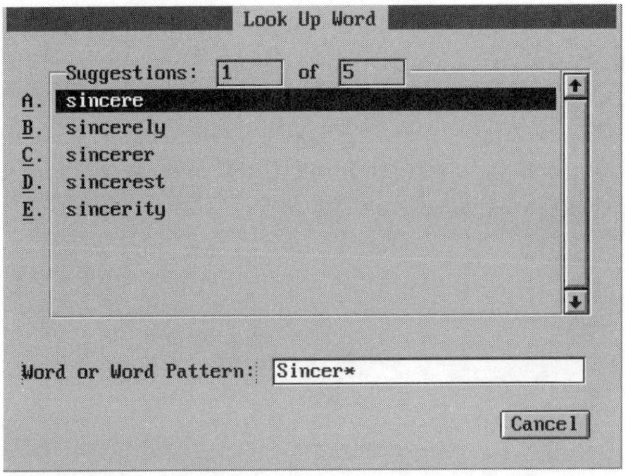

Figure 5.5 *The Look Up Word suggestions dialog box.*

Characters in the position where the wildcard appears are ignored. Using the letters *Sincer**, means that matching words must begin with the letters *Sincer*, but it doesn't match what letters follow. As a result, WordPerfect finds five possible matching words. Select the word **Sincerely**. It asks you if you want it to automatically insert the matching word in the text.

To automatically insert the word, select **Yes**, otherwise, select **No**.

Spell Checker's Wildcards

Using the asterisk wildcard, you can ignore one or more characters that appear in a specific character position when you perform a word look up. In addition to the asterisk wildcard, WordPerfect lets you use the question mark wildcard (?). When you use the question mark, you direct WordPerfect to ignore only one character. Here's why you might need two different wildcards. Assume that you want to know the spelling of the word receive (i before e, except for something). Using the asterisk wildcard, you can look up the spelling using the following letters, *rec*ve*. In this case, WordPerfect matches over a dozen words as shown in Figure 5.6.

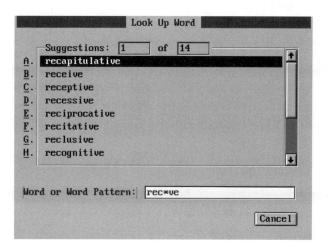

Figure 5.6 *Using the Look Up Word feature.*

All of the words listed in Figure 5.6 match your specified wildcard combination. Because you are really only confused by the *i* and *e* you can use the question mark wildcard—*rec??ve*. WordPerfect display the correct spelling.

Understanding Supplemental Dictionaries

When WordPerfect does not find a word in its dictionary, it displays the word as a possible misspelling. If the word is spelled correctly, you can direct WordPerfect to add the word to its dictionary. The next time it encounters the word, WordPerfect knows the spelling is correct. Depending on your profession, you may find it convenient to purchase one or more supplemental dictionaries. WordPerfect supports dictionaries for the medical, legal, computer, and even religous professions. By starting with a supplemental dictionary, you can avoid having to build your own by continually adding dictionary words. If you purchase a supplemental dictionary, you must tell WordPerfect about the dictionary before it can use it. To inform WordPerfect of a supplemental dictionary, select the **Setup** option that appears in the Speller dialog box.

Correcting Words in the Supplemental Dictionary

When WordPerfect identifies a word that is not in its dictionary, you can direct it to add the word. Over time, you may inadvertently add a misspelled word to your dictionary. To remove the word from the dictionary:

1. Open the Tools menu and select **Writing Tools**.
2. Select **Speller**.
3. From the Speller dialog box, select **Edit Supplemental Dictionary**.
4. Select the dictionary you want to correct and choose **Edit**.
5. In the Edit Supplemental Dictionary dialog box, select the incorrect word and choose **Edit** or **Delete**.

Understanding What a Spell Checker Won't Catch

Spell checkers only identify possible misspelled words—they do not identify misused words. For example:

```
It was greet to sea ewe this weekend. The kids wear
so big. Their just sew much fun. Tell everyone we
said high!
```

Because all of the words are spelled correctly, the spell checker does not identify any errors.

Summary

Every time you create a document, you should use the spell checker to examine and correct the document's spelling. WordPerfect makes it very easy to spell check a document, or even a specific page of the document. It identifies words that are not in its dictionary as possible misspellings. When WordPerfect displays a possible misspelling, you can replace the word with one of the suggestions; you can edit the word; you can tell WordPerfect to skip the word; or, if the word is spelled correctly, you can tell WordPerfect to add the word to its dictionary. Using the spell checker, you can even look up words as you work. After WordPerfect displays the desired word, you can direct it to automatically insert the word at the current cursor position. The spell checker truly is a tool that improves the quality of your writing.

New Terms

- ◆ **Supplemental dictionary.** A dictionary that contains additional words and acronyms, possibly specific to a profession or hobby.
- ◆ **Wildcard.** A symbol you can include in a Word Look Up to specify *don't care* characters. There are two such wildcards:
  - The asterisk (*) directs WordPerfect to ignore one or more characters.
  - The question mark (?) directs WordPerfect to ignore only one character.

Chapter 6

Customizing Your Working Environment

In this chapter you:

- ◆ Use the Setup menu
- ◆ Specify your mouse type
- ◆ Select your video display type
- ◆ Customize environment settings
- ◆ Select a keyboard layout
- ◆ Specify the directories WordPerfect should search for files
- ◆ Customize your screen colors

Setup Options

When you install WordPerfect, the installation program configures your system hardware, screen colors, and directories. In this section you learn how to view your system's current configuration and how to customize different settings. If you are happy with your system, you can skip this chapter. As you work more with WordPerfect, you may later turn to this chapter to learn how to customize different options in your work environment.

Each of the configuration settings discussed in this chapter are accessed by first selecting the File menu and choosing **Setup**. WordPerfect will cascade the Setup menu.

Selecting a Mouse

To specify your mouse type to WordPerfect, select **Mouse** from the Setup dialog box. WordPerfect displays the Mouse dialog box, shown in Figure 6.1.

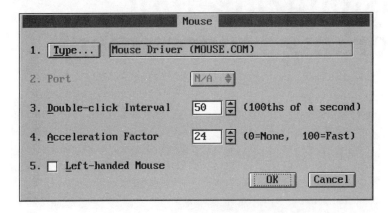

Figure 6.1 The Mouse dialog box.

Type **T** to select the **Type** button. WordPerfect displays its list of known mouse types. Using your Arrow keys, highlight the desired mouse and type **S** to choose **Select**.

If you are using a serial mouse (a mouse that connects to a serial port on the back of your PC such as COM1), use the **Port** option to specify the correct port.

After you work with your mouse, you may find that you want to fine-tune the mouse's double-click responsiveness or the speed at which the mouse moves across the screen. To set a faster double-click, *decrease* the double-click Interval. Likewise, to make the mouse pointer move faster across your screen, *increase* the acceleration Factor.

If you are left handed and you want to reverse the mouse buttons, type **L** or click on the **Left-handed Mouse** button, placing an X in the box. After you have customized the mouse options, select **OK**.

Selecting the Video Display Type

When you install WordPerfect, one of the first screens asks you whether or not you can see the red, green, and blue colored boxes. If you select **Yes**, WordPerfect knows you have a color system. WordPerfect then checks your system's video hardware to determine the video display type (such as EGA or VGA). In most cases, WordPerfect correctly identifies your video display type. You probably won't need to change the video type selection. However, you may want to customize WordPerfect's screen colors.

To choose a video display type or to customize the screen colors, select **Setup**, **Display**. WordPerfect shows the Display dialog box, as shown in Figure 6.2.

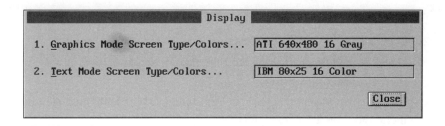

Figure 6.2 The Display dialog box.

The Display dialog box lets you select the display modes and screen colors WordPerfect uses in graphics and text modes. If you select **Graphics Mode**, WordPerfect displays the **Graphics Mode Screen Type/Colors** dialog box, shown in Figure 6.3.

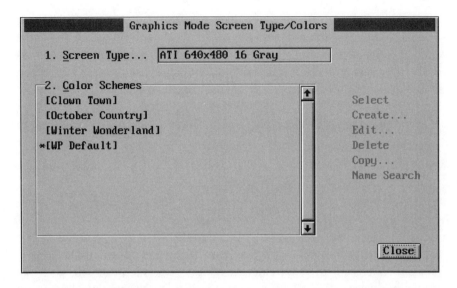

Figure 6.3 *The Graphics Mode Screen Type/Colors dialog box.*

WordPerfect predefines several color schemes. To try a color scheme, highlight the scheme and type **S** or click on **Select**. You may want to try each color scheme. In addition, WordPerfect lets you edit one of the existing color schemes or create your own. To create your own color scheme:

1. Type **2** or click on **Color Schemes**.

2. Type **2** (again) or click on **Create**.

3. When WordPerfect prompts you for a color scheme, type in a meaningful name and press **Enter**.

4. In the Edit Graphics Screen Colors dialog box, highlight a screen element and type **1** to assign a color.

5. In the Colors dialog box, use your Arrow keys to highlight a color or click on the color using your mouse. Type **S** or click on the **Select**.

6. Repeat Steps 3 and 4 for each screen element.

7. Select **OK**.

Customizing Your Work Environment

WordPerfect groups several different custom options under the Environment option. When you select **Environment**, WordPerfect displays the Environment dialog box, as shown in Figure 6.4.

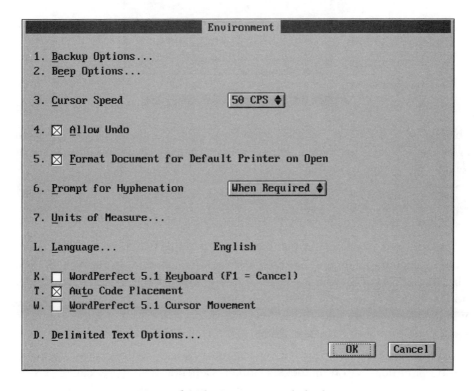

Figure 6.4 *The Environment dialog box.*

Chapter 7 discusses WordPerfect's backup options in detail. The Beep options let you control when your computer's built-in speaker sounds. If you select **Beep Options**, WordPerfect displays the Beep Options dialog box, shown in Figure 6.5.

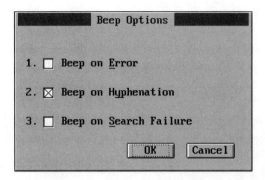

Figure 6.5 *The Beep Options dialog box.*

The dialog box lets you specify when you want WordPerfect to beep. If an event box contains an X, WordPerfect beeps when the event occurs. To set or remove the X, type the event number or click on the event box.

WordPerfect's Cursor Speed option lets you specify how fast WordPerfect repeats a character when you hold down a key. If you select the **Cursor Speed** option, WordPerfect displays a list of possible character speeds.

As you edit your documents, there may be times when you delete a sentence, paragraph, or figure and then wish that you hadn't. In most cases, you can use Undo to undo your last operation. The **Allow Undo** controls whether or not WordPerfect lets you undo such operations. If the box contains an X, WordPerfect supports undo operations, otherwise it does not. To set or remove the X, type **A** or click on **Allow Undo**.

When you open a document, WordPerfect formats the document so that it can be print quickly on the default printer. Depending on the document's size, the format operation may consume some time. If you don't normally print every document you open, you may not want WordPerfect to format these documents. To disable automatic document formatting when you open a file, type **F** or click on **Format Document for Default Printer on Open**.

As you type, there may be times when WordPerfect needs to hyphenate a word that appears at the end of the line. The **Prompt for Hyphenation** option lets you specify whether or not WordPerfect should prompt you for assistance. When you select **Prompt for Hyphenation**, WordPerfect displays a list of options.

By default, WordPerfect uses inches as its unit of measure. If you look at the cursor position indicator that appears in the status bar, you will find it appears in inches. When you set your document margins, you will find WordPerfect uses inches. Not all users work with inches, however, especially those users outside of the United States. The **Units of Measure** option lets you select WordPerfect's default unit of measure. When you select this option, WordPerfect displays the Units of Measure dialog box as shown in Figure 6.6.

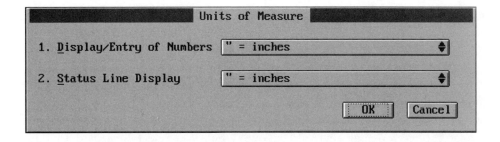

Figure 6.6 *The Units of Measure dialog box.*

Display/Entry of Numbers controls which units of measure WordPerfect displays in dialog boxes and uses for the default when you type in a value. The Status Line Display controls the units WordPerfect uses to display cursor positioning information. If you select either entry, WordPerfect displays a list of available units of measure:

To help you create documents for languages other than English, WordPerfect sells language modules. If you have purchased additional language modules, select **Language** to find the desired language.

If you have upgraded from WordPerfect 5.1 and you like 5.1's keyboard and Arrow keys, select **WordPerfect 5.1 Keyboard** and **WordPerfect 5.1 Cursor Movement** to support similar keystrokes:

When you work with WordPerfect's formatting codes, it may automatically move certain codes to the start of your document or to the start of the current paragraph. Such processing is called *auto code placement.* **Auto Code Placement** controls if WordPerfect moves the codes or leaves the codes where you placed them. If the check box is selected, WordPerfect moves the codes as it best sees fit. If the box is not selected, WordPerfect does not move the codes.

WordPerfect merge operations define records of data, such as a mailing label and fields within the label, such as name, street, city, state, and zip. To help you define such entries, WordPerfect lets you select specific characters that distinguish one part of the entry from another. WordPerfect refers to these special characters as *delimiters*. Delimited Text Options lets you define these characters. When you select this entry, WordPerfect displays the Setup Delimited Text Options dialog box. Most users will not have a reason to change the default delimiters.

Selecting the Keyboard Layout

WordPerfect's keyboard layout defines the operations that it performs when you press various keyboard combinations. By default, WordPerfect uses its original keyboard layout. As you begin working with WordPerfect macros, you may want to assign macros to different keyboard combinations. To do so, you can create or select a specific keyboard layout. WordPerfect does not let you assign a macro to its original keyboard layout. When you select Keyboard Layout, WordPerfect displays the Keyboard Layout dialog box, as shown in Figure 6.7.

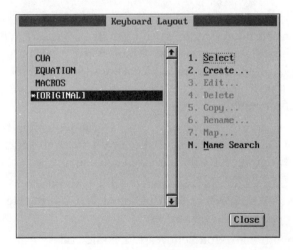

Figure 6.7 The Keyboard Layout dialog box.

In the Keyboard Layout dialog box, you can select an existing keyboard layout, make changes to the layout, or copy an existing layout so you can edit and create your own custom key definitions.

Defining the Location of WordPerfect Files

When you install WordPerfect, the installation program creates three directories on your disk:

◆ **WP60** contains your WordPerfect executable programs, macros, keyboard files, and styles.

◆ **WPC60DOS** contains WordPerfect's writer tools, such as the grammar checker.

◆ **WPDOCS** is the subdirectory in which WordPerfect places your document files unless you specify otherwise.

To control the directories in which WordPerfect stores or searches for specific files, open the Setup menu, an select **Location of Files**. When you select this option, WordPerfect displays the Location of Files dialog box, as shown in Figure 6.8.

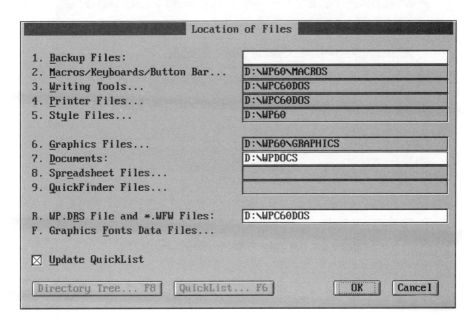

Figure 6.8 *The Location of Files dialog box.*

To change the directory in which WordPerfect stores or searches for specific files, type the number that corresponds to the directory or click on the directory box. Next, type in the directory path you desire. You may want to create a directory named WPBACKUP and direct WordPerfect to use the directory to store its backup files. In addition, if you normally store your WordPerfect document files in a specific directory, you can use the Documents directory entry to specify the desired path. By default, WordPerfect uses the directory path C:\WPDOCS.

Selecting a Color Printer Palette

If you are using a color printer, WordPerfect lets you customize its color palette. To specify the color printer palette, open the Setup menu and select **Color Palette**. WordPerfect displays the Color Printing Palettes dialog box, shown in Figure 6.9.

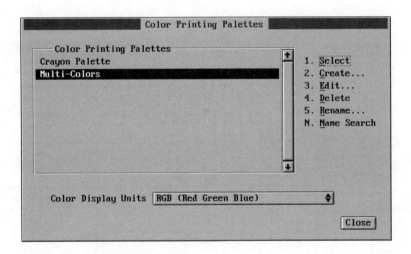

Figure 6.9 *The Color Printing Palettes dialog box.*

In this dialog box, you can select a predefined palette, make changes, or create your own palette. In addition, WordPerfect lets you select the units used to describe color values (in terms of RGB, HLS, or CYMK). To select a color printer palette, highlight the desired palette and type **S** or click on **Select**.

Summary

This chapter presented several different ways customize your WordPerfect working environment. As you work and learn more about WordPerfect, you may want to refer to this chapter to see how you can take advantage of different configuration options. Customizing your work environment often requires some trial and error. Don't be afraid to experiment. None of the options presented in this section can damage your system.

New Terms

- **Auto code placement.** WordPerfect's automatic movement of different formatting codes at the start of the document or current paragraph.

- **Color scheme.** A collection of colors that WordPerfect uses to display various screen elements.

- **Customization.** The process of selecting the options that best meet your needs and desires.

- **Delimiters.** Special characters used to differentiate items. Many lists use commas to delimit the list entries.

- **Undo.** The process of reversing the previous edit operation. If you delete a word, undoing the operation puts the word back into the document.

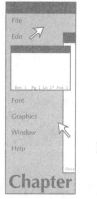

Chapter 7

Using Automatic Backups

In this chapter you:

◆ Learn how automatic backups prevent data loss

◆ Customize WordPerfect's automatic backups

◆ Use a backup file to recovery your document

◆ Save your original file contents before a Save operation

◆ Learn the importance of regularly backing up your disk

Understanding Timed Backups

In Chapter 2 you learned that the more often you save your document changes, the less work you may lose in the event of a power loss or system failure. To help protect those who don't always protect themselves, WordPerfect automatically makes a backup copy of your document file every ten minutes. If you experience a loss of power or a system error, you may be able to use the backup copy WordPerfect has created to restore (most of) your edits

Controlling Automatic Backups

When you install WordPerfect, the installation program configures it to automatically perform the backups every ten minutes. If you want to change the time interval, either increasing or decreasing it, or to ensure the automatic backup operation is active, open the File menu and choose **Setup**.

Type **E** or click on the **Environment** option. WordPerfect displays the Environment dialog box, shown in Figure 7.1.

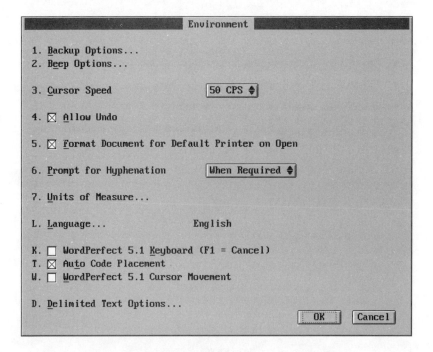

Figure 7.1 *The Environment dialog box.*

Type **B** or click on **Backup Options**. WordPerfect displays the Backup dialog box, shown in Figure 7.2.

```
┌─────────────────────────────────────────────────────────────┐
│▓▓▓▓▓▓▓▓▓▓▓▓▓▓▓▓▓▓▓▓▓▓▓▓▓▓   Backup   ▓▓▓▓▓▓▓▓▓▓▓▓▓▓▓▓▓▓▓▓▓▓▓▓│
│                                                             │
│  1. ⊠ Timed Document Backup                                 │
│  2. Minutes Between Backups:      ┌──────────────┐          │
│                                   │ 10           │          │
│                                   └──────────────┘          │
│  3. ☐ Back Up Original Document (.BK!) on Save or Exit      │
│                                                             │
│  ┌──────┐                          ┌──────┐  ┌──────────┐  │
│  │ Help │                          │  OK  │  │  Cancel  │  │
│  └──────┘                          └──────┘  └──────────┘  │
└─────────────────────────────────────────────────────────────┘
```

Figure 7.2 The Backup dialog box.

Enabling the Automatic Backup Operations

If you want WordPerfect to perform automatic backup operations, the **Timed Document Backup** field should contain an X.

To place an X in the box, type **1** or click your mouse in the box.

WordPerfect can normally perform its automatic backup operations fast enough that they don't interfere with your word processing operations. In most cases, the small delay you experience when a backup operation occurs is a small price to pay if your computer loses power or experiences a system error. If you choose to turn off WordPerfect's automatic backup operations, make sure that your regularly save your edits.

Changing the Automatic Backup Time Interval

By default, WordPerfect performs its automatic document backup operations every ten minutes. If you want to change the time interval, type **2** or click on the **Minutes Between Backups** box and type in the desired interval in minutes.

The Automatic Document Backups

WordPerfect performs automatic backups whether or not you use the **Save** option to save your edits. If you experience a system error or power loss, you can recover your edits, at least up to the last ten minutes, using the automatic backup file.

Saving Your Original Document

As you have learned, when you edit and save your document, the document file's previous contents on disk are lost. The next time you open the document file, your new edits are shown. There may be times after you edit and save changes to a document, that you wish you had not changed the original document.

To prevent the loss of the document's original contents, WordPerfect saves your original document to a different file each time you choose **Save**. Assume, for example, that you open the file AIRGIZMO.LTR and make changes. WordPerfect writes the original document to the file AIRGIZMO.BK!, and saves your edited document to AIRGIZMO.LTR. If you decide later that you don't want the changes, you can delete the file AIRGIZMO.LTR, and rename AIRGIZMO.BK! as AIRGIZMO.LTR.

WordPerfect always uses the BK! file extension for backup files. If you edit and save the contents of a document named BUDGET93.DOC, WordPerfect stores the original document in the file BUDGET93.BK!.

WordPerfecs installation program does not enable original document save operations. To turn on such operations, open the Backup dialog box, type **3** or click on the **Back Up Original Document**.

WordPerfect disables automatic backups of your original documents because each document you edit and save is stored on disk, as well as the copy of original contents. Because each document may end up with two files (the current and previous original) you can consume a great deal of disk space. If disk space is low on your system, you may want to disable automatic save operations. In addition, you may periodically want to check your WordPerfect directory for files with the BK! extension and delete them to free up disk space.

Understanding The Concept of the Original Document

It is important to understand that each time you save a document, WordPerfect considers the most recently saved contents as the original document. Assume you edit a document and remove a paragraph. If you save the file, WordPerfect stores your original document (the one with all paragraphs) with the file extension BK!, placing the document's new contents in the specified file. Next, you edit the document and remove a second paragraph. If you save the document, WordPerfect considers the previously saved document (the document minus one paragraph) as the original and writes that document to the file with the BK! extension. The actual original document, with all paragraphs, is lost.

Recovering from a Power Loss or System Error

When automatic backups are enabled, WordPerfect backs up your document at specified time intervals. It writes the document to a file with the name WP{WPC}.BKn, where *n* is a number, such as WP{WP}.BK1 or WP{WCP}.BK2, depending on the number of documents you currently have open. Normally, if you successfully exit WordPerfect, saving your files, it automatically deletes these files. If you experience a power loss, the files are not deleted. When WordPerfect starts, it checks if any of these files exist. If it finds a file, it knows an error or power loss occurred. If it finds a backup file, it displays the Backup File Exists dialog box, shown in Figure 7.3.

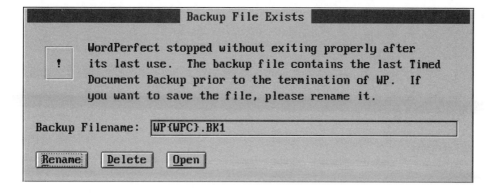

Figure 7.3 *The Backup File Exists dialog box.*

There are three options for dealing with the backup file.

1. **Rename** assigns a more meaningful name. Renaming the file lets you later examine the document's contents, while eliminating the WP{WPC}.BKn filename that causes WordPerfect to display this dialog box.
2. **Delete** removes the file without letting you examine its contents.
3. **Open** allows you to the document view contents. After viewing the contents use **Save As** to save the contents. If you select **Close**, WordPerfect displays a dialog box asking if you want to save the file's contents. If you chose **No**, it removes the backup file from your disk.

If you select **Save As** to backup the document using the document's filename, WordPerfect prompts you to insure that you want to overwrite the document file's current contents. Before you overwrite a file, examine its current contents. This way you can determine if the original file or the backup file contains the most recent edits.

Controlling Where WordPerfect Places Your Backup Files

By default, WordPerfect places your backup files in the current directory. To better organize your files, you may want to create a directory named C:\WPBACKUP and direct WordPerfect to place its backup files in this directory. If you want WordPerfect to place the backup files in a specific directory:

1. Select **Setup**.
2. Select **Location of Files**.
3. Select **Backup Files** and type in the directory path in which you want the backup files stored.

Summary

In this chapter you learned how to enable and customize WordPerfect's automatic backup operations. By allowing WordPerfect to periodically backup your documents, you reduce the possibility of lost work due to a power loss or system error. In addition, you learned how to direct WordPerfect to save a copy of your document's original file contents to a file with the BK! extension, each time you select **Save**. If you save your document's original contents in this way, you should periodically delete the backup files from your directory to reduce the amount of disk space consumed by backup files you probably won't need.

New Terms

- ◆ **Automatic backup.** A backup of your document's current content to a file on disk that WordPerfect automatically performs at specified time intervals.

- ◆ **Automatic backup file.** A file created by WordPerfect that writes the contents of your document at specified time intervals.

- ◆ **Original document.** The contents of your document immediately before the most recent **Save** operation.

- ◆ **Original document backup.** A document file containing the contents of your document immediately before the most recent **Save** operation.

Chapter 8

Getting Started with Fonts

In this chapter you:

- ◆ Select a specific font attribute such as bolding, italics, or underlining
- ◆ Change font sizes
- ◆ Use superscripting to create characters such as x^2
- ◆ Use subscripting to create characters such as H_2O
- ◆ Select a specific font

Understanding Fonts

A *font* provides a way to display characters. Each font includes a *typeface* such as Courier or Times Roman, a weight such as **bold** or *italic*, and a point size. Many books refer to italics, bolding, and underlining as font *attributes*. A point is 1/72 of an inch. This book's text uses an 11-point font (each character has a vertical width of up to 11/72 of an inch). Figure 8.1 illustrates different point sizes.

This is 11 point.

This is 18 point.
This is 24 point.

This is 48 point.

72 point is big.

Figure 8.1 Different point sizes.

As you create documents, using different fonts sizes and attributes significantly improves your document's appearance and readability. Consider the memo presented in Figure 8.2.

```
Office Memo

To: All Employees

Subject: Office Fiesta!

From: E. Conroy

========================================================

Early Bird Airlines, Inc. is very happy to
announce our Summer Fiesta! Everyone is encour-
aged to bring their families. We'll have hot
dogs, burgers, beer, margaritas, bosses and
plenty of H₂0.

    Where: Airport Park

    When: Saturday, July 4

If you need a map of Airport Park, please come by
and see me. We look forward to seeing everyone
there!

Ed
```

Figure 8.2 *Font attributes in a memo.*

In the next section, you create this memo using WordPerfect.

Selecting Font Attributes

When you create a document you can select the font size and attributes you want to use for the text. As you type, WordPerfect makes it very easy for you to use different font attributes. To select the font attribute you want to use next, select the Font menu and choose the desired attribute. For example, to bold a word you would perform these steps:

1. Open the Font menu and choose **Bold**.

2. Type the desired word.

3. Open the Font menu and choose **Normal**.

Most of the font attributes may be selected from the Font menu, as displayed in Figure 8.3.

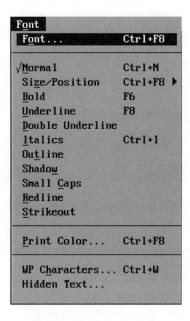

Font	
Font...	Ctrl+F8
√Normal	Ctrl+N
Size/Position	Ctrl+F8 ▶
Bold	F6
Underline	F8
Double Underline	
Italics	Ctrl+I
Outline	
Shadow	
Small Caps	
Redline	
Strikeout	
Print Color...	Ctrl+F8
WP Characters...	Ctrl+W
Hidden Text...	

Figure 8.3 *The Font menu.*

Creating the Fiesta Memo

To create the Fiesta memo previously shown in Figure 8.2, open a new document. The first words in the Fiesta memo appear in bold. Before you type these words, open the Font menu and choose **Bold**. Type the following text:

```
Office Memo
To:
```

The words *All Employees* appears in a normal font. Open the Font menu and choose **Normal**. Type *All Employees* and press **Enter** twice. Using this technique to select the **Bold** and **Normal** font attributes:

```
Subject: Office Fiesta!
From: E. Conroy
========================================================
```

The Office Memo is displayed in Figure 8.4.

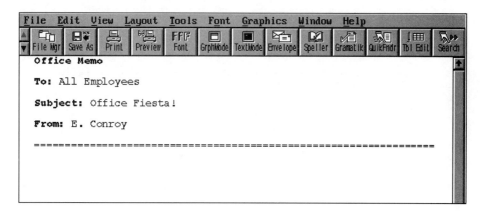

Figure 8.4 *Using Font attributes.*

The words *very happy* use the Italic attribute. Likewise, the word *Everyone* is Double Underlined and the bosses uses Strikeout. To type the **2** in H_2O, open the Font menu and select **Size/Position**. WordPerfect cascades the Size/Position menu.

Select **Subscript** and type **2**. Open the **Size/Position** menu a second time, select **Normal Position** and type the **O**. Use the bold and normal fonts as needed to complete your document. Figure 8.5 displays the Fiesta memo.

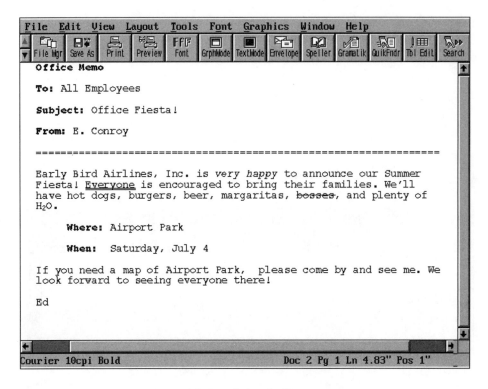

Figure 8.5 *Completing the Fiesta memo.*

Selecting a Font Size

Font sizes are normally expressed in terms of *points*, where a point is 1/72 of an inch. Most of the letters, memos, and reports you create will use an 11- or 12-point font. When you place section titles or other key information in your document, there may be times when you want to use a larger font. When you work with fonts, you normally first select a typeface, such as Courier. The typeface that you select often dictates the sizes you can use. Different typefaces support different font sizes. A Courier font, for example, may only support the font sizes 8, 10, and 12 point. If you want to use a different point size, you must select a different typeface.

If the current typeface supports multiple point sizes, you can quickly select a relative font size by using the cascading **Size/Position** options from the Font

If the current typeface supports multiple point sizes, you can quickly select a relative font size by using the cascading **Size/Position** options from the Font menu.

Size/Position lets you quickly select a Normal, Fine, Small, Large, Very Large, and Extra Large font size. If you select one of these options and the text type does not change in appearance, your current typeface does not support the relative point size. In the next section, you learn how to select a different type-face and how to display the point sizes the typeface provides. WordPerfect defines each relative font size as a percentage of the normal font size. Table 8.1 lists the relative size percentages.

Table 8.1 WordPerfect's relative font size settings.

Relative size	Percent of normal font size
Fine	60
Small	80
Large	120
Very Large	150
Extra Large	200
Super/Subscript	60

Each font typeface supports a specific number of font sizes, which vary from one typeface to the next. In many cases, if you want to use a unique font size within your document, you must first determine the typefaces that support the point size. Using **Size/Position**, you can quickly increase or decrease the size of the current font, provided the typeface supports different font sizes. When you select a font size, the size remains in effect for all text you type until you change to a different size.

Selecting a Font

When you select a font, you essentially choose a typeface, size, and attributes. Fonts come in two types, hard and soft. *Hard fonts* are built into your printer or a printer font cartridge. *Soft fonts* are files that reside on your disk that you can load into your printer's memory. Depending on your printer type, WordPerfect provides different soft fonts it loads in your printer as required. To select a font, open the Font menu and select **Font**. WordPerfect displays the Font dialog box shown in Figure 8.6.

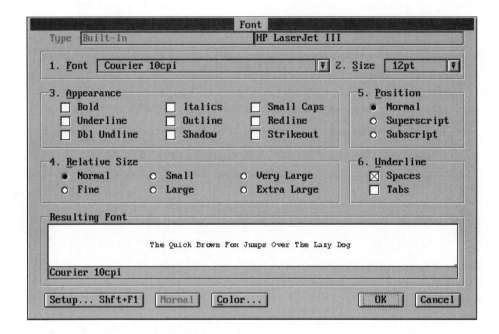

Figure 8.6 *The Font dialog box.*

In the Font dialog box, you can select a typeface, size, and attributes.

Selecting a Typeface

A font's typeface defines the shape of characters. Figure 8.7 shows several typefaces:

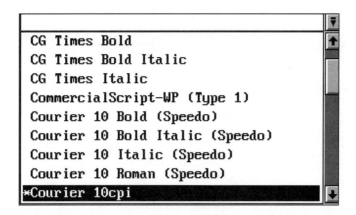

Figure 8.7 Examples of typefaces.

To select a font, type **1** in the Font dialog box or click on **Font**. WordPerfect displays a list of available fonts.

As you highlight different typefaces, WordPerfect displays an example of the typeface's use in the Resulting Font box.

A font consists of a typeface, point size, and attributes. You can select specific font settings. To chose a font:

1. Open the Font menu and choose **Font**.
2. Select the desired typeface.
3. Select the desired point size.
4. Select the desired options:
    - Position
    - Relative Size
    - Underlining
5. Select **OK** to close the Font dialog box.

Selecting a Font Size

Depending on the typeface you select, the available point sizes will differ. To select a point size, type **2** or double click on the **Size** box. WordPerfect displays a list of available point sizes:

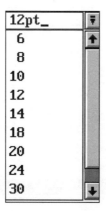

Figure 8.8 *Point sizes.*

As you highlight different point sizes, WordPerfect displays a sample of the font's use in the Resulting Font box. To select a point size, highlight the size using the Arrow keys, press **Enter**, or double click on **Size**.

Selecting the Desired Attributes

The Font dialog box lets you select one or more font attributes you want WordPerfect to apply to the font. To select or remove a font attribute, type **3** or click on **Appearance**. WordPerfect places numbers next to each attribute.

	Appearance				
1 ☐	Bold	4 ☐	Italics	7 ☐	Small Caps
2 ☐	Underline	5 ☐	Outline	8 ☐	Redline
3 ☐	Dbl Undline	6 ☐	Shadow	9 ☐	Strikeout

Figure 8.9 *The Font Attributes.*

To select or remove a specific attribute, type the attribute's number or click on the attribute.

Selecting the Font's Relative Size

To specify the font's relative size type **4** or click **Relative Size**. WordPerfect displays numbers next to each size option.

```
┌─Relative Size─────────────────────────────────────┐
│  1 ● Normal    3 ○ Small     5 ○ Very Large        │
│  2 ○ Fine      4 ○ Large     6 ○ Extra Large       │
└────────────────────────────────────────────────────┘
```

Figure 8.10 *Selecting a relative size.*

To select a relative size, type the corresponding number or click on the size.

Selecting Font Position

You can specify the desired font position: normal, superscript, or subscript. To select a font position, type **5** or click on **Position**. WordPerfect displays numbers next to each position option:

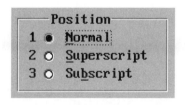

Figure 8.11 *The Position option.*

To select a position, type the corresponding number or click on the position.

Controlling Underlining

When you underline text, there may be times when you only want words underlined, while other times you may want the spaces that appear between the words underlined as well. Underline lets you control whether WordPerfect underlines spaces and white space created by a Tab. To control underlining, type **6** or click on **Underline**. WordPerfect displays numbers next to each option.

Figure 8.12 *The Underline option.*

If an entry's box contains an X, WordPerfect underlines the entry. To set or remove an X, type the entry's number or click on the entry's box.

Selecting Font Colors for a Color Printer

If you have a color printer, WordPerfect lets you assign a color to the current font. To assign a font color, select the **Font** option. Type **C** or click on the **Color** button. WordPerfect displays the Color Selection dialog box shown in Figure 8.13.

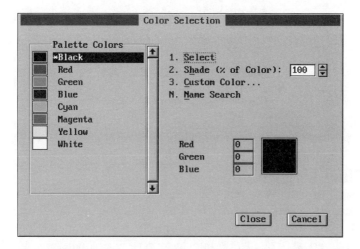

Figure 8.13 *The Color Selection dialog box.*

To assign a color to the current font, highlight the desired color and type **1** or click on **Select**.

Advanced Font Setup

As you become more familiar with fonts and acquire additional font printer cartridges or soft fonts, you need to inform WordPerfect of the font's availability. To manage your fonts, select the **Font** option. When WordPerfect displays the Font dialog box, press **Shift-F1** or click on the **Setup** button. WordPerfect displays the Font Setup dialog box as shown in Figure 8.14.

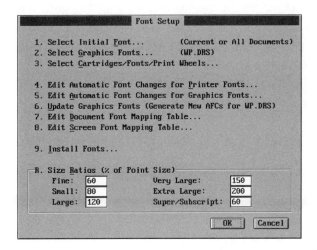

Figure 8.14 The Font Setup dialog box.

As you can see, the dialog box provides options for selecting, editing, and updating fonts. You can also use the dialog box to change the size ratios WordPerfect associates with its relative size settings.

Summary

A font consists of a typeface, point size, and attributes. By using different fonts in your documents, you can quickly draw the reader's attention to key elements.

To change font attributes, open the Font menu and select the desired settings. If you want to change the typeface and size, you can use WordPerfect's Font dialog box. After you change a font, the font remains in effect for all text you type.

New Terms

◆ **Font.** A typeface, point size, and weight that describes the appearance of printed characters.

◆ **Font weight.** An attribute of the font, such as bold or italics.

◆ **Typeface.** A complete set of characters in a particular design or style. Typefaces of different weights (such as, light, regular, and bold) make up a family of fonts.

◆ **Point.** 1/72 of an inch. Font sizes are typically expressed in terms of points, such as a 10-point font.

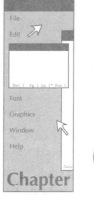

Chapter 9

Running Tutorial Lesson 1

In this chapter you:

- ◆ Learn how to use WordPerfect's built-in tutorial
- ◆ Review the lessons you learned in Chapters 1 through 8

Using WordPerfect's Built-In Tutorial

To help you become productive more quickly, WordPerfect provides an on-line tutorial that you can run from within WordPerfect. The tutorial presents essential WordPerfect concepts and techniques. The time you spend with the tutorial is time very well spent. This lesson walks you through the steps you need to perform to start the tutorial. The tutorial presents five different lessons. In this case, you will only perform Lesson 1, which reviews all of the concepts you have learned in Chapters 1 through 8 of this book. The tutorial lesson takes about fifteen minutes to complete.

To begin, press **Alt-H** or click on the **Help** menu. The Help menu is displayed in Figure 9.1.

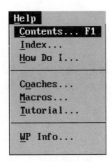

Figure 9.1 *The Help menu.*

Type **T** or click on **Tutorial**. The dialog box displayed in Figure 9.2 welcomes you to the WordPerfect tutorial.

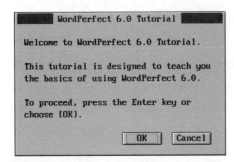

Figure 9.2 *The WordPerfect 6.0 Tutorial dialog box.*

Press **Enter** to select **OK**. A dialog box is displayed, asking you if you will be using a mouse within the tutorial. If you are using a mouse, click on **Yes**. Otherwise, select **No**. WordPerfect then displays the Tutorial's Main Menu, shown in Figure 9.3.

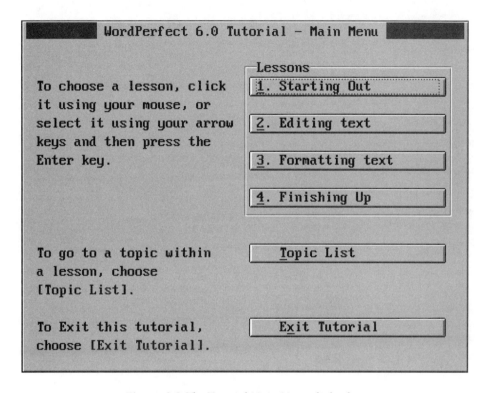

Figure 9.3 The Tutorial Main Menu dialog box.

Type **1** or click on **Starting Out**. WordPerfect displays the first dialog box for the Lesson 1 tutorial, shown in Figure 9.4.

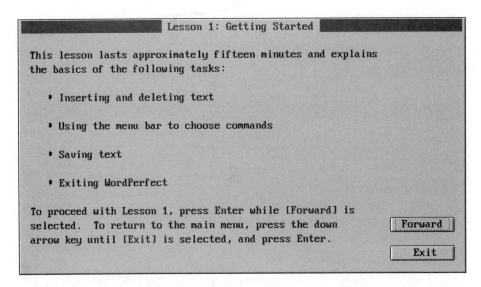

Figure 9.4 Lesson 1: Getting started.

As the tutorial runs, simply the follow the instructions that are displayed on your screen. When you complete the instructions, you normally select the **Forward** button. You can end the lesson at any time by selecting **Exit**. When you complete or exit the lesson, WordPerfect returns you to the tutorial's Main Menu. To return to WordPerfect select. **Exit Tutorial**.

Using Other Lessons

Obviously, you can use the tutorial to run any of the lessons at any time you want. However, to avoid possible confusion, you may want to use the tutorial lessons to review concepts presented in this book. As you finish learning the concepts that are presented in a tutorial lesson, this book directs you to run the corresponding lesson. From time to time, you may want to return to the tutorial to review concepts you may have forgotten.

Creating a Custom Fax Cover Sheet

With everyone using faxes these days, you will probably want to create your own custom fax cover sheet. To help you do so, the companion disk that accompanies this book provides a document file you can edit. Figure 9.5 illustrates the companion disk fax cover sheet.

FAX COVER SHEET

Company Name
Company Slogan

To: _____ From: _____
Company: _____ Pages: _____
Fax: _____ Fax: (999) 999-9999
Phone: _____ Phone: (999) 999-9999

Comments: _____
_____
_____
_____
_____
_____
_____
_____
_____
_____
_____
_____
_____

Figure 9.5 The companion disk Fax Cover Sheet.

To use the fax cover sheet:

1. Open the File menu, select **Open** and type **FAXCVR.DOC** .
2. Edit the document to include your company name, slogan, phone number and fax numbers.
3. Select **Save** from the File menu to save your changes.

Next, you can either print several copies, so you can hand write fax cover sheets as you need them, or you can open this document, and type in the cover sheet information. If you choose to type in the cover sheet information, you must move the cursor to the next line in the comments section. The document does not wrap text in the comments section from one line to the next. Instead, use the Arrow keys to advanced the cursor. After you type in the information, use the **Print/Fax** option to print the cover sheet and then, if necessary, use the **Save As** option to save the cover sheet to a document file on disk.

Summary

In this chapter you learned how to use WordPerfect's built-in tutorial to review and learn key WordPerfect concepts and techniques. As you read through the chapters of this book, you may be instructed to use specific tutorial lessons for a hands on review.

New Terms

◆   **On-line tutorial.** A computer program you can run that provides hands-on instruction for one or more topics.

Chapter 10

Displaying Document Information

In this chapter you:

◆ Type in a document summary to describes a document's contents

◆ Customize the document summary fields

◆ Print the document summary

◆ Display statistics about your document

Understanding the Document Summary

When you share documents with other office workers or when you create a large number of documents, you should take advantage of WordPerfect's *document summary* information. A document summary is simply a page of information that WordPerfect associates with your document. Items in the document summary normally include the following:

◆ The author of the document.

◆ The subject of the document.

◆ The date the document was created.

◆ The date the document was last changed (revised).

◆ The typist of the document.

◆ A descriptive name for the document.

◆ A descriptive document type.

◆ A client name for whom the document was prepared.

◆ The document's security classification.

To enter document summary information for the current document, open the File menu and choose **Summary**. The Document Summary dialog box is displayed in Figure 10.1.

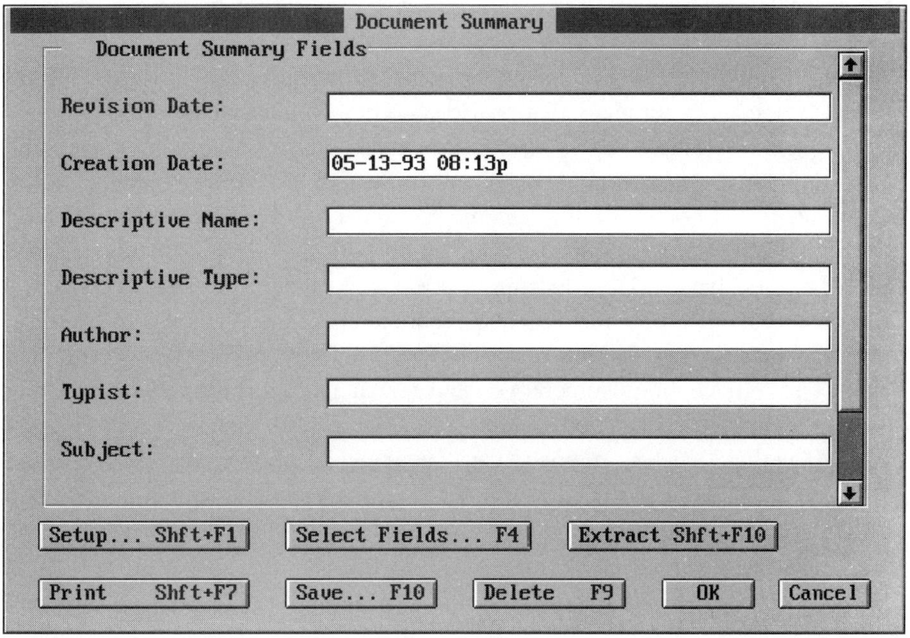

Document Summary		
Document Summary Fields		

Revision Date:	
Creation Date:	05-13-93 08:13p
Descriptive Name:	
Descriptive Type:	
Author:	
Typist:	
Subject:	

Setup... Shft+F1   Select Fields... F4   Extract Shft+F10

Print   Shft+F7   Save... F10   Delete   F9   OK   Cancel

Figure 10.1 *The Document Summary dialog box.*

Using WordPerfect's Document Summary

To help you record information about a document's contents or creation, such as who created the document, when, and why, WordPerfect provides a document summary. When you enter document summary information, WordPerfect stores the summary in your document file. To access the document summary:

1. Open the File menu and choose **Summary**.

2. Type in the information for the desired fields and, press **Tab** after each entry to move the cursor to the next field.

3. After you have completed the entries, press **Esc**, highlight **OK** and press **Enter**. If you are using a mouse, simply click on **OK**.

Pressing **Tab** advances the cursor to the next document summary field. If you press **Shift-Tab** WordPerfect moves the cursor back to the previous field.

WordPerfect stores the document summary information in the document.

When to Use the Document Summary

If you work in an office where document exchange is common, you should always complete a document summary that provides users with information about the document's origin. If multiple copies of a document are created, users can examine the document summary to determine which document file is the most recent. If you use WordPerfect at home, use the document summary to record specifics about the document. As the number of document files on your disk increases, there will be times when you have trouble locating a specific document file. WordPerfect lets you search your document files for document summary information. For example, if you type a memo to your boss regarding Product distribution to Mexico, and you later need to retrieve the document, you can search all your documents for the one whose summary contains specific text (See Chapter 19). The few minutes you spend typing the document summary can save you a lot of time later on.

Get in the habit of completing the document summary information for every document you create.

Printing the Document Summary

Normally, you will only view the document summary on your screen so you can look up specific details. However, if you have a question about a document that was created by another user, you might want to print a copy of its summary information. Figure 10.2 illustrates how a typical document summary prints.

```
Revision Date:
Creation Date:       05-13-93
Descriptive Name:    Office Fiesta Invitation
Descriptive Type:    Office Memo
Author:              Mary Smith
Typist:              Ed Conroy
Subject:             Office Fiesta
Account:
Keywords:            Party
Abstract:            Office Fiesta, July 4, Airport Park
```

Figure 10.2 A printed document summary.

To print a document summary:

1. Open the File menu and choose **Summary**.
2. Press **Shift-F7** or click on the **Print** button.
3. WordPerfect displays a dialog box asking you if you want to print the document summary. Select **Yes**.

Customizing the Document Summary

When you install WordPerfect, everyone is assigned the same set of document summary fields. You will probably want to customize the document summary fields to better suit your needs. When you customize document fields, you can do so for the current document summary only, or you can customize the default summary that WordPerfect displays for every document. To customize the document summary, select **Summary**. WordPerfect displays the Select Summary Fields dialog box, shown in Figure 10.3. Press **F4** or click on the **Select Fields** button.

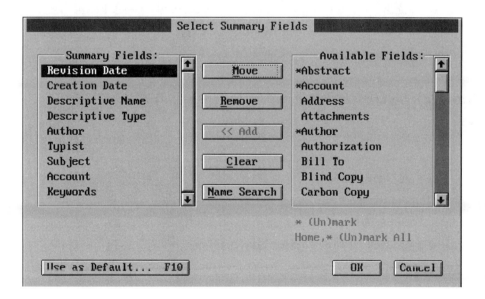

Figure 10.3 *The Select Summary Fields dialog box.*

In the dialog box, you can remove, add, or reorder document summary fields.

Adding a Document Summary Field

To add a document summary field:

1. If Summary Fields and Available Fields are not preceded by a 1 and 2, press **Esc**.
2. Type **2** to select **Available Fields** or click your mouse in the box.
3. Using the Arrow keys, highlight the desired field or click on the field.
4. Press **Enter** or click on the **Add** button.
5. Repeat steps 3 and 4 for each field you want to add.

Removing a Document Summary Field

To remove a document summary field:

1. If Summary Fields and Available Fields are not preceded by a 1 and 2, press **Esc**.
2. Type **1** to select Summary Fields or click your mouse in the box.
3. Using the Arrow keys, highlight the desired field or click on the field.
4. Press **Alt-R** or click on the **Remove** button.
5. Repeat steps 3 and 4 for each field you want to remove.

Moving a Document Summary Field

WordPerfect lets you rearrange your document summary fields. To move a field:

1. If the Summary Fields and Available Fields are not preceded by a 1 and 2, press **Esc**.
2. Type **1** to select **Summary Fields** or click your mouse in the box.
3. Using the Arrow keys, highlight the desired field or click on the field.
4. Type **Alt-M** or click on the **Move** button.
5. Using the Arrow keys, move the field to the desired location and press **Enter**.
6. Repeat Steps 3 through 5 for each field you want to move.

Saving Your Customized Document Field

When you change the document summary fields, WordPerfect customizes it for the current document by default. If you want to use the customized document summary for each document you create, select the **Use as Default** button.

Prompting for a Document Summary

By default, you create a document summary by selecting the File menu **Summary** option. Since WordPerfect does not remind you to create a summary for every document it is easy to forget. You can display the Document Summary dialog box when you first save a document file. This way, you are more likely to remember to complete the summary. To automatically prompt for a document summary:

1. Choose **Summary**.
2. When WordPerfect displays the Document Summary dialog box, press **Shift-F1** or click on the **Setup** button. WordPerfect displays the Document Summary Setup dialog box displayed in Figure 10.4.

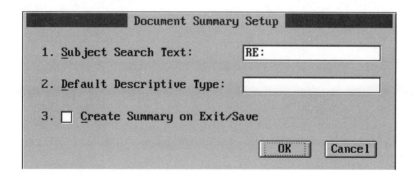

Figure 10.4 The Document Summary Setup dialog box.

3. Type **3** or click on **Create Summary on Exit/Save**. An X is placed in the box.
4. Press **Enter** or click on **OK**.

Displaying Document Statistics

If you are using WordPerfect to create reports or journal articles, you often have to make sure it meets a length criteria. For example, at least five hundred words or no more than three thousand words. To help you determine statistics about a document, use the Document Information dialog box displayed in Figure 10.5.

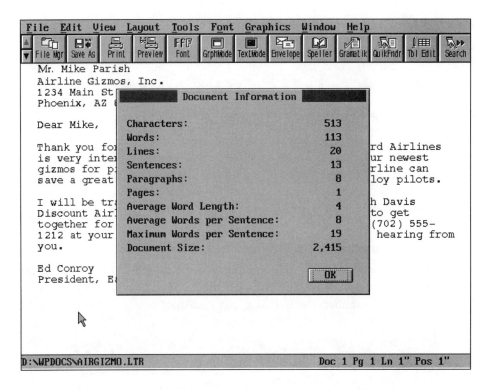

Figure 10.5 *The Document Information dialog box.*

To display the Document Information dialog box:

1. Open the Tools menu and choose **Writing Tools**. The Writing Tools dialog box is displayed.

2. Type **4** or click on **Document Information**. The information about your current document is displayed.

Creating a Travel Checklist

If you are a business traveler who is on the road a lot, you may have a packing ritual you go through before every trip. To make sure you pack the items you need, the companion disk that accompanies this book provides a travel checklist. Actually, the companion disk provides two checklists, one for a woman and one for a man, shown in Figure 10.6 and 10.7, respectively.

WOMEN'S TRAVEL CHECKLIST

CLOTHING

❏	Blouses	❏	Skirts
❏	Coats	❏	Slacks
❏	Hosiery	❏	Suits
❏	Jackets	❏	Sweaters
❏	Shoes	❏	Underwear

ACCESSORIES

❏	Belts	❏	Hats
❏	Gloves	❏	Jewelry
❏	Handkerchiefs	❏	Scarfs

TOILETRIES

❏	Brush/comb	❏	Mouthwash
❏	Curlers	❏	Perfume/cologne
❏	Curling iron	❏	Razor
❏	Deoderant	❏	Shampoo/conditioner
❏	Hairdryer	❏	Skin care products
❏	Hairspray/styling lotion	❏	Toothbrush
❏	Makeup	❏	Toothpaste

LEASURE & RECREATION

❏	Book	❏	Running suit
❏	Casual shoes	❏	Shorts
❏	Pajamas	❏	Suntan lotion
❏	Robe	❏	Swimsuit

MISCELLANEOUS

❏	Business cards	❏	Road maps
❏	Credit cards	❏	Travel tickets
❏	Flashlight	❏	Travelers checks
❏	Notebook & pen	❏	Umbrella

Figure 10.6 *The companion disk Travel Checklist for women.*

MEN'S TRAVEL CHECKLIST

CLOTHING

❏	Coats	❏	Shoes
❏	Jackets	❏	Socks
❏	Neckties	❏	Suits
❏	Pants	❏	Sweaters
❏	Shirts	❏	Underwear

ACCESSORIES

❏	Belts	❏	Handkerchiefs
❏	Gloves	❏	Jewelry

TOILETRIES

❏	Aftershave/cologne	❏	Shampoo/conditioner
❏	Brush/comb	❏	Shaving razor
❏	Deoderant	❏	Shaving cream
❏	Hairspray/styling lotion	❏	Toothbrush
❏	Mouthwash	❏	Toothpaste

LEASURE & RECREATION

❏	Book	❏	Running suit
❏	Casual shoes	❏	Shorts
❏	Pajamas	❏	Suntan lotion
❏	Robe	❏	Swimsuit

MISCELLANEOUS

❏	Business cards	❏	Road maps
❏	Credit cards	❏	Travel tickets
❏	Flashlight	❏	Travelers checks
❏	Notebook & pen	❏	Umbrella

Figure 10.7 The companion disk Travel Checklist for men.

To use the travel checklist:

1. Select **Open** from the File menu.
2. Type in the document name **MANTRV.DOC** or if you want the women's list, type **WOMANTRV.DOC**.
3. Change the list contents to suit your needs. Use the File menu **Save** option to save your changes.
4. Select **Print/Fax** to print a copy of the document.

After you examine the list's contents, you might want to add, remove, or edit entries. Before you travel, you can print a copy of the document and check off items as you pack.

Summary

The document summary lets you record key facts about a document or information you can use later to you locate a document file on disk. You should complete a document summary for every document file you create. To better suit your needs, WordPerfect lets you customize the document summary to include specific information fields.

As you create different documents, there may be times when you need to know such specifics as the number of characters, words, or sentences your document contains. Likewise, you may need to know average word or sentence length. WordPerfect lets you quickly display statistics about your document.

New Terms

- ◆ **Default document summary.** The document summary that WordPerfect uses for every document you create unless told to do otherwise.
- ◆ **Document statistics.** Specifics about your document such as the number of characters, words, sentences and average paragraph word length.

◆ **Document summary.** An informational page WordPerfect stores in your document file that describes who created the document, the date the document was created and last changed, and possibly many more fields.

◆ **Revision date.** The date the document was last changed (revised).

Chapter 11

Understanding Block Operations

In this chapter you:

- ◆ Select a block of text
- ◆ Apply a specific font to a block of text
- ◆ Delete a block of text
- ◆ Move a block of text
- ◆ Copy a block of text
- ◆ Print a block of text
- ◆ Select a sentence, paragraph, or page
- ◆ Understand the clipboard
- ◆ Perform Lesson 2 of WordPerfect's online tutorial

Understanding Block Operations

All of the document editing to this point has been done a character or possibly a word at a time. Many times, however, you may want to work with a group of words, sentences, or paragraphs—in other words, with a block of text. For example, there may be times when you want to move, copy, or delete a block of text. Likewise, you might want to assign a specific font to a passage of your text, or change the margins for a given part of your document. WordPerfect defines such operations as *block operations*. So that you have a document with which you can perform your block operations, open the File menu, choose **New** and type in the following names and phone numbers:

```
David Smith      (702) 555-4567
John Abbott      (602) 555-5678
Joanne Baker     (303) 555-6789
Alice Tamber     (206) 555-7890
Bambi Wyatt      (212) 555-1212
David Smith      (702) 555-4567
John Abbott      (602) 555-5678
```

Selecting a Block of Text

To perform a block operation:

1. Select a block of text.
2. Move the cursor to the first item in the block. In this case, move the cursor to the start of the first name in the list.
3. Open the Edit menu displayed in Figure 11.1.

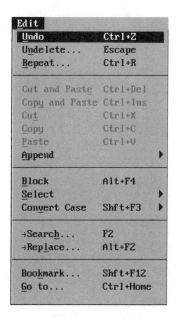

Figure 11.1 *The Edit menu.*

4. Select the **Block** option. Notice your status bar has changed to include the words *Block on*.

5. Press the **Down Arrow** key to move the cursor to the end of the list. As you move the cursor, WordPerfect highlights the block by displaying it in reverse video as displayed Figure 11.2.

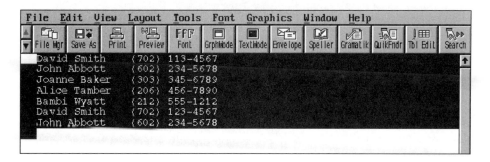

Figure 11.2 *WordPerfect displays selected text in reverse video.*

6. After the text is selected open the Font menu and choose **Italics**. WordPerfect immediately displays the previously selected names using italics. Note that after you perform the operation (in this case assigning italics), WordPerfect removes the block highlight and the words *Block on,* from your status bar.

Canceling a Block Selection

If you select the wrong text, or decide you don't want to perform a block operation, you can cancel the selection by performing any one of the following:

◆ Press **Esc**.

◆ Open the Edit menu and choose **Block.**

◆ Click on the mouse.

When you cancel the block operation, WordPerfect turns off the reverse video highlight and removes the words *Block on* from your status bar.

Applying a Font Attribute

In Chapter 8 you learned how to use fonts by selecting a font and then typing. If text already exists in your document, and you want to apply a specific font:

1. Move the cursor to the start of the desired text.

2. Open the Edit menu and choose **Block**.

3. Move the cursor to the end of the text, highlighting the text in reverse video.

4. Open the Font menu and choose the desired attribute.

Selecting Text Using Your Mouse

If you are using a mouse, WordPerfect lets you quickly select text by performing a *drag operation*. To drag your mouse:

1. Aim the mouse pointer at the start of the desired text.

2. Hold down the mouse button and move the mouse pointer to the end of the text.

3. As you move the mouse with the button depressed, WordPerfect selects the corresponding block, displaying the block in reverse video. As before the words   are displayed in your status bar.

4. To cancel a selection, click your mouse.

Performing Block Operations

After you select a block, you can quickly delete, copy, move, print or even change the case of words (to all uppercase or lowercase).

Deleting a Block

To delete text, you have used the **Del** or **Backspace** keys to erase text one character at a time. If you want to delete a block of text:

1. Select the desired block.

2. Press the **Del** or **Backspace** key.

If you examine the list of names and phone numbers that appear in your current document, you will find that David Smith and John Abbott appear twice. Using the Edit menu **Block** option or a mouse drag operation, select the last occurrence of these two names. Next, press **Del**. WordPerfect removes the block (the two names) from your document.

If you inadvertently delete the wrong block, you may be able to recover the block by opening the Edit menu and choosing **Undelete**. When you select Undelete, WordPerfect restores the deleted text and displays a dialog box asking you if you want to restore the deletion. Select **Restore**.

Printing a Block of Text

If your document is large, there may be times when you only want to print a specific section. To print a selected block of text:

1. Select the block.

2. Open the File menu and choose **Print**.

3. In the Print dialog box, select the **Blocked Text** and choose **Print**.

Changing the Case of a Block

WordPerfect lets you covert the characters in a block to upper or lowercase, or you can capitalize only the first letter of each word. In this case, covert the names in your phone list to uppercase by selecting the names and then opening the Edit menu **Convert Case** option. The Convert Case menu is displayed in Figure 11.3.

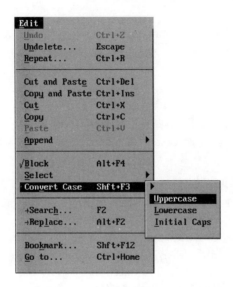

Figure 11.3 *The cascaded Convert Case menu.*

Moving a Block of Text

Moving a block is often called a *cut-and-paste* operation because conceptually, you are cutting the block out of your document, and pasting it back in at a different location. If you examine your list of names and phone numbers, you find that the name David Smith is not in alphabetical order. To move David Smith to the correct location:

1. Select the line containing the name David Smith and his phone number.

2. Open the Edit menu and choose **Cut**. The block is removed from view.

3. Move the cursor to the correct location, in this case, the start of the line containing the name Alice Tamber.

4. Open the Edit menu and choose **Paste**. WordPerfect inserts the name at the correct location.

If WordPerfect does not advance the name Alice Tamber to the start of the new line, but leaves the name to the right of David Smith's phone number, press **Enter** to move Alice down one line. WordPerfect leaves the previous name on the same line if you do not select the paragraph marker (at the end of the line) that followed David Smith's phone number.

When you perform a Cut and Paste operation, the selected text temporarily removed from the document. It places the text into a storage location that it calls the *clipboard*. If the clipboard previously contained other information, the old information is overwritten by the selected block. If you perform a Paste operation later, a copy of the clipboard's contents are placed at the current cursor position.

Copying a Block of Text

Copying text is very similar to the Cut and Paste operation. The difference is WordPerfect does not remove the selected text from your document as it copies the text to the clipboard. For example, you need two copies of your phone list. To copy the names and numbers:

1. Select the block.

2. Open the Edit menu and choose **Copy**.

3. Move the cursor to the end of the phone list.

4. Select **Paste**.

When you work with multiple documents, a common operation is to copy text from one to the other. If you use the **Copy** option, you can copy the desired text to the clipboard. Then, you can select the second document, position the cursor, and use the Edit menu **Paste** option to copy the text from the clipboard.

When you paste text from the clipboard, WordPerfect does not remove the clipboard's contents. If you use the **Paste** option three times, WordPerfect inserts three copies of the clipboard's contents into your text.

NOTE

Select **Paste** a second time to place a third copy of the names and numbers into your document. Before you continue, delete the second and third copies of the names and numbers by performing a block operation.

 Understanding the Clipboard. WordPerfect uses a *clipboard* to temporarily hold information during a cut and paste operation. It has only one clipboard. Each time you perform a cut or copy operation, WordPerfect overwrites the clipboard's previous contents with the newly selected block. When you perform a Paste operation it does not erase or remove the clipboard contents. If you need five copies of the clipboard's contents, use **Paste** option five times.

Cut-and-Paste and Copy-and-Paste Options

In addition to the **Cut**, **Copy**, and **Paste** options, WordPerfect provides **Cut and Paste** and **Copy and Paste** options. The Cut and Paste option combines the steps you need to perform in order to move selected text. When you select **Cut and Paste** the selected text is removed from your screen. It displays a message in your status bar.

When you position the cursor and press **Enter**, WordPerfect moves the block as desired. The Copy and Paste options are similar exceptions since they do not remove the selected block from your screen.

Appending a Block of Text

Cut and **Copy** options, you can move or copy selected text to the clipboard and overwrites the clipboard's contents. You may want to use the clipboard to build a list. For example, to list your names and numbers sorted by area code:

1. Select **Alice Tamber**.
2. Open the Edit menu and select **Copy** to copy the name and number to the clipboard.
3. Select **Bambi Wyatt**.
4. Choose **Append** from cascaded menu displayed in Figure 11.4.

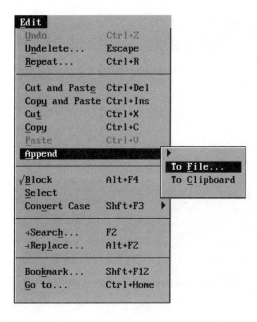

Figure 11.4 *The Cascading Append menu.*

5. Select the **To Clipboard**. WordPerfect copies the selected text from your document, appending it to the contents of your clipboard. It does not remove the selected text from your document. By selecting and appending each name and number in this way, you can build the sorted list within the clipboard.

6. When the list is done, you can use **Paste** to place the list in the document.

Other Operations

Many of the operations discussed throughout this book can be performed on the current document or on selected text. For example, you can save selected text to a file, you can Spell Check selected text, or you can apply a specific margin or text alignment to a block of text.

As you edit your documents, there will be times when you want to select the current sentence, paragraph, or page. To help you perform such operations, choose the **Select** option. The cascaded Select menu is displayed in Figure 11.5.

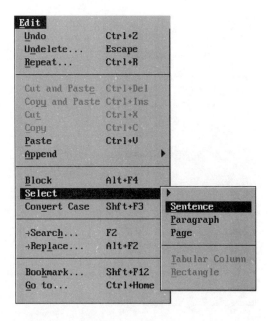

Figure 11.5 *Cascading the Select menu.*

If you choose the Sentence, Paragraph, or Page option, WordPerfect selects the corresponding item.

Understanding the Delete Buffer

The clipboard is a temporary storage location WordPerfect uses to hold a block of text during a move (cut-and-paste) or copy operation. In a similar way, WordPerfect uses three *delete buffers*. When you delete information from your document, it stores the information in a delete buffer. The first item you delete is placed in the first delete buffer. The second item you delete is placed in the second delete buffer and so on. If you delete a fourth item, it overwrites the contents of the first delete buffer, replacing it with the fourth item. In this way, WordPerfect always keeps track of your last three deletions. If you later decide you want undelete previously erased text, you can do so, provided the text is still in one of the delete buffers.

To better understand how the delete buffers work, select and delete John Abbott's name and phone number. The deleted line is placed in a delete buffer.

To better understand how the delete buffers work, select and delete John Abbott's name and phone number. The deleted line is placed in a delete buffer. Select and delete the line containing the name Joanne Baker and David Smith.

To undelete the text, open the Edit menu and choose **Undelete**. Your last deletion is shown in reverse video on your screen. The Undelete dialog box is displayed in Figure 11.6.

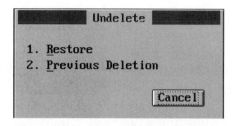

Figure 11.6 *The Undelete dialog box.*

To undelete this text, type **R** or click on the **Restore** option. If you select the **Previous Deletion** option, WordPerfect displays your second text deletion, and so on. Using the **Undelete** option, you can quickly recover inadvertently deleted text.

The Undo Option

When you perform block operations, there may be times when you perform the wrong operation on a block of text. You can select **Undo** to reverse the operation's effect.

Running Tutorial Lesson 2

In Chapter 9 you performed the tutorial's first lesson. Perform these steps to run the tutorial's second lesson:

1. Select the Help menu and choose **Tutorial**.
2. When the introductory screen is displayed select **OK**.

3. Select **Yes** or **No** to indicate whether or not you want to use a mouse.

4. Type **2** or click on **Editing Text**

5. Perform the instructions that appear on your ,screen to run lesson 2.

6. To exit type **X** or click **Exit Tutorial**

Summary

Operations that you perform on one or more characters are called *block opera-tions*. Common block operations include moving, copying, deleting, or printing specific text. Before you can perform a block operation, you must identify the desired text. Moving a block of text is often called a cut-and-paste operation. To move or copy a block, WordPerfect uses a temporary storage location called the clipboard. As you move text to the clipboard, WordPerfect overwrites the clip-board's previous contents. Using the Edit menu Paste option, you can place as many copies of the clipboard's contents into your document as you desire.

New Terms

◆ **Block**. One or more characters (and graphic images) you select for use in a specific operation.

◆ **Block operation**. An operation performed on a selected block of text. Typical block operations include moving, copying, deleting, and print-ing.

◆ **Clipboard.** A temporary storage location to which WordPerfect moves text during a cut and paste operation, or copies text during a block copy.

◆ **Cut-and-paste.** The process of removing a block from one location in your document (cutting) and placing the block in another (pasting).

12

Searching for and Replacing Text

In this chapter you:

◆ Search your document for a specific word or phrase

◆ Search for specific formatting codes

◆ Replace occurrences of a word or phrase

◆ Replace one formatting code with another

Searching Your Document for a Specific Word or Phrase

When your documents are small, you can normally view their contents by performing one or two **PgDn** operations. As the size of your documents increase, locating specific text within the document can become more time consuming. To help you locate specific text ,you can search for a word or phrase. To better understand the search operations, create the following letter:

Dear Jeff,

I wanted to make sure that you ordered the correct paper for the party invitations. As you will recall, we planned on using black print on a white paper. Please make sure that you order 250 sheets. We need to get the invitations out this week. Invitations will take about a week through the mail. Don't forget to get enough envelopes. Call me later.

Mike

Searching for a Word or Phrase

To search your document for a specific word or phrase:

1. Open the Edit menu and choose **Search**. The Search dialog box is displayed in Figure 12.1.

```
┌──────────────────────────────────────────────────────────────┐
│▓▓▓▓▓▓▓▓▓▓▓▓▓▓▓▓▓▓▓▓▓▓▓▓▓▓▓▓▓ Search ▓▓▓▓▓▓▓▓▓▓▓▓▓▓▓▓▓▓▓▓▓▓▓▓▓▓│
│                                                                │
│  Search For: ┌──────────────────────────────────────────────┐ │
│              └──────────────────────────────────────────────┘ │
│                                                                │
│    □ Backward Search          □ Find Whole Words Only          │
│    □ Case Sensitive Search    □ Extended Search (Hdrs, Ftrs, etc.) │
│                                                                │
│  ┌ Codes... F5 ┐ ┌ Specific Codes... Shft+F5 ┐   ┌ Search F2 ┐ ┌ Cancel ┐ │
│  └─────────────┘ └───────────────────────────┘   └───────────┘ └────────┘ │
└──────────────────────────────────────────────────────────────┘
```

Figure 12.1 *The Search dialog box.*

2. Type **Jeff** and press **F2** or click on **Search**. If you have just typed the document, and the cursor is at the end of the document, WordPerfect displays the Not found dialog box.

When you perform a Search, WordPerfect, by default, searches your document from the current cursor position toward the end of the document. If it does not find the text by the time it reaches the end of the document, it displays the Not found dialog box.

3. Press **F2** to direct WordPerfect to display the Search dialog box.

4. When the dialog box appears, search backward, toward the start of the document. Press **Esc**.

5. Numbers are displayed before each of the dialog box options. Type **2** or click on the **Backward Search** box.

As a rule try to search forward in your document, from the start toward the end. Searching backward, especially in a large document can be very time consuming.

In the above example the cursor is placed immediately after the name Jeff, which appears in the document's first line. Each time matching text is successfully located, the cursor is placed immediately to the right of the text. In many cases, the text occurrence WordPerfect locates may not be the occurrence that you desire. Assume you want to move the cursor to the word *sure* that appears in the text, *Please make sure,* in the third line. If you search from the start of the document, WordPerfect first locates the word *sure* in the first line of the document, in the text *to make sure.* Because the occurrence found is not the one you desired, you can repeat the search operation (by pressing **F2** twice) from the current cursor position. The next occurrence of the word *sure,* is the one you desire.

To quickly repeat a search of the same word or phrase, press **F2** twice in fast succession. The first time displays the Search dialog box that contains the text for which you just searched. The second time directs WordPerfect to search for the text. Because you are not changing the search text, you can press **F2** very quickly, without having to use the Search dialog box.

Using the Button to Search. If you have enabled the button bar, you can display the Search dialog box by clicking on the **Search** button.

Understanding Case Sensitive Searches

By default, when a search operation is performed, it ignores the case of words–meaning WordPerfect doesn't care if letters appear in uppercase or lowercase. There may be times, when you can move the cursor to a specific location by performing a case dependent search. For example, assume that the cursor is at the start of the previous letter. If you want to locate the word *Invitations* that starts the fourth sentence and you search for *invitations,* it finds matches in the first and third sentences, before locating the text you desire. To perform a case dependent search operation, you must type in the text using the exact uppercase and lowercase letters and then select **Case Sensitive Search** in the Search dialog box.

Understanding Whole Word Searches

When WordPerfect searches for text, by default, it matches each occurrence of your text, even if the text occurs inside a second word. If the cursor is at the start of the previous letter and you are searching for the word *order,* the word *ordered* is matched first, because *ordered* contains the word *order.* If you only want to match whole word occurrences (as opposed to occurrences that appear in another word), select **Find Whole Words Only** in the Search dialog box

Understanding Extended Searches

The text that appears in a header or footer is considered distinct from the document text. Depending on how you are editing your document, there may be times when you want to search these document objects. A search that extends beyond the document's standard text is called an *extended search.* To perform an extended search, select **Extended Search** in the Search dialog box.

Searching for Document Codes

Formatting codes are placed throughout a document. Normally, you aren't aware that these formatting codes are used. If you bold a word, a code is inserted that tells it where to turn bolding on, and where to turn bolding off. When you select a different font size, WordPerfect inserts a formatting code. Chapter 38 discusses formatting codes in detail. When you become more conversant with such codes, there may be times when you want to search for a specific code. For example, you might want to search your document for italic text.

To search for formatting codes:

1. Display the Search dialog box and press **F5** or click on the **Codes** button. The Search Codes dialog box is displayed Figure 12.2.

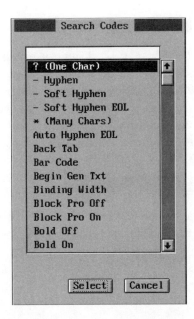

Figure 12.2 The Search Codes dialog box.

2. Using the Arrow keys or the scroll bar, highlight the desired code and choose the **Select** button.

To search for specific codes that change the size, type, or location of a code:

1. Select the Search dialog box and press **Shift-F5** or click on **Specific Codes**. The Specific Codes dialog box is displayed in Figure 12.3.

Figure 12.3 *The Specific Codes dialog box.*

2.   Highlight the desired code and choose the **Select** option.

Replacing One Word or Phrase with Another

As your document size increases, you may find that simple operations such as replacing one word or phrase throughout your document becomes time consuming. To simplify such operations, Search and Replace operations are provided. To better understand search and Replace operations:

1.   Move the cursor to the start of the previous letter.
2.   Open the Edit menu and choose **Replace**, or press **Alt-F2**. The Search and Replace dialog box is displayed in Figure 12.4.

```
┌──────────────────────────────────────────────────────────────┐
│ ▓▓▓▓▓▓▓▓▓▓▓▓▓▓▓▓▓▓      Search  and  Replace      ▓▓▓▓▓▓▓▓▓▓▓▓ │
│                                                                │
│  Search For:   ┌──────────────────────────────────────────┐  │
│    ·           │ _                                        │  │
│                └──────────────────────────────────────────┘  │
│  Replace With: ┌──────────────────────────────────────────┐  │
│                │ <Nothing>                                │  │
│                └──────────────────────────────────────────┘  │
│                                                                │
│        ☐ Confirm Replacement      ☐ Find Whole Words Only     │
│        ☐ Backward Search          ☐ Extended Search (Hdrs, Ftrs, etc.) │
│        ☐ Case Sensitive Search    ☐ Limit Number of Matches:  │
│                                                                │
│   ┌─────────────┐ ┌────────────────────────┐  ┌──────────┐ ┌────────┐ │
│   │ Codes... F5 │ │ Specific Codes... Shft+F5 │  │ Replace F2 │ │ Cancel │ │
│   └─────────────┘ └────────────────────────┘  └──────────┘ └────────┘ │
└──────────────────────────────────────────────────────────────┘
```

Figure 12.4 *The Search and Replace dialog box.*

3. In the Search For field, type in the word **invitations** and press **Tab**.

4. The cursor advances to the Replace With field. Type in the word **invites** and press **F2** or click on **Replace. Each** occurrence of the word is replaced, displaying a dialog box showing the number of replacements made:

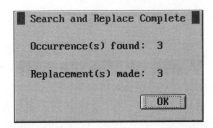

Figure 12.5 *The Search And Replace Complete dialog box.*

Unless told to do otherwise, WordPerfect replaces each occurrence of the word it locates between the current cursor position and the end of your document. In many cases, you only want to replace specific instances of a word or phrase. To perform selective replacements:

1. Select the **Confirm Replacement** box in the Search and Replace dialog box.

2. In the Confirm Replacement dialog box, a matching occurrence is highlighted, displaying the Confirm Replacement dialog box.

3. To replace the highlighted text, select **Yes**.

4. To leave this occurrence unchanged, select **No**.

5. To replace each remaining occurrence, select the **Replace All** option.

6. To end the replacement operation, select **Cancel**.

In later chapters, you learn how to add the search and replace option to a button bar button.

Restricting the Number of Replacements

Depending on your document's contents, there may be times when you want to replace the first five or ten occurrences of a word. You can select the **Limit Number of Matches** option from the Search and Replace dialog box. WordPerfect displays a small box letting you type in a number from 1 through 9999.

If you want to change the first two occurrences of the word *invitations* to *invites*, move to the start of the letter and then use the **Limit Number of Matches** option.

Deleting a Word or Phrase throughout Your Document

There may be times when you want to remove each occurrence of a word or phrase. Using your letter about the party invitations, remove each occurrence of the word *that*:

1. Open the Search and Replace dialog box.

2. In the Search For field, type in the word **that** and press **Tab**.

3. In the Replace With field, remove all the text. In this way, you are replacing the word *that* with nothing. As a result, each occurrence of the word is removed.

Replacing Formatting Codes

WordPerfect makes extensive use of formatting codes throughout your documents. When you begin working with formatting codes, there may be times when you want to replace one code with another. Assume your document contains three occurrences of the word *happy*, one that appears in italics. You want to replace the italicized word with the same word in bold, leaving the other occurrences unchanged.

1. Open the Search and Replace dialog box.
2. In the Search For field, select **Codes** to access the Search Codes dialog box.
3. Select the **[Italic On]** code.
4. Type the word **happy.**
5. Using the Search Codes dialog box, select the **[Italic Off]** code.
6. Using these same techniques, you replace the text using the following codes:

Figure 12.6 *Replacing text in code.*

Because the italicized word only has two matches, the other two occurrences of the word happy remain unchanged.

Other Search and Replace Options

The Search and Replace operations combine a search operation discussed at the start of this chapter with an optional text replacement. Many of the dialog box options that appear in the Search and Replace dialog box are identical in function to those previously discussed for search operations.

Summary

As you edit large documents, finding a specific word or phrase in the document can be quite time consuming. To help you perform such operations, WordPerfect searches the document for specific text. You must remember that by default, WordPerfect searches from the current cursor position to the end of the document. If the word or phrase you are searching appears above the current cursor position, it may not be found. If WordPerfect successfully matches the text, it stops the search operation, placing the cursor immediately after the last matching letter. If the occurrence WordPerfect finds is not the occurrence that you desire, you can quickly repeat a search operation by pressing **F2** twice in quick succession.

As your documents increase in length, there may be times when you want to replace one word or phrase with another, or remove each occurrence of the word or phrase that appears throughout your document. WordPerfect provides a Search and Replace operation that lets you quickly do just that. Each matching occurrence is replaced without asking you to verify the replacement. If you only want to replace a specific number of occurrences, or if you want to individually specify the occurrences it changes, you must use the Search and Replace dialog box to select operations.

New Terms

- ◆ **Case sensitive search.** A search operation for which WordPerfect must match exactly, the uppercase and lowercase letters of the specified word or phrase with a corresponding word or phrase in the document.

- ◆ **Extended search.** A search operation that searches text beyond that normally classified as document text, such as headers, footers, and so on.

- ◆ **Formatting code.** A special code placed in your document that controls some aspect of the document's formatting. For example, WordPerfect uses the formatting codes [Bold On] and [Bold Off] to control when it turns bolding on and off. Normally, the formatting codes are not visible on your screen.

Chapter 13

Justifying Text

In this chapter you:

- ◆ Left, right, and fully justify a paragraph
- ◆ Center text in your document

Understanding Text Justification

Justification controls how text appears in your margins. All of the letters and memos you have created throughout this book have been left justified only, meaning that the text aligns along the left margins. The text along the right margin, however, is probably jagged. Consider the following text (the preamble to the Constitution):

```
We the people of the United States, in order to form
a more perfect Union, establish justice, insure
domestic tranquillity, provide for the common
defense, promote the general welfare, and secure the
blessings of liberty to ourselves and our posterity,
do ordain and establish this Constitution for the
United States of America.
```

In this case, the text appears *left justified*, meaning text that appears along the left margin is aligned. When you prepare a memo or letter, you will normally use left justification. In the opposite way, right justification, aligns text to the right margin, possibly leaving the text's left margin jagged:

```
We the people of the United States, in order to form
        a more perfect Union, establish justice, insure
            domestic tranquillity, provide for the common
   defense, promote the general welfare, and secure the
    blessings of liberty to ourselves and our posterity,
            do ordain and establish this Constitution for the
                        United States of America.
```

Right justification is the least commonly used form of justification. Most reports, school papers, and even books use *full justification*, which aligns text along both the right and left margins:

```
We  the  people  of  the  United  States,  in  order  to  form
a  more  perfect  Union,  establish  justice,  insure
domestic  tranquillity,  provide  for  the  common
defense,  promote  the  general  welfare,  and  secure  the
blessings  of  liberty  to  ourselves  and  our  posterity,
do  ordain  and  establish  this  Constitution  for  the
United  States  of  America.
```

When you *center justify* text, the text appears equal distance from the right and left margins. Center justification can be used for poems, invitations, and other free-form text, however, its most common use is to center a title:

```
        The  Constitution  of  the  United  States
```

```
We  the  people  of  the  United  States,  in  order  to  form
a  more  perfect  Union...
```

Justifying Text

WordPerfect makes it very easy for you to justify text. As with fonts, you can select a justification and then type the corresponding text, or you can type the text, and later select and assign the desired justification. To better understand text justification, open the File menu **New** option to create a new document.

Typing Justified Text

Center justification is most often used for titles. To center the text, *The Constitution of the United States*:

1. Open the Layout menu and select **Justification**. The Justification menu cascades as displayed in Figure 13.1.

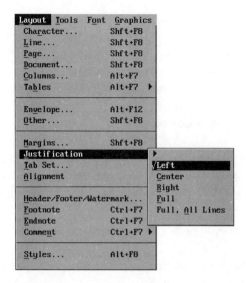

Figure 13.1 *The Cascading Justification menu.*

2. Select left, right, full or centered justification.

3. A check mark is placed in front of the current justification technique.

4. Select the **Center** option. The cursor moves to the center of your screen.

5. Type in the text **The Constitution of the United States** and press **Enter**.

When you select left, right, center, or full justification, it remains in use until you change it. Using the Justification menu, select **Full** justification and type:

```
We the people of the United States, in order to form
a more perfect Union, establish justice, insure
domestic tranquillity, provide for the common
defense, promote the general welfare, and secure the
blessings of liberty to ourselves and our posterity,
do ordain and establish this Constitution for the
United States of America.
```

The text is displayed in Figure 13.2.

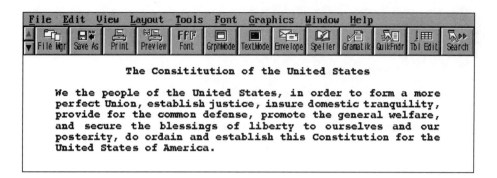

Figure 13.2 *Justifying document text.*

Use the File menu **Print** option to print your document. Take a close look at your print out. When you fully justify text, it aligns the left and right margins. To align the text, extra space is periodically inserted between words. Depending on the font, document settings, and the text itself, the additional characters may be very noticeable, or possibly hard to detect. To fully justify text, however, the spacing is manipulated between words.

Applying Justification

Justification is applied as you type. If the text you want to justify already exists in your document:

1. Select the text by performing a block operation.
2. Open the Layout menu and select **Justification**.
3. Choose the justification you desire. The justification will only affect the selected block of text.

Understanding Full, All Lines Justification

If you examine the Justification menu shown in Figure 13.1, you will find that it provides options for Full and Full, All Lines justification. When you select **Full** justification, it justifies lines up to the last line that probably does not contain enough words to justify the text. If you select **Full, All Lines** justification, it justifies even the last line. Figure 13.3 illustrates the Full, All Lines justification options.

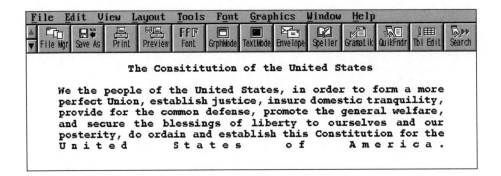

Figure 13.3 The Full, All Lines Justification.

Justifying Existing Text

If you want to change the justification of text that is already typed in a document:

1. Select the desired text using a block operation
2. Open the Layout menu and choose **Justification**.
3. Select the justification technique you desire.

Using these three steps, select the preamble text that appears on your screen and left justify the text. Next, experiment with the justification, selecting center and then right justification. As you can see, justifying your text is very easy.

Summary

Justification controls how your text appears between the document's margins. When you create a letter or memo, you normally use left justification. For reports or other documents, however, you will probably fully justify the text. When you want to center text, such as a title, you can use center justification. You can justify text in two ways. First, using the Layout menu Justification option, you can select the justification you desire and then type. When you select a justification, the it remains in effect until you change it. Second, if the text is already in your document, you can select the text using a block operation, and the choose the desired justification. In

New Terms

◆ **Center justified**. The alignment of document text so that the text appears at the center of the page, equal distance from the right and left margins.

◆ **Full justification.** The alignment of document text so that the text at both the right and left margins is aligned.

◆ **Justification.** The alignment of document text between the margins of a page. Common justifications include, left, right, center, and full.

◆ **Left justified.** The alignment of document text so that the text along the document's left margin is aligned. The text along the document's right margin may appear jagged.

◆ **Right justified.** The alignment of document text so that the text along the document's right margin is aligned. The text along the document's left margin may appear jagged.

Date Text, Codes, and Drag-and-Drop Operations

In this chapter you:

- ◆ Use WordPerfect's date text and format options
- ◆ Select the date format you desire
- ◆ Learn how to perform the drag-and-drop operations

Getting Started with Date Operations

When you create a letter or dated document, WordPerfect provides you with three options for inserting the date.

1. You can type in the date, using any format you desire. If you have a calendar near your desk, you may often type in the date for memos and other simple notes.

2. You can direct WordPerfect to insert the current date for you. The advantage of using this technique is that you don't have know the current date, and it always uses a consistent date format.

3. You can direct WordPerfect to insert a date code. When you create a letter or report, you probably are less concerned with the date at the time you started the document, than the date at the time the document is printed. When you use the date code, it automatically inserts the current date in the document. For example, if on Sunday, July 4, you start a letter and don't finish the letter until the following Sunday (July 11), a date of July 11 is inserted.

To access the date options, open the Tools menu and select **Date**. The Date menu is displayed in Figure 14.1.

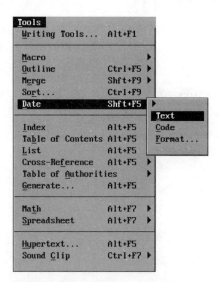

Figure 14.1 *The cascading Date menu.*

To insert the current date as *text,* select the Date menu **Text** option. Because the date is inserted as normal text characters, you can edit the date as you desire.

To insert a *date code*, open the Date menu and select **Code**. The date is displayed in your document. However, because the date is a date code and not text, you cannot edit it.

Customizing Your Date Format

You can select the date format you desire from one of many predefined formats. In addition, you can define your own format. To select one of the predefined date formats, select the Tools menu **Date** option and choose **Format**. The Date Formats dialog box is displayed in Figure 14.2.

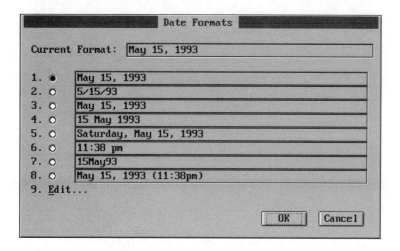

Figure 14.2 *The Date Formats dialog box.*

To select a specific date and time format, type the number that precedes the format, or click on format.

When you select a date format, the format will remain in use from one session to the next until you change it.

Creating A Custom Format

If none of the predefined date formats meet your needs, you create your own custom format. To create a custom date and time format, select the Tools menu **Date** option and choose **Format**. When the Date Format's dialog box is displayed, type **E** or click on the **Edit** option. The Edit Date Format dialog box is displayed in Figure 14.3.

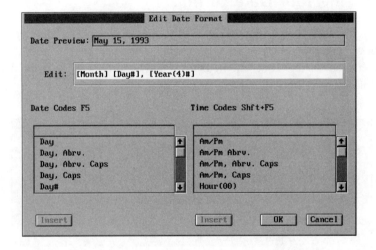

Figure 14.3 *The Edit Date Format dialog box.*

Using the Edit Date Format dialog box, you can customize the date by displaying the full or abbreviated day name (Saturday or Sat.), the full or abbreviated month name, and various numeric combinations for the day month and year. You can also include the current time (in hours and minutes).

To create a custom date format:

1. Place the cursor at a specific location in the Edit field.

2. Press **F5** or **Shift-F5** to select the Date or Time codes, or click on the corresponding box.

3. Highlight the field you desire and select **Insert**.

4. To remove a field from the date, place the cursor in front of the field and press **Del**. As you build your date, a sample in the Date Preview field is displayed.

5. After your format is created, select **OK**.

Understanding Drag-and-Drop Operations

If you are using a mouse, the cut-and-paste operations are simplified by letting your drag selected text and later dropping it a new location. To better understand drag-and-drop operations:

1. Type:

    ```
    This order sentence is out of.
    Chapter 14 of this book discusses drag-and-drop.
    This is Chapter.
    ```

2. Use your mouse to select the word *order* (and the space that appears before it). The text is displayed in reverse video.
3. Aim the mouse pointer at the highlighted text.
4. Hold down the mouse button and move the pointer to the end of the sentence, aiming the pointer between the *f* in *of* and the period.
5. Two small boxes are displayed at the end of the mouse pointer that tells you are dragging text.
6. Release the mouse button and the selected text is moved as desired:

    ```
    This sentence is out of order.
    ```

Drag-and-drop operations also let you copy text from one location to another. To perform a Copy operation:

1. Select text as above.
2. Select the number **14** (and the space that appears before it).
3. Aim the mouse pointer at the selected text.
4. Hold down **Ctrl** as you drag the text to the end of the third sentence. When you release the mouse select button, the text is copied.

    ```
    Chapter 14 of this book discusses drag-and-drop.
    This is Chapter 14.
    ```

As you can see, drag-and-drop operations let you quickly (and easily) move or copy text.

Summary

It's a very good habit to date every memo, letter, or document you create. To help you do this, WordPerfect inserts the current date for you. When the date is inserted as text characters you can later edit the text. When a date code is used, the current date is displayed in the document. If you work with the document over a several day period, it automatically changes the date so that it matches the current date. In this way, the date shown in your printed documented reflects the date the document was printed, not necessarily the date you began work on the document.

If you have a mouse, you can use the drag-and-drop operations that let you quickly move or copy text from one location to another in a document.

New Terms

◆ **Date Code.** A special symbol (code) that is inserted in your document that replaces the current date any time the document is open.

◆ **Date text.** Text characters inserted in your document that contains the current date.

◆ **Drag-and-drop.** A mouse operation that drags (moves or copies) selected text to a new location. To drag selected text, you must hold down the mouse button while moving the mouse pointer.

Chapter 15

Using WordPerfect's Thesaurus

In this chapter you:

- ◆ Look up words using the built-in thesaurus
- ◆ Replace a selected word with a more descriptive word
- ◆ Understand adjectives, adverbs, antonyms, and synonyms

Getting Started

When you create documents there may be times when one of the words you are using just isn't right. For such times, WordPerfect provides a built-in thesaurus. To use the thesaurus:

1. Open the Tools menu and choose **Writing Tools**. The Writing Tools dialog box is displayed in Figure 15.1.

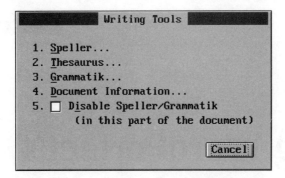

Figure 15.1 *The Writing Tools dialog box.*

2. Type **T** or click on **Thesaurus**. The Thesaurus dialog box is displayed.

3. Type in the word of interest in the Word field:

Figure 15.2 *The Word field.*

4. Type **happy**. WordPerfect displays a list of *synonyms* (words that mean the same but are spelled differently), as displayed in Figure 15.3.

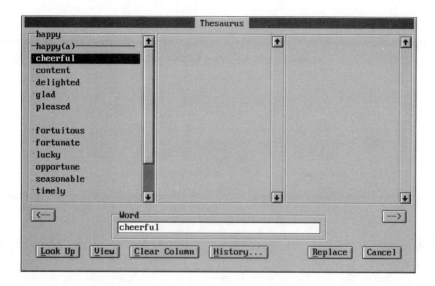

Figure 15.3 *Thesaurus synonyms for the word happy.*

As you examine the list of thesaurus words, you find that one or more words may be preceded by a dot. These words are *headwords*, which mean they have there own thesaurus entries.

To display a headword:

1. Highlight the word using the Arrow keys and press **Enter** or double click on the headword.
2. The headword's entries is displayed.

For example, if you select the headword **lucky**, the alternative words are displayed.

Depending on the headwords you select, you may encounter words that are followed by letters within parenthesis such as (v) or (n). These letters indicate the word's type, such as a verb or noun. Table 15.1 describes the symbols you may encounter.

Table 15.1 Symbols used in the thesaurus.

Symbol	Meaning	Definition
(a)	Adverb	A word that describes a verb.
(adj)	Adjective	A word that describes a noun.
(ant)	Antonym	A word with the opposite meaning.
(n)	Noun	A person, place, or thing.
(v)	Verb	An action word.

NOTE **Take Advantage of WordPerfect's Thesaurus.** Because WordPerfect makes it so easy for you to make changes to your document, you should always try to spend an extra few minutes reading your document to make sure you are using the best and most meaningful words. If you aren't sure about a specific word, take advantage of WordPerfect's built-in thesaurus. By viewing different synonyms (alternatives) for the word, you may find just the right word.

Working with Multiple Columns

If you view the entries for several headwords, your previous entries are scrolled to the left, to make room for the new entries. There may be times when you want to review the entries that are no longer visible. To bring the entries into view, press the **Right Arrow** and **Left Arrow** keys, or click on the **Right Arrow** and **Left Arrow** buttons that appear in the Thesaurus dialog box.

In addition to cycling through the entries in this way, you can type **H** or click on the **History** button. The History dialog box that tracks your headword selection for the current session is displayed in Figure 15.4.

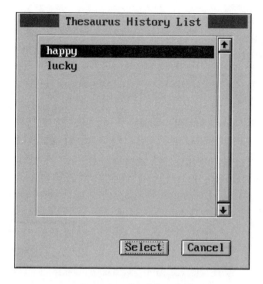

Figure 15.4 *The History dialog box.*

To quickly display an entry listed in the History dialog box, highlight the entry using the **Arrow** keys and press **Enter**, or double click on the entry.

If you no longer need the entries for a specific headword, place the cursor in the column containing the entries and type **C** or click on the **Clear Column** button. WordPerfect removes the column, bringing a column previously hidden, back into view.

Replacing a Word in a Document

In many cases, you may have a specific word you want to replace. To replace a word:

1. Type in the following sentence:

    ```
    John, make sure you order the computer immediately.
    ```

2. To look for an alternative for the word *immediately*, place the cursor anywhere in the word.

3. Start the thesaurus. The thesaurus displays the alternative words for *immediately*.

4. To use the words *right now*, highlight them using the Arrow keys or mouse.

5. Type **R** or click on the **Replace** button. The word is immediately replaced in the document, removing the thesaurus dialog box from your screen.

Replacing specific words in a document in this way is the most common way to use the thesaurus.

Summary

To help you choose more descriptive words in your documents, WordPerfect provides a built-in thesaurus. Using the thesaurus, you can look up and optionally replace a specific word in your document. The thesaurus displays alternatives for selected words. If you find an alternative word that you desire it can instantly replace the word in your document

As you view words in the thesaurus, you may find that many words are preceded by a dot, which indicates the words are headwords, which contain their own thesaurus entries

New Terms

◆ **Thesaurus.** A collection of synonyms and antonyms.

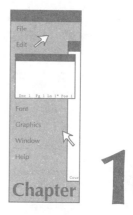

Chapter 16

Checking a Document's Grammar

In this chapter you:

- ◆ Use Grammatik to check your document's grammar
- ◆ Understand Grammatik's statistics
- ◆ Configure Grammatik to meet your needs

Getting Started with Grammatik

When you create a report or important letter, you should check your document's grammar. To help you do just that, WordPerfect provides a grammar checking tool called *Grammatik*. To better understand the process of checking your document's grammar, the companion disk that accompanies this book provides the document file GETTADDR.DOC, displayed in Figure 16.1, which contains the Gettysburg Address.

Four score and seven years ago our fathers brought forth, upon this continent, a new nation, conceived in liberty, and dedicated to the proposition that all men are created equal.

Now we are engaged in a great civil war, testing whether that nation, or any nation, so conceived, and so dedicated, can long endure. We are met here on a great battle-field of that war. We have come to dedicate a portion of it as a final resting place for those who here gave their lives that that nation might live. It is al together fitting and proper that we should do this.

But in a larger sense we can not dedicate—we can not consecrate—we can not hallow this ground. The brave men, living and dead, who struggled here, have consecrated it far above our poor power to add or detract. The world will little note, nor long remember, what we say here, but can never forget what they did here. It is for us, the living, rather to be dedicated here to the unfin ished work which they have, thus far, so nobly carried on. It is rather for us to be here dedicated to the great task remaining before us—that from these honored dead we take increased devotion to that cause for which they here gave the last full measure of devotion—that we here highly resolve that these dead shall not have died in vain; that this nation shall have a new birth of freedom; and that this government of the people, by the people, and for the people, shall not perish from this earth.

Figure 16.1 *The Gettysburg Address.*

To open the document file so you can check its grammar:

1. Choose the File menu **Select** option and type in the document file name **GETTADDR.DOC**.

2. Select **Writing Tools** from the Tools menu. The Writing Tools dialog box is displayed in Figure 16.2.

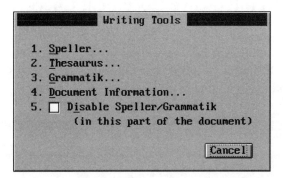

Figure 16.2 *The Writing Tools dialog box.*

3. Type **3** or click on **Grammatik**. The Grammatik screen is displayed in Figure 16.3.

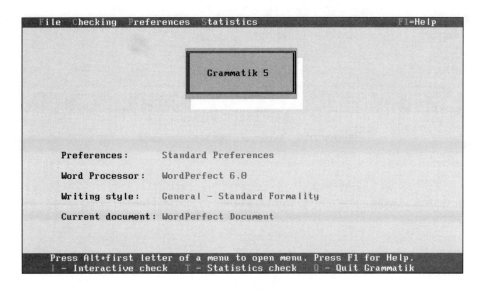

Figure 16.3 *Grammatik's opening screen.*

The Grammatik lets you work in one of two ways:

1. You can direct Grammatik to interactively show you document errors.

2. You can direct Grammatik to mark up your document, much like an English teacher would, so you can print and review the corrections

Performing an Interactive Document Check

To walk through each of your document errors, type **I** or click on the **Interactive** check option. Grammatik divides your screen into two parts, displayed in Figure 16.4, so you can see the sentence containing the error as well the error type and the recommended correction.

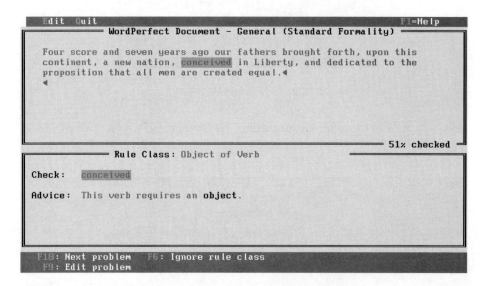

Figure 16.4 *Viewing a grammar correction.*

Grammatik examines your document by applying a set of standard tests and rules. In some cases, the error Grammatik displays may not actually be a mistake. You need to consider Grammatik's suggestions as just that, suggestions. You will probably respond to many of the suggestions, but not all of Grammatik's suggestions are correct.

In the case of the document containing the Gettysburg address, you can see that all of Grammatik's suggestions are not correct. When Grammatik displays an error, you can ignore the error, skipping to the next problem, or you can edit your document to correct the error. Press **F10** each time Grammatik displays an error, or click on the **Next Problem** option.

Directing Grammatik to Mark Up Your Document

If your document is long and you don't want to interactively correct it, Grammatik can mark up your document, much like an English teacher would. To mark up your document:

1. Open the Checking menu displayed in Figure 16.5 and select **Mark**.

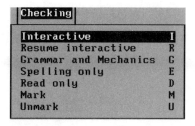

Figure 16.5 *The Checking menu.*

2. The corrections are written into your document.

3. To exit open the File menu and select **Quit** to return to your document or to print corrections. Grammatik's suggestions for Gettysburg Address are displayed in Figure 16.6

|--(LONG SENTENCES CAN BE DIFFICULT TO READ AND UNDER-
STAND. CONSIDER REVISING SO THAT NO MORE THAN ONE COM-
PLETE THOUGHT IS EXPRESSED IN EACH SENTENCE.)--|Four
score and seven years ago our fathers brought forth,
upon this continent, a new nation, |--(THIS VERB
REQUIRES AN_OBJECT_.)--|conceived in liberty, and dedi-
cated to the proposition that all men |--(THIS IS_PAS-
SIVE VOICE_. CONSIDER REVISING USING_ACTIVE VOICE_. SEE
HELP FOR MORE INFORMATION.)--|are created equal.

|--(USUALLY A PARAGRAPH SHOULD HAVE MORE THAN ONE SEN-
TENCE.)--|Now we are engaged in a great civil war,
testing whether that nation, or any nation, so con-
ceived, and so dedicated, can long endure. |--(THIS
IS_PASSIVE VOICE_THIS IS_PASSIVE VOICE_. CONSIDER
REVISING USING_ACTIVE VOICE_. SEE HELP FOR MORE INFOR-
MATION.)--|We are met here on a |--(SPELLING ERROR.)--
|great battle-field of that war. We have come to dedi-
cate |--(TRY TO SIMPLIFY; BE MORE SPECIFIC IF YOU
CAN.)--|a portion of it as a final resting place for
those who here gave their lives |--(DELETE DOUBLED
'THAT'.)--|that that nation might live. It is |--
('ALTOGETHER' IS AN_ADVERB_ MEANING "COMPLETELY". YOU
MAY MEAN 'ALL TOGETHER', MEANING "IN A GROUP" OR "IN
UNISON". IF SO, TRY SIMPLY 'TOGETHER'.)--|altogether
fitting and proper that we should do this.

|--(TRY TO USE 'BUT' SPARINGLY TO BEGIN A SENTENCE.)--
|But in a larger sense we |--(THE PREFERRED FORM IS
'CANNOT'.)--|can not |--(SPELLING ERROR.)--|dedicate—we
|--(THE PREFERRED FORM IS 'CANNOT'.)--|can not |--
(SPELLING ERROR.)--|consecrate—we |--(THE PREFERRED FORM
IS 'CANNOT'.)--|can not |--(SPELLING ERROR.)--|hallow
this ground. The brave men, living and dead, who

struggled here, have consecrated it far above our
poor power to add or detract. The world will lit-
tle note, nor long remember, what we say here,but
can never forget what they did here. It is for
us, the living, |--(THIS WORD USUALLY ADDS LITTLE
AND SHOULD BE OMITTED.)--|rather to be dedicated
here to the unfinished work |--(UNLESS YOU COULD
SUBSTITUTE 'WHICH ONE'('S') FOR 'WHICH' HERE, YOU
SHOULD PROBABLY USE 'THAT' INSTEAD. WHEN 'WHICH'
BEGINS A _CLAUSE_, IT IS USUALLY PRECEDED BY A
COMMA. USE HELP KEY FOR MORE INFORMATION.)--
|which they have, thus far, so nobly carried on.
|--(LONG SENTENCES CAN BE DIFFICULT TO READ AND
UNDERSTAND. CONSIDER REVISING SO THAT NO MORE
THAN ONE COMPLETE THOUGHT IS EXPRESSED IN EACH
SENTENCE.)--|It is |--(THIS WORD USUALLY ADDS
LITTLE AND SHOULD BE OMITTED.)--|rather for us to
be here dedicated to the great task remaining
before |--(SPELLING ERROR.)--|us—that from these
honored dead |--(THE _SUBJECT PRONOUN_ 'WE'
SHOULD NOT BE USED IN THE _OBJECT_ POSITION.
CHECK ALSO FOR MISSING WORDS OR PUNCTUATION.)--
|we take increased devotion to that cause for
which they here gave the last full measure of |--
(SPELLING ERROR.)--|devotion—that we here highly
resolve that these dead shall not have died in
vain; |--(A SEMICOLON USUALLY JOINS 2 _INDEPEN-
DENT CLAUSE_S. CHECK TO SEE IF YOU SHOULD HAVE
USED A COMMA HERE INSTEAD.)--|that this nation
shall have a new birth of freedom; |--(TRY TO USE
'AND' SPARINGLY TO BEGIN A SENTENCE.)--|and that
this government of the people, by the people, and
for the people, shall not perish from this earth.

Figure 16.6 *The suggestions for the Gettysburg Address.*

NOTE

Grammatik places corrections directly into your document. To remove the correction marks, invoke Grammatik a second, and open the Checking menu, and choose **Unmark**. Grammatik removes the correction marks.

Using Grammatik's Statistical Information

In addition to marking up your document's possible errors, you are provided with an analysis of your document that tells you the document's ease (or difficulty) of reading and the grade level a reader must have to understand your document. To view your document's analysis after Grammatik has examined the text, type **T** from Grammatik's opening screen or click on the **Statistics** check option. The analysis is displayed in Figure 16.7.

```
                                                     ⟨F1: Help⟩

    Statistics for:  WordPerfect Document

    ┌ Readability Statistics ──────────────────────────────────────
    Flesch Reading Ease:  68           Flesch-Kincaid Grade Level: 10
    Gunning's Fog Index:  13

    ┌ Paragraph Statistics ────────────────────────────────────────
    Number of paragraphs: 4            Average length:   3.0 sentences

    ┌ Sentence Statistics ─────────────────────────────────────────
    Number of sentences:  12           Short (< 12 words):   3
    Average length:       22.4 words   Long  (> 30 words):   2
    End with '?':         0
    End with '!':         0

    ┌ Word Statistics ─────────────────────────────────────────────
    Number of words:      269          Average length:      4.24 letters
                                       Syllables per word:  1.37


        ⟨Enter: Next Screen⟩                  ⟨Esc: Done⟩
```

Figure 16.7 *The analysis of your document.*

The Readability Statistics tell you how difficult your document is to read and understand–as well as the reading level required to understand your document. In the case of the Gettysburg Address, readers must read at a tenth grade level to understand the passage. Your goal is to reduce, not increase the reading level. The better your document is written, the lower the required reading level. Using Grammatik is an iterative process. You use Grammatik to detect errors, correct the errors, and then you run it again. You repeat this process until no errors or a small number of errors is found. As you correct errors, you may find that your document's reading level decreases (becomes easier to read).

If you press **Enter** or click on the **Next Screen** option, a screen is displayed that explains the meaning of your document's statistical values, as shown in Figure 16.8.

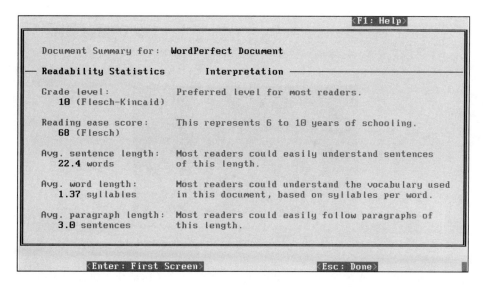

Figure 16.8 *Grammatik's explanatory screen.*

Get in the habit of using Grammatik to check a document's grammar. After you have corrected errors for three or four documents, you may find that you have fewer grammatical errors in the documents created. You learn how to improve your grammar simply by working with Grammatik. To correct a document using Grammatik:

1. Open the Tools menu and choose **Writing Tools**.
2. Select **Grammatik**.
3. Type **I** or click on the **Interactive** check option.
4. Edit the document to correct each error displayed.

Setting up Grammatik for a Specific Document Type

Depending on the type of document you are creating, you can apply different editing rules. In other words, the rules applied when correcting a children's book are different from those used for an article written for a medical journal. You can turn the rules on and off for different testing. To apply the rules for a specific document style:

1. Open Grammatik's Preferences menu and choose **Writing Style**. The Select Writing Style screen is displayed in Figure 16.9.

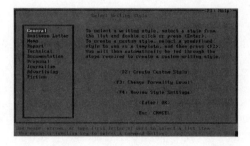

Figure 16.9 The Select Writing Style screen.

2. Using the Arrow keys, highlight the option that best describes the document's contents.

3. Press **Enter** or click on the option. For most documents, you can use the General style.

4. In the Select Writing Style screen, press **F2** or click on the **Create Custom Style** option.

5. A screen is displayed asking you to select a custom style.

6. Using the Arrow keys, highlight a style name and press **Enter** or click on the style name. A dialog box is displayed asking you for the name of style, shown in Figure 16.10.

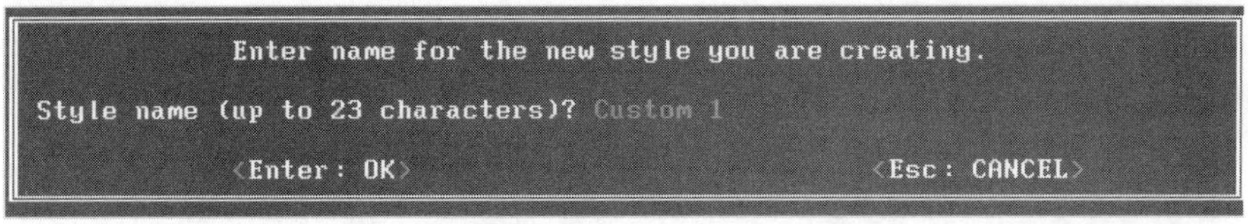

```
┌────────────────────────────────────────────────────────────────┐
│         Enter name for the new style you are creating.           │
│                                                                  │
│  Style name (up to 23 characters)? Custom 1                      │
│                                                                  │
│         <Enter: OK>                        <Esc: CANCEL>         │
└────────────────────────────────────────────────────────────────┘
```

Figure 16.10 *The prompt for a custom style name.*

7. Type in name you desire or press **Enter** to select the default name. The Grammar Rules screen is displayed in Figure 16.11.

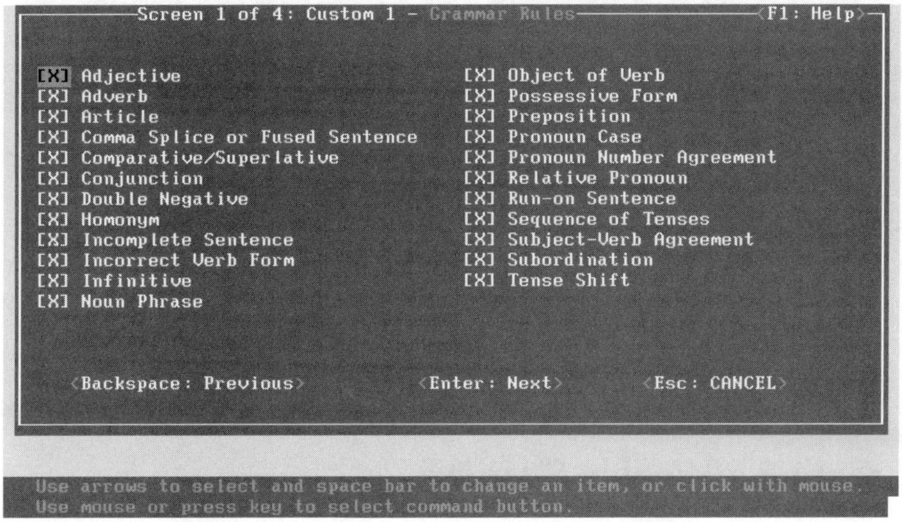

```
┌──────Screen 1 of 4: Custom 1 - Grammar Rules──────<F1: Help>─┐
│                                                              │
│   [X] Adjective                    [X] Object of Verb        │
│   [X] Adverb                       [X] Possessive Form       │
│   [X] Article                      [X] Preposition           │
│   [X] Comma Splice or Fused Sentence [X] Pronoun Case        │
│   [X] Comparative/Superlative      [X] Pronoun Number Agreement │
│   [X] Conjunction                  [X] Relative Pronoun      │
│   [X] Double Negative              [X] Run-on Sentence       │
│   [X] Homonym                      [X] Sequence of Tenses    │
│   [X] Incomplete Sentence          [X] Subject-Verb Agreement │
│   [X] Incorrect Verb Form          [X] Subordination         │
│   [X] Infinitive                   [X] Tense Shift           │
│   [X] Noun Phrase                                            │
│                                                              │
│                                                              │
│   <Backspace: Previous>    <Enter: Next>    <Esc: CANCEL>    │
│                                                              │
├──────────────────────────────────────────────────────────────┤
│ Use arrows to select and space bar to change an item, or click with mouse. │
│ Use mouse or press key to select command button.            │
└──────────────────────────────────────────────────────────────┘
```

Figure 16.11 *The Grammar Rules screen.*

All of the rules applied are selected with an X. To turn testing for a rule on or off:

1. Highlight the rule and press the **Spacebar** or click on the rule.

2. Press **Enter** until Grammatik displays its threshold settings displayed in Figure 16.12.

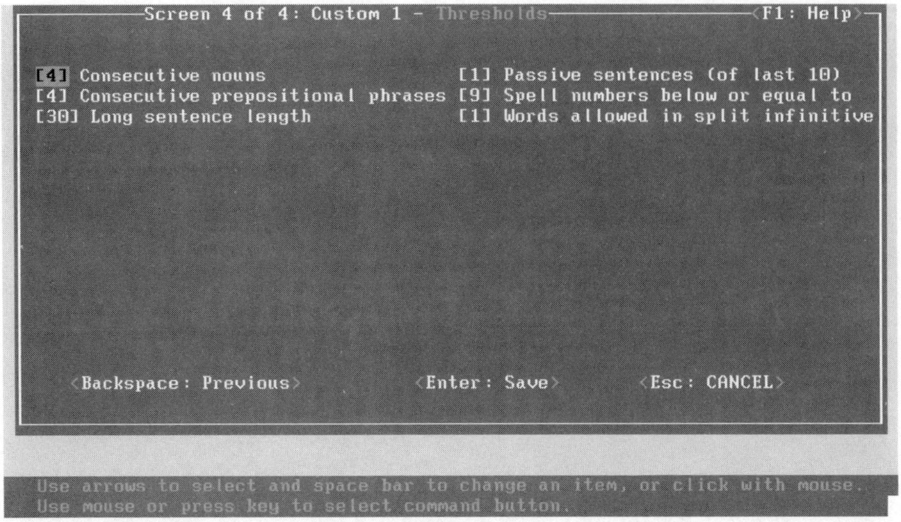

Figure 16.12 *Grammatik's threshold values.*

3. Change any threshold values you desire and press **Enter** or click on **Save**.

4. Select **OK** for any other dialog boxes displayed.

Creating a Weekly Planner

If you have a busy schedule, you probably find yourself running from one meeting or deadline to the next. To help you better manage your busy schedule, the companion disk that accompanies this book provides a Weekly Time Planner document, displayed in Figure 16.13.

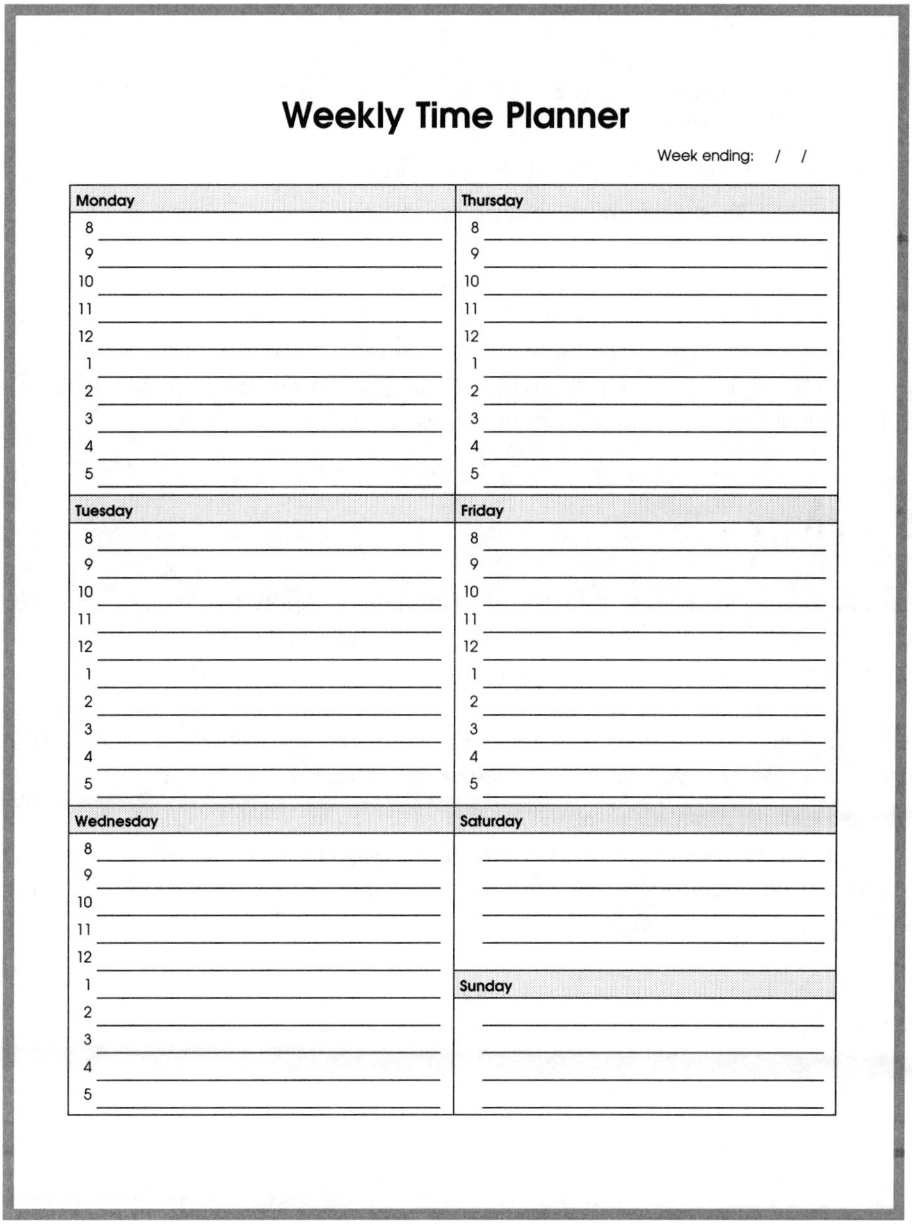

Weekly Time Planner

Week ending: /   /

Monday		Thursday	
8		8	
9		9	
10		10	
11		11	
12		12	
1		1	
2		2	
3		3	
4		4	
5		5	

Tuesday		Friday	
8		8	
9		9	
10		10	
11		11	
12		12	
1		1	
2		2	
3		3	
4		4	
5		5	

Wednesday		Saturday
8		
9		
10		
11		
12		
1		**Sunday**
2		
3		
4		
5		

Figure 16.13 *The companion disk Weekly Time Planner.*

To use the weekly time planner:

1. Select **Open** from the File menu. Type in the document filename **WEEKLY.DOC**.

2. Type in your appointments for the week.

3. Select **Save As** from the File menu to save your schedule using a meaningful file name.

You can print the document and hand write your appointments or you can retrieve the document, type in your appointments and then save (optionally printing) the document to a different file on disk. To move the cursor from one appointment time to the next, use the Arrow keys.

Summary

To improve a document's quality, use Grammatik. Apply the built-in grammar checker right after you finish spell checking. Grammatik examines the document, applying a specific set of grammar rules. If an error is suspected, it is highlighted, the error is described, and a recommended solution is displayed. After Grammatik examines the document, you can display statistics about the document that help you determine its ease (or difficulty) of reading.

Remember, Grammatik applies a set of grammar rules to check the document. In some cases, the errors Grammatik displays may not actually be errors at all. You need to consider each error message Grammatik displays, implementing only those that are correct.

New Terms

◆ **Grammar.** A set of rules that describe how you should use a language.

◆ **Grammar checker.** A software program that applies rules of grammar to a document, displaying possible language usage violations.

Chapter 17

Working with Multiple Open Documents

In this chapter you:

- ◆ Open multiple documents
- ◆ Quickly switch between document windows
- ◆ Minimize, maximize, cascade, and tile windows
- ◆ Move and size windows
- ◆ Copy text from one document to another

179

Opening Multiple Documents

There may be times when it is convenient to have more than one document open at a time. For example, assume that you have three document files that contain monthly budget information. The first contains expenses, the second accounts payable, and the third accounts receivable. If you are creating a document containing your monthly summary, it would be convenient to be able to quickly view the contents of one of the other documents from time to time. A document you created sometime in the past may contain a table, image, or text you want to include in your current document. Rather than having to retype the information, you can open the old document, copy the information to the clipboard, and then paste the information into your current document.

You can open up to nine documents at one time. When you open multiple documents, each document displays its contents in a window. A *window* is really nothing more than a framed region on your screen. By default, each time you open a document, the previous document's window is covered with that of the new window. As a result, just by looking at the screen, you may not be aware that more than one document (window) is open. WordPerfect lets you size and move windows. You can display all of the open documents, as shown in Figure 17.1.

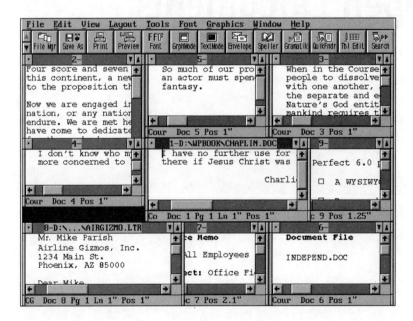

Figure 17.1 Displaying multiple document windows.

Opening more than one document at a time is really no different than opening a single document. In this chapter, you will work with three open documents. To work with multiple document:

1. Open the File menu and choose **New**.
2. Type the following text:

    ```
    I don't know who my grandfather was; I am much
    more concerned to know what his grandson will be.
    ```

    ```
                              Abraham Lincoln (1809-1865)
    ```

3. Use the **Save As** option to save the document as LINCOLN.DOC.
4. Select **New**. A new document window is displayed
5. Type in the following text:

    ```
    So much of our profession is taken up with pre-
    tending, that an actor must spend at least half
    his waking hours in a fantasy.
    ```

    ```
                                  Ronald Reagan (1911-)
    ```

6. **Save** this document to the file REAGAN.DOC.
7. Repeat this process a third time, creating a new document and typing the following text:

    ```
    I have no further use for America. I wouldn't go
    back there if Jesus Christ was President.
    ```

    ```
                              Charlie Chaplin (1889-1977)
    ```

8. **Save** this document to the file CHAPLIN.DOC.

As you know, you just created three documents, however, only one of the documents is in view. To view your open documents, open the Window menu, displayed in Figure 17.2.

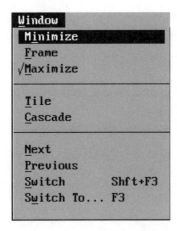

Figure 17.2 The Window menu.

9. Select the **Tile** option. Your open document windows are sized and arranged(like mosaic tiles) so each window's contents is partially visible on the screen, displayed in Figure 17.3

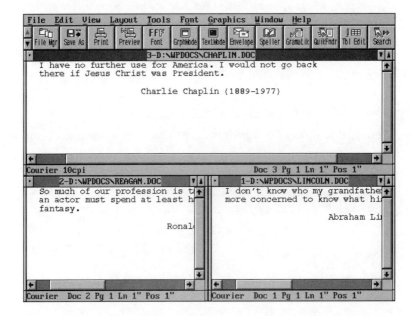

Figure 17.3 Tiling open windows on your screen.

Notice that the name of each document is displayed in the title bar that appears at the top of the document window. If you have not yet saved an open document, WordPerfect displays the text Untitled in the title bar.

WordPerfect displays one title bar in color and the rest are dimmed. The color title bar indicates the active document window. If you begin typing, the text you type is placed in the active window.

Selecting the Active Document Window

When you work with multiple document windows, you need a way to select the window in which you want to work. If you are using a mouse, you can select a window by clicking in the window. If you are not using a mouse, select the Window menu previously shown and choose **Switch To**. The Switch to Document dialog box is displayed in Figure 17.4.

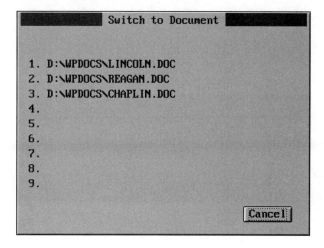

Figure 17.4 *The Switch to Document dialog box.*

Type the number of the document you desire. WordPerfect switches to the desired document.

Cascading Open Document Windows

When you tile open document, the windows are sized and arranged so that a portion of each open document appears on your screen. You can cascade, or overlay one window on top of another, so that each window's title bar remains

overlay one window on top of another, so that each window's title bar remains visible. To cascade your current document windows:

1. Open the Window menu and choose **Cascade**. It cascades your windows as displayed in Figure 17.5.

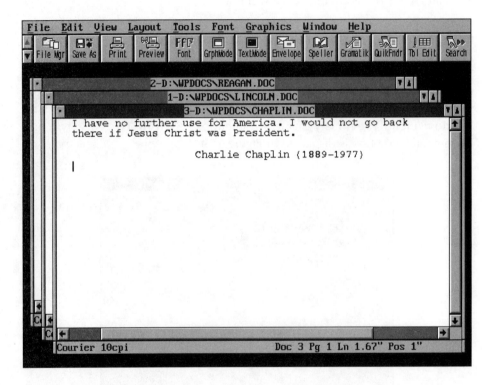

Figure 17.5 *Cascading open document windows.*

The advantage of cascading windows is that you can view a larger portion of the active document while still seeing the title bars of your open documents. If you are using a mouse, you can select a window by clicking in the window's title bar.

Sizing a Document Window

Depending on the content of your document windows, there may be times when you want to change a window's size. You can display more of the window's contents, or reduce the window so you can see more of another window.

dow's contents, or reduce the window so you can see more of another window. There are two ways to size windows:

1. You can minimize or maximize the window.
2. You can drag the window's frame with your mouse until the window is the desired size.

Minimizing and Maximizing a Document Window

If you look to the far right of the window's title bar, you find two arrows, one facing up and one down. These arrows are the window's *maximize* (▲) and *minimize* (▼) buttons. If you click on the maximize button, it expands the window's size so that the window consumes your entire screen display. When you maximize one window, your other open document windows are hidden from view. If you click on the downward facing button, WordPerfect minimizes the window to the window's smallest possible size.

If you have a mouse, minimize each of your open document windows. If you don't have a mouse, select each window, one window at a time and use the Window menu **Minimize** option to reduce the window size. The windows are displayed in Figure 17.6.

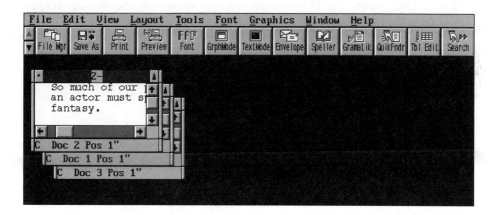

Figure 17.6 *Minimizing document windows.*

Select one of the document windows and click on the M**aximize** button or use the Window menu **Maximize** option. WordPerfect restores the window to its previous size. If you maximize the window a second time, it expands the window to fill the entire screen. When a window is maximized, it does not display the window frame or the title bar.

Incrementally Sizing a Window

When you maximize and minimize a window, you basically have two size choices, big and small. If you want finer control over your window size, you can size the window by dragging the window frame (the box that surrounds the window) using your mouse. If the frame is not visible (you have maximized the window), open the Window menu and choose **Frame**. To incrementally size the window:

1. Aim the mouse pointer at the thin vertical bar along the window's left and right sides, or at the status bar that appears at the bottom of the window.
2. Hold down the mouse button.
3. As you move the mouse pointer, it displays a dashed rectangle that represents the current window size.
4. Push the frame towards the windows center, the window will shrink. Likewise, if you pull the frame, the window will grow.
5. If you drag the small rectangular box that appears in the bottom corners of the window, you can change the window's height and width at the same time.

Moving a Document Window

To move a window (without changing the size), aim the mouse pointer at the window's title bar and hold down the mouse button. As you move the mouse pointer, it moves the window.

A Quick Way to Close a Window

If you are working with a framed window, you will see a small box to the left of the title bar that contains a small triangle. If you click your mouse in this box, it closes the window. If you have made changes to the document's contents, it discloses the window. If you have made changes to the document's contents, it displays a dialog box asking you if you want to save the changes.

Cutting and Pasting between Documents

When you work with multiple documents, there will be times when you want to copy or move information from one document to another. To do this you use the cut-and-paste operations similar to those discussed in Chapter 11. The only difference now is that you cut information from one document and paste it into another. To better understand this process:

1. Open the File menu and choose **New**.
2. Open the Window menu and choose **Tile**. WordPerfect displays each of your open documents.
3. Select the window containing the Lincoln quote.
4. Open the Edit menu and choose the **Select** option. When the menu cascades, choose **Page**. It selects the entire document.
5. Open the Edit menu and choose **Copy**. The text is copied to the clipboard.
6. Select the empty document you just created.
7. Open the Edit menu and select **Paste**. WordPerfect pastes the text from the clipboard into the document.
8. Repeat these steps to copy the other two quotes to the new document.

As you will find, WordPerfect makes it very easy to move or copy text from one document to another.

Exiting with Multiple Open Documents

If you exit WordPerfect with multiple documents open, it displays each document's name in the Exit WordPerfect dialog box, displayed in Figure 17.7.

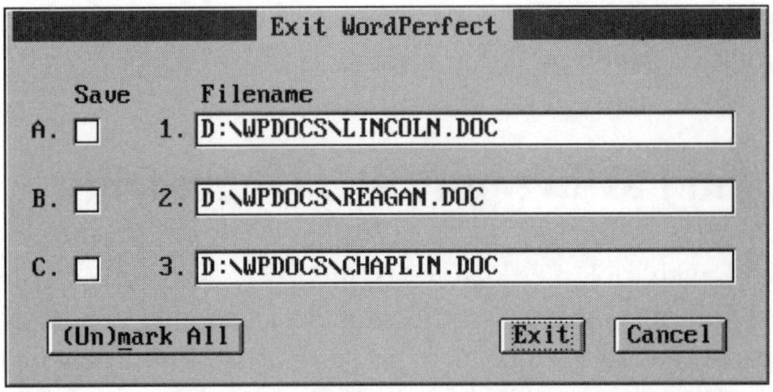

Figure 17.7 Multiple documents in the Exit WordPerfect dialog box.

To save the changes to a document, place an **X** in the Save check box.

Summary

WordPerfect lets you open up to nine documents at one time. When you are working with multiple documents, it displays each document in its own window. There may be times when you want to view the contents of all documents at once. To do this you can tile the document windows so that a portion of each window is visible. Regardless of the number of open documents, only one document is active. Any operations you perform or text you type only affects the active document. To help you manage your screen appearance, WordPerfect lets you size and move your documents. If you minimize a document, it reduces the document window to its smallest possible size. If you maximize a document, it expands the document to fill your screen display. To simplify minimize and maximize operations, WordPerfect places two buttons at the far right the window's title bar. You can incrementally change a document window's size or move a window.

New Terms

◆ **Cascading windows.** The display of open document windows that successive windows overlay each other, allowing only the display of the previous window's title bar. The active window is displayed on top with its contents in view.

◆ **Document window.** The rectangular framed region in which WordPerfect displays a document.

◆ **Maximizing a window.** Enlarging a window to fill your screen display.

◆ **Minimizing a window.** Reducing window to its smallest possible size.

◆ **Tiling windows.** The display of open windows such that windows are sized and arranged so a portion of each window's contents is visible.

WordPerfect's Online Help

In this chapter you:

- ◆ Learn how to take advantage of WordPerfect's online Help
- ◆ Get quick step-by-step answers to your "How do I? "questions
- ◆ Use WordPerfect's Coaches to walk you through a task
- ◆ View the information you should know when calling WordPerfect technical support

Putting WordPerfect's Online Help to Use

WordPerfect provides an extensive built-in Help facility that you can use to find the answers to most of your questions and in many cases, the step-by-step instructions you must perform. This chapter looks at several different features provided by WordPerfect's online Help. Take the time to experiment as you read this chapter. Once you are comfortable using the online Help, the answers to your WordPerfect questions are very easy to find. To start WordPerfect's online Help, open the Help menu shown in Figure 18.1.

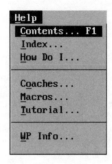

Figure 18.1 *The Help menu.*

You have used the Help menu Tutorial option to run the online tutor. In this chapter, you use the options listed here:

◆ **Contents** lists the online Help table of contents.

◆ **Index** displays an alphabetical listing of online Help topics.

◆ **How Do I** provides step-by-step answers to your How do I do . . . questions.

◆ **Coaches** walks you through the steps you must perform for a specific operation.

◆ **WP Info** displays key information you should have before calling WordPerfect technical support.

To begin, open the Help menu **Contents** option. WordPerfect displays the online Help table of contents displayed in Figure 18.2.

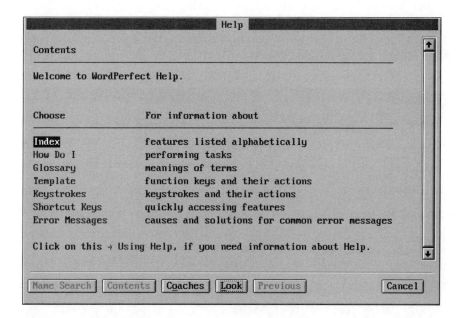

Figure 18.2 *The online Help table of contents.*

From the table of contents:

◆   You can access the Help index of alphabetical topics as well as the step-by-step answers to your How Do I questions.

◆   You can display the glossary definitions for various terms and view the functions of different keystrokes.

If WordPerfect displays an error message on your screen, you can use the Error Messages option to display the meaning of the messages as well as the steps you should perform to resolve the errors.

As previously discussed, the online Help is like having an expert at your side. To end a Help session at any time, you can press **Esc** or click on the **Cancel** button.

Using the Online Help Index

To use online Help:

1. From in the Help table of contents, select the **Index** option by high-
    lighting the option and pressing **Enter**, or by double clicking on the
    option. An alphabetical listing of Help topics is displayed in Figure 18.3.

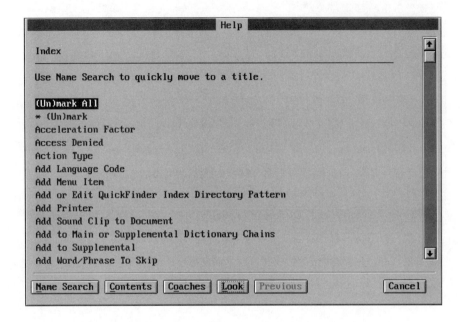

Figure 18.3 The index of online Help topics.

2. Using the Arrow keys, or using your mouse in the vertical scroll bar,
    move through the Help topics.

3. Highlight the **Backup** topic and press **Enter** or double click on the
    topic. WordPerfect displays Help text about its backup file processing,
    shown in Figure 18.4.

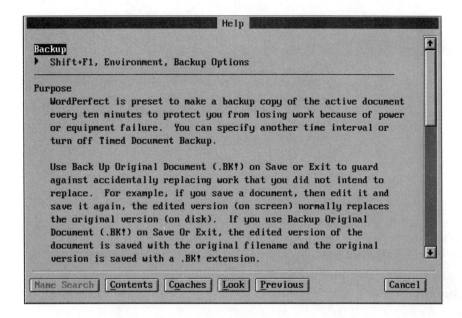

Figure 18.4 *Online Help text about backups.*

4. Using the Arrow keys or the vertical scroll bar, you can move through the Help text.

As you view the Help text, you may encounter words that appear in bold or are underlined. The bold words correspond to topics that are discussed in greater detail elsewhere. If you highlight the word and select the **Look** option, it displays the corresponding Help text.

The words that appear underline are defined in the Help glossary. If you highlight an underlined word and select **Look**, it displays the word's definition. For example, Figure 18.5 shows the definition of the word *block*.

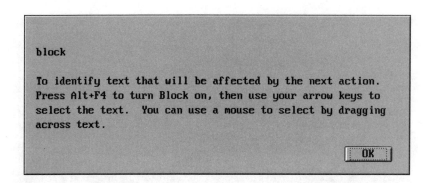

Figure 18.5 The glossary definition of the word block.

As you move through Help topics, there may be times when you want to review the previous topic. At such times, type **P** or click on the **Previous** button.

If you want to return to the Help Table of Contents, type **C** or click on the **Contents** button.

Quickly Locating a Specific Topic

If the topic you desire begins with a letter near the end of the alphabet, scrolling through the index of topics can be quite time consuming. To quickly move to a specific topic in the list, type **N** or click on the **Name Search** button. A box is displayed in which you can type the desired topic name:

Figure 18.6 The Name Search box.

As you type in the Name Search box, WordPerfect displays the topic words that match the letters typed. For example, if you want Help on searching for text, you could begin typing the letters **search**. WordPerfect, in turn, displays letters beginning with *s* then those with *se, sea,* and so on as you type. Once the desired word is displayed, press **Enter**. It returns you to the index, highlighting the topic name. To display the topic text, select **Look**.

Using Online Help. When you work with software, it is very frustrating to have to stop working and chase down a manual before you can complete your next step. To eliminate this frustration, WordPerfect provides extensive online Help. In online Help you find answers and explanations for topics ranging from Printing or Saving Your Document, to Applying Binding Offsets. If you need to know how to do it, chances are you can find the answers in the online Help.

Getting Answers to Your How Do I Questions

Almost every WordPerfect question you have begins with the three words, How do I. For example, How do I spell check, change margins, assign page numbers, and so on. With these three words in mind, the online Help provides answers to the most common questions. From the online Help Table of Contents, select **How Do I**. A screen is displayed containing the questions to which it provides answers, shown in Figure 18.7.

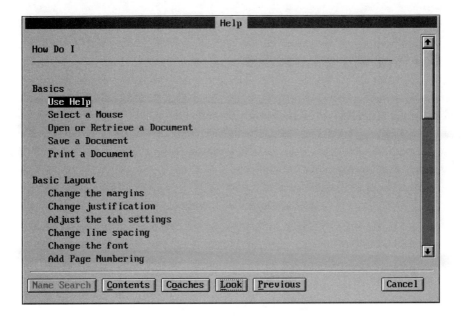

Figure 18.7 *The How Do I questions.*

If you highlight a topic and press **Enter**, it displays the step-by-step instructions you need to perform. For example, if you select **Print a Document**, WordPerfect lists the steps you must perform to print a document, as shown in Figure 18.8.

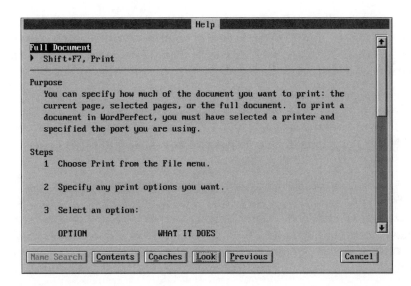

Figure 18.8 Steps to print your document.

Understanding Coaches

One of the most powerful feature of the online Help is its built-in Coaches. A WordPerfect *Coach* is an expert that not only lists the steps you must perform for an operation, but if you ask, actually performs the steps for you. When you select **Coaches**, it displays the Coaches dialog box, in Figure 18.9, which lists the topics that are available to help you.

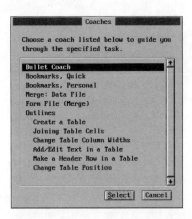

Figure 18.9 The Coaches dialog box.

If you highlight a topic and choose **Select**, Coach walks you through the steps you must perform. If you select the Coach's **Show Me** button, the Coach performs the operation for you.

Technical Support Information

If you can't find the solution to your problem in online Help and you are going to call WordPerfect's technical support, open the Help menu and choose **WP Info**. It displays information you need to provide to the technical support specialist, as shown in Figure 18.10.

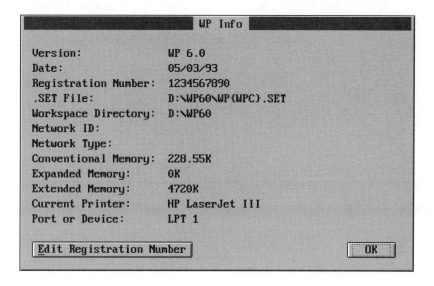

Figure 18.10 *WordPerfect's technical support information.*

Summary

WordPerfect provides a powerful and complete online Help facility that probably contains the answers to all your WordPerfect questions. Get in the habit of using the online Help today—the Help facility is like having an expert at your side.

New Terms

◆ **Coach.** An interactive word processing expert built into the online Help. It tells you the step-by-step operations you must perform to accomplish a task, and in many cases, can perform the steps for you.

◆ **Online Help.** A Help facility built into software that provides step-by-step instructions for common operations.

Chapter 19

Using the File Manager

In this chapter you:

◆ Use the File Manager to find document files

◆ Use the File Manager to print, copy, rename, or delete one or more files

◆ Copy a document to a floppy disk so you can give the document to another user

◆ Create one or more quick lists of commonly used subdirectories

◆ Search documents for specific text

◆ Use the QuickFinder to locate a file

Understanding the File Manager

When you create a document, you store the document in a file on disk so you can later refer back to the document or make changes. If you create three to four documents a day, it takes you less than a year to have over one thousand documents! To help you manage these files, WordPerfect provides a File Manager. Using the File Manager, you can list your document files, search them for specific text, select one or more files you want to print, copy, rename, or delete, and much more. The File Manager is very powerful. This chapter presents those File Manager operations you may perform on a regular basis.

Each time you select the File menu **Open** option, WordPerfect displays the Open Document dialog box shown in Figure 19.1.

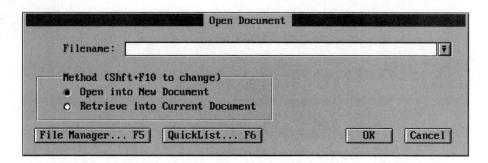

Figure 19.1 *The Open Document dialog box.*

If you can't remember the name of the document file you want to open, you can press **F5** or click on the **File Manager** option. WordPerfect displays the Specify File Manger List dialog box shown in Figure 19.2.

Figure 19.2 *The Specify File Manager List dialog box.*

When you store document files on your disk, the files are placed in *subdirectories*, which are similar to drawers of a filing cabinet. In general, a subdirectory is really nothing more than a list of filenames. When the Specify File Manager List dialog box is displayed, it is asking you to name the subdirectory whose files you want to list. As discussed in Chapter 6, WordPerfect uses the directory WPDOCS as the default subdirectory for your documents. WordPerfect normally displays WPDOCS as the default directory name. If you press **Enter** or click on **OK**, it displays a list of the files contained in the default directory. If you want to view the files contained in a different directory, type in that directory name and press **Enter**. The list of filenames is displayed in its File Manager screen in Figure 19.3.

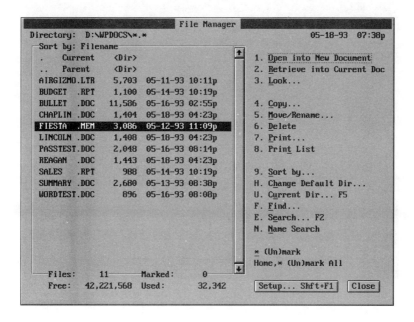

Figure 19.3 The File Manager screen.

Using the Arrow keys or the vertical scroll bar and your mouse, scroll through the list of document filenames. Note that the File Manager displays a count of the number of files listed, the amount of free (available) disk space as well as the amount the files listed consume

As you highlight a filename, the File Manager enables different options.

Open, Retrieve, and Look Operations

Using the Open or Retrieve options directs the File Manager to open a new document window to display the current file or to retrieve the file's contents into the current document.

If you want to view the document's contents, without actually opening the document, select the **Look** option.

When you highlight a file and select **Look**, WordPerfect displays the documents contents, as shown in Figure 19.4.

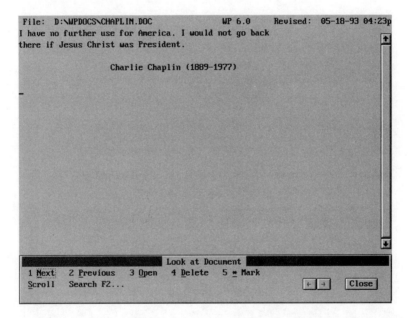

Figure 19.4 Looking at a document's contents using the File Manager.

If the file contains the document you desire, you can open, delete, mark the file for a print, copy, or rename operation. You can also view the contents of the file that precedes or follows the current document in the directory list.

Copy, Rename, Delete, and Print Operations

The File Manager lets you copy, rename, delete, or print the highlighted document.

Copying the Selected File

If you exchange documents with other users, there may be many times when you need to copy a file to a floppy disk. To copy a specific file, highlight the file in the File Manager List and type **4** or click on the **Copy** option. The Copy dialog box is displayed in Figure 19.5.

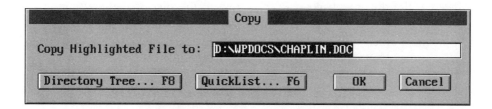

Figure 19.5 *The Copy dialog box.*

Type in the location to which you want the document file copied. To copy the file CHAPLIN.DOC to a floppy disk in drive A, for example, you would type **A:CHAPLIN.DOC** and press **Enter**.

Moving the Selected File

As the number of document files on your disk increases, create additional subdirectories in which you can place related files. For example, you might create a directory for letters, one for reports, and one for memos. There may be times when a document's contents change enough that you want to rename the file. If you need to move a file to a different directory or need to rename a file, highlight the file in the file list and type **5** or click on the **Move/Rename** option. The Move/Rename dialog box is displayed in Figure 19.6, asking you to type in the desired location or new document file name.

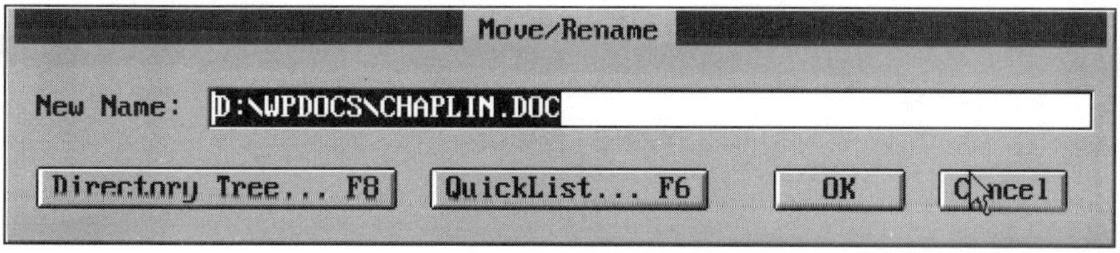

Figure 19.6 *The Move/Rename dialog box.*

If you are moving the selected file, type in the complete pathname of the subdirectory in which you want the file placed. If you are renaming the file, simply type the desired name and press **Enter**.

Deleting the Selected File

Over time, you no longer need many of the documents that reside on your disk. By deleting the document files, you can free up the disk space they consume. Before you delete a document file, use the File Manager Look option to ensure the document does not contain information that you need. Next, select the **Delete** option. The Delete dialog box is displayed in Figure 19.7.

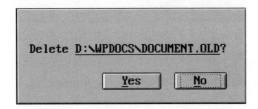

Figure 19.7 The Delete dialog box.

To delete the document, select **Yes**. To leave the document on your disk, select **No**.

Printing the Selected Document

To print an open document use the File menu **Print/Fax** option. In a similar way, the File Manager lets you print the contents of a selected file. Type **7** or click on the **Print** option. The Print Multiple Pages dialog box, displayed in Figure 19.8, specifies the pages you want to print.

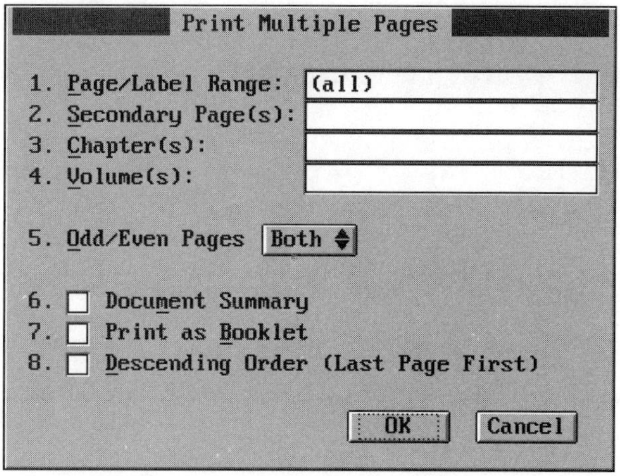

Figure 19.8 *The Print Multiple Pages dialog box.*

To print the entire document, select **OK**.

The File Manager also provides a Print List option. If you select this option, it prints the names and directory information for all of the files listed in the current directory list.

Directory Listing Options

The File Manager provides several options that let you select the filenames the list contains as well as the order and appearance of the names in the list.

Sorting the Directory List

By default, WordPerfect displays filenames in the file list sorted by name. If you are having trouble locating a specific file, you may want to display the files sorted by size, extension, or date. To change the sort order, type **9** or click on **Sort**. The File Manager Setup dialog box is displayed in Figure 19.9.

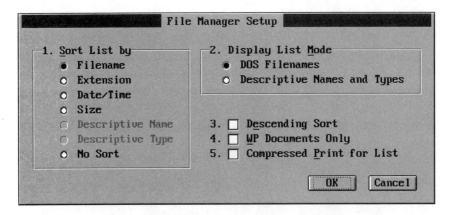

Figure 19.9 *The File Manager Setup dialog box.*

To change the sort order, type **1** or click on the **Sort List by** option. Select the field on which you want to sort the files

In Chapter 10 you learned that WordPerfect's Document Summary dialog box lets you type in a descriptive name for your document, such as 1993 Tax Information for the IRS or Letter to New York Regarding Distribution. If you assign such descriptive names to your documents, you can direct WordPerfect to display them instead of the document's DOS filenames.

To sort the document names from highest to lowest, restrict the file list to document files only, or to print the directory listing using a compressed font to save paper, select the corresponding check box.

After you make your directory sort and mode selections, choose **OK**.

Changing the File Manager's Default Directory

WordPerfect normally uses the directory WPDOCS as its default for File Manager operations. To use a different directory as the default, type **H** or click on the **Change Default Dir** option. The Change Default Directory dialog box is displayed in Figure 19.10.

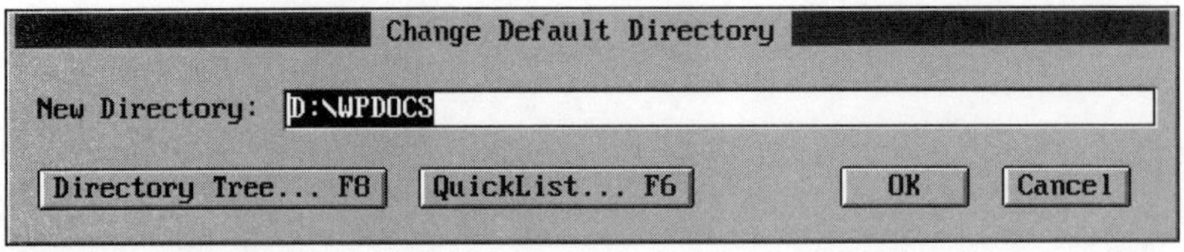

Figure 19.10 *The Change Default Directory dialog box.*

Type in the name of the directory you want to use as the default and press **Enter**.

Changing the Current Directory for the File List

The File Manager displays the files contained in a specific directory, to change the directory, type **U** or click on **Current Dir**. The Specify File Manager List dialog box as previously shown in Figure 19.2. Type in the desired directory name and press **Enter**.

Searching for a Specific Document File

As the number of document files on your disk increase, so does the difficulty of finding a specific document. To help you locate files, the File Manager provides several different options. To begin, type **F** or click on the **Find** option. The Find dialog box is displayed in Figure 19.11.

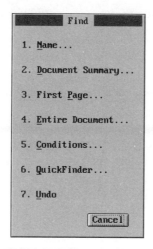

Figure 19.11 The Find dialog box.

Searching for a Document Name Pattern

Depending on the number of files in the list, the Name option may let you reduce the number of files you must examine by typing in a wildcard combination. When you select the **Name** option, the Find Name dialog box is displayed, as in Figure 19.12.

Figure 19.12 *The Find Name dialog box.*

If you want to restrict the list to only those files whose names begin with the letter B, you can type in the wildcard combination **B*.*** and press **Enter**.

Searching for Specific Text

If you can't remember a document's name, but you can remember specific text that appears in the document, you can search for the text:

◆ **Document Summary** searches each file's document summary for specific text.

◆ **First Page** lets you search the first page of each document for specific text.

◆ **Entire Document** searches the entire document (for each file) for the specified text.

When you search for specific text, you can reduce the number of matching files you must later search by providing specific search conditions. For example, you might locate a file that contains the words *Pay Raise* in the document summary and *Cheap Boss* in the document text. To define such conditions, type **C** or click on the **Conditions** option. The File Manager Find Conditions dialog box is displayed in Figure 19.13.

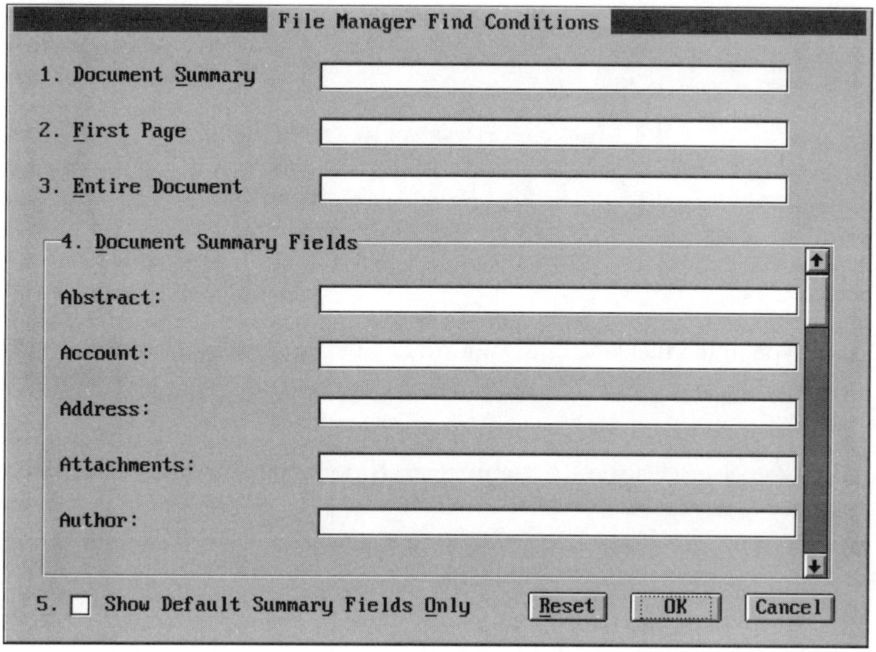

Figure 19.13 *The File Manager Find Conditions dialog box.*

In each section of the dialog box, type in the text that you want the File Manager to search and select **OK**. Use **Tab** to move the cursor from one field to the next.

Searching for a Specific Document Name

To locate and highlight a specific file in File Manager:

1. Press **F2** or click on the **Search** option. The Search for Filename dialog box is displayed in Figure 19.14.

Figure 19.14 The Search for Filename dialog box.

2. Type in the filename or a wildcard combination and press **Enter**.

3. The matching file is highlighted or a dialog box is displayed stating a match was not found.

4. Type **N** or click on the **Name Search** option. The Name Search dialog box is displayed.

5. As you type in the Name Search dialog box, the cursor advances to the first file whose name matches the letters typed.

Selecting Multiple Document Files for an Operation

The File Manager lets you print, copy, move, and delete document files. In many cases you may want to perform such operations on two or more files. The File Manager lets you mark the files you want to use in an operation.

The (Un)mark options work like a toggle switch. If a file is not marked and you select the option, the File Manager marks (selects) the file. If you select the option a second time, it unmarks the file. The (Un)mark All option lets you quickly mark or unmark all files.

To print a copy of every file in the directory mark all of the files and select **Print**. As you mark files, the File Manager displays a count of the number of files currently marked.

Understanding QuickLists

To organize your document files it is easy to select and display files when you create several different directories. A QuickList is simply a name you assign to a commonly used directory. When you select **Open** from the File menu, it displays the Open Document dialog box. The Open Document dialog contains the QuickList button that lets you view the names of your commonly used directories. The QuickList option displays the QuickList dialog box, shown in Figure 19.15.

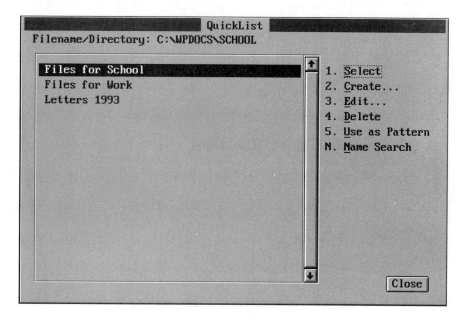

Figure 19.15 The QuickList dialog box.

If you have previously defined a QuickList, you can select it to display the list of files the corresponding directory contains. To define a QuickList:

1. Type **2** or click on the **Create** option.

2. A dialog box is displayed prompting you for the QuickList's description name and the corresponding directory path.

3. Type in both names and select **OK**.

Using the Directory Tree

The File Manager lets you display the files a directory list contains. There may be times when you can't recall the name of the directory that contains your files.

When you select the Directory Tree options, a visual representation of the directories that reside on your disk are displayed in Figure 19.16.

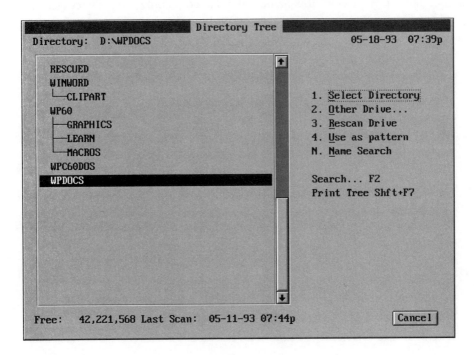

Figure 19.16 *The Directory Tree.*

Using the Arrow keys or mouse, you can scroll through the available directory names. When you locate the directory you desire, type **1** or click on the **Select Directory** option. The File Manager displays the names of the files that reside in the directory.

Changing the Default Drive

There may be times when you need to search for files that reside on a different disk. To display a directory tree for a different drive, type **2** or click on the **Other Drive** option. The File Manager list of available drives is displayed in Figure 19.17.

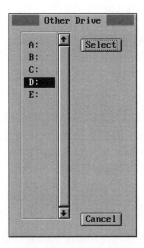

Figure 19.17 *A list of available disk drives.*

Using the Arrow keys, highlight the drive letter you desire and press **Enter**, or double click on the drive letter.

Understanding the QuickFinder

The QuickFinder File Indexer is very powerful and very complex. Most users do not need to use it. You may want to skip the following discussion.

The File Manager lets you define commonly used subdirectories as QuickLists. When you select a QuickList, the File Manager displays the files that reside in the directory list. If you are working on a large project, you may have files that reside in several different directories. Using QuickLists to locate a specific file can be a matter of trial and error. For such cases, the File Manager lets you define a QuickFinder File Index. A *file index* is a list of related document files. The files can reside in multiple directories on your disk. For example, for to write this book, I might create a QuickFinder File Index called *teach yourself WP 6.0* that contains the names of each file containing a chapter as well as the directory that contains each file.

To use a QuickFinder File Index:

1. Define an index.

2. Select the **Use QuickFinder** option the Specify File Manager List dialog box. The QuickFinder File Indexer dialog box is displayed in Figure 19.18.

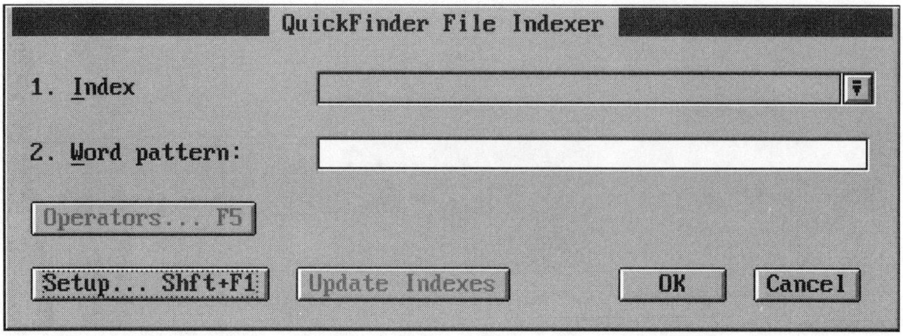

Figure 19.18 *The QuickFinder File Indexer dialog box.*

3. Type **Shift-F1** or click on the **Setup** option. The QuickFinder File Indexes Setup dialog box is displayed in Figure 19.19.

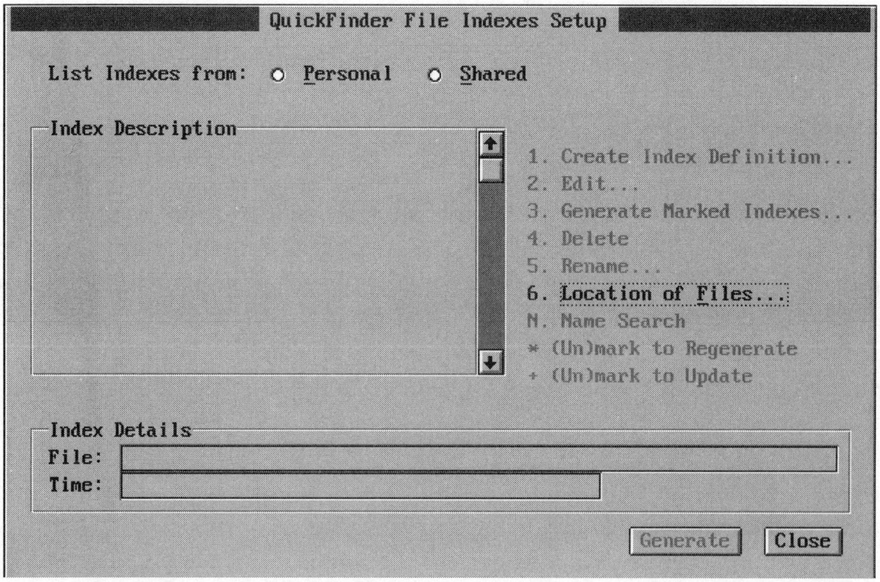

Figure 19.19 *The QuickFinder File Indexes Setup dialog box.*

4. Type **P** or click on the **Personal** button.

5. Type **1** or click on the **Create Index Definition** option. A dialog box asking you for the index description is displayed.

6. Type in an index name, such as Teach Yourself WP 6.0.

7. The index filename is created and displayed.

8. Select **OK**. A dialog box is displayed asking you for a filename pattern you want associated with the index.

In the case of this book, my document files began with the letters CHAP (such CHAP19), so I would use CHAP*.DOC. In the Create Index Definition dialog box, you can add multiple directories and file patterns to index. To include the document files containing appendices, for example, I would include the document pattern APPX*.DOC. If the desired files do not reside in the WPDOCS directory, select the **Location of Files** option to tell it the correct directory.

To search indexed files for a word pattern:

1. Select **QuickFinder** from the File Manager. The QuickFinder File Indexer dialog box is displayed in Figure 19.20.

Figure 19.20 *The QuickFinder File Indexer dialog box.*

2. In the Word Pattern field, type in the word you want to search.

3. Select the **Update Indexes** option to make sure the File Manager can correctly identify the corresponding files.

4. Select **OK**.

5. The indexed files are searched for the corresponding text, displaying a list of matching files or a dialog box containing a message that the text was not found.

Summary

As the number of document files on your disk increases, so does the difficulty in locating a specific file. To help you better manage your files, a File Manager is provided. The File Manager lets you view the files a directory contains to help locate the file you desire. It also lets you perform common file operations such as copy, move, rename, delete, and print operations. The File Manager is a very powerful and convenient way to access your document files. Take time to experiment with the File Manager. The time you spend now may save you more time in the future when you need to locate a specific document file.

New Terms

◆ **QuickFinder File Index**. A list of related document files may reside in the same or different directories. To help you quickly search related files for specific text, the File Manager lets you define a QuickFinder File Index. The files that hold the chapters of a book or a large report might be combined to create a QuickFinder File Index.

◆ **QuickList.** A name you assign to a commonly used subdirectory.

◆ The **File Manager** tracks and lets you display the files contained in a QuickList.

Chapter **20**

Customizing
the Button Bar

In this chapter you:

- ◆ Assign new buttons to the button bar
- ◆ Remove button bar buttons that you don't use
- ◆ Select a different button bar
- ◆ Control the button bar's appearance

Adding and Removing Button Bar Entries

After you have used WordPerfect for a short time, you begin to identify the operations that you perform on a regular basis. If the operations are not available on the button bar, you can add them to the bar, in the location that is most convenient. By placing commonly used operations on the button bar, the operations are only a mouse click away, as displayed in Figure 20.1

Figure 20.1 *The Button bar with Icons.*

If the button bar is not currently visible, select the View menu and choose **Button Bar**. There may be button bar buttons that you use on a regular basis, some you don't use, and some you wish that you had. For example, if you use the italic or bold font attributes on a regular basis, you may want to place buttons in the button bar for each. To add a button bar button:

1. Select the View menu and choose **Button Bar Setup**. WordPerfect cascades the menu shown in Figure 20.2.

Figure 20.2 *Cascading the Button Bar Setup menu.*

2. Choose the **Edit** option. The Edit Button Bar dialog box is displayed in Figure 20.3.

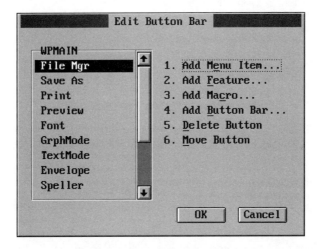

Figure 20.3 *The Edit Button Bar dialog box.*

3. From the Edit Button Bar dialog box, create a new button by selecting one of the menu items.

The Add Feature is a capability that allows you to choose options that may not appear on a menu, such as searching for the next matching word or phrase. In addition, you can add, delete, or move buttons, and make Macros.

Adding Button Bars

In Chapter 14, you learned how to insert the current date in your document as text. Because most users create dated letters and memos on a regular basis, you may want to add a date button to your button bar. To add a date text button:

1. Type **1** or click on the **Add Menu Item** button.
2. Select the desired menu option at the prompt, and press **F7**.
3. Choose **Date** from the Tools menu. The Date menu is cascaded.
4. Choose **Text**.

5. The menu is removed from your screen and the text DateText is added to your button list.

6. Press **F7** or click on **OK**.

If you want to create buttons for other menu options, do so before pressing **F7**.

In Chapter 30 you learn how to create Macros that let you perform specific operations. If you create a macro that performs a common operation, you may want to add the Macro to the button bar. To add a Macro to the button bar:

1. Open the View menu and choose **Button Bar Setup**.

2. Choose **Edit**

3. Type **3** or click on **Add Macro**.

4. Highlight the Macro you desire and press **Enter** or double click on the Macro.

5. Select **OK** to exit.

Viewing Buttons That Don't Appear on Your Screen. There is only a limited amount of screen space in which you can display your button bar buttons. If you assign many buttons to the bar, it wraps the buttons off the screen. To view buttons that don't appear on your screen, click on the **Up Arrow** or **Down Arrow** at the far left end of the button bar. The **Up Arrow** displays the previous screen's button bar, while the **Down Arrow** displays the buttons that appear on the following screen.

Removing Button Bar Buttons

If you have buttons on the button bar that you don't use, you can remove the buttons to make room for others. To remove a button from the button bar:

1. Open the View menu and choose **Button Bar Setup**.

2. When the menu cascades , choose **Edit**. The Edit Button Bar dialog box, shown in Figure 20.3, is displayed.

3. Using the Arrow keys, highlight the name of the button you want to remove, or click on the name.

4. Type **5** or click on the **Delete Button** option

5. To remove the button from the bar, select **Yes**.

6. To leave the button bar unchanged, select **No**.

Moving a Button Bar Button

Because of the limited amount of space to display buttons on your screen, you may have to page through the buttons using the Arrow buttons. To reduce the number of button bar scroll operations you must perform, place your most commonly used buttons at the start of the button bar. To move a button bar button:

1. Open the View menu and choose **Button Bar Setup**.

2. Choose **Edit**.

3. Use the Arrow keys to highlight the name of the button you want to move, or click on the name.

4. Type **6** or click on the **Move Button**.

5. Using the Arrow keys, highlight the name of the button *before which* you want the button placed.

6. Type **P** or click on the **Paste** button.

Controlling the Button Bar Display

By default, WordPerfect displays the button bar at the top of the screen. Depending on your preferences, you may want it to appear at the left, right, or bottom of your screen. The name and picture icon for each button are also displayed by default. To display only the button name or picture can reduce the amount of space the screen uses, as shown in Figures 20.4 and 20.5.

Figure 20.4 *The Button Bar with pictures only.*

Figure 20.5 *The Button Bar with text only.*

To control how the button bar is displayed, select the View menu and choose **Button Bar Setup**. When the menu cascades, choose **Options**. The Button Bar Options dialog box is displayed in Figure 20.6.

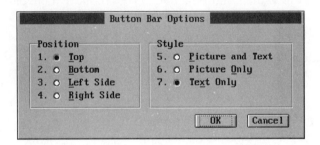

Figure 20.6 *The Button Bar Options dialog box.*

The Position field lets you place the button bar along any edge of the screen. The Style field lets you control the appearance of the button bar.

Changing Button Bars

WordPerfect provides several predefined Button Bars, each of which contains buttons that correspond to related operations. Following is a brief description of each button bar:

- ◆ **WPMAIN** is the main or default button bar.
- ◆ **FONTS** contains buttons for each font attribute.

- ◆ **LAYOUT** contains buttons for document formatting.
- ◆ **MACROS** contains buttons for WordPerfect's predefined macros.
- ◆ **OUTLINE** contains buttons for outlining operations.
- ◆ **TABLES** contains buttons for common table operations.
- ◆ **TOOLS** contains buttons for tools such as the Spell Checker, Thesaurus and Macro recorder.

You can only display one button bar at a time. To switch between bars:

1. Open the View menu and choose **Button Bar Setup**.
2. Choose **Select**.
3. Use the Arrow keys to highlight the desired button bar name or click on the name.
4. Type **1** or click on **Select**.

Spend a few moments now selecting and viewing WordPerfect's predefined button bars.

Adding a Button Bar as a Button

If you have two or three button bars you work with on a regular basis, you might consider placing buttons on each button bar that let you quickly select a different button bar. For example, if you place a Fonts button on the main button bar, selecting that button displays the Fonts button bar. To add a button bar as a button:

1. Open the View menu and choose **Button Bar Setup**.
2. Choose **Edit**.
3. Type **4** or click on **Add Button Bar**.
4. In the Button Bar List, use the Arrow keys to highlight the name of the desired button bar or click on the button bar name.
5. Press **Enter** or click on **Select**.

Summary

To make common operations easy and fast for you to perform, WordPerfect provides a button bar. By default, it displays the button bar at the top of your screen, but it lets you move the bar to the left, right, or bottom of your screen. Also by default, WordPerfect displays a graphic icon and includes a text name in each button. you can display only the text or graphic, which reduces the amount of screen space the button bar consumes. As you work with WordPerfect, you identify the operations you perform on a regular basis. If the operations don't have buttons, you can add a button for the operation. If the buttons you commonly use aren't easy to access, you can move or delete buttons you don't use. Depending on the operations you are currently performing, you may want to use one of the predefined button bars, such as the Outline or Tables button bar.

New Terms

◆ **Button bar.** One or more icons displayed on the screen that you can click on to perform a common operation.

Chapter **21**

Headers, Footers, and Watermarks

In this chapter you:

- ◆ Assign headers and footers to your document
- ◆ Assign a watermark to a document
- ◆ Edit an existing header, footer, or watermark

227

Understanding Headers and Footers

When you create reports and other long documents, you normally place the document's name at a position on the page that falls outside the document text. Likewise, you might print the date the document was created at the bottom of your page. To display information outside of your document text in this way, you use headers and footers. For example, if you look at the top of the pages of this book, you will see the headers. When you create a header, WordPerfect places the text at the first usable line beneath the top margin. The footer text is placed immediately above the bottom margin, as in Figure 21.1.

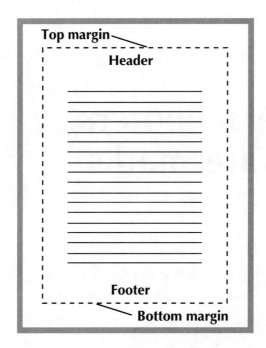

Figure 21.1 *Headers and footers.*

Depending on your document, you may want to display a different header and footer on odd and even pages. WordPerfect lets you define headers named *Header A* and *Header B* and two footers named *Footer A* and *Footer B*. You might, for example, assign the header and footer you want to appear on even pages to Header A and Footer A, and the header and footer for odd pages to pages to Header A and Footer A, and the header and footer for odd pages to Header B and Footer B.

When you assign headers and footers to your document, WordPerfect begins the headers and footers on the current page. If you want the headers and footers to appear on every page, move your cursor to the start of your document before assigning the header or footer.

Most documents do not display a header or footer on the opening page. Move the cursor to page two of your document before assigning the header and footer.

N O T E

To create a header or footer, open the Layout menu and choose **Header/Footer/Watermark**. The Header/Footer/Watermark dialog box is displayed in Figure 21.2.

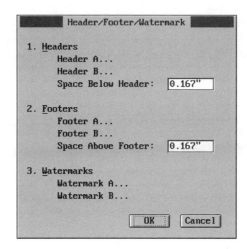

Figure 21.2 *The Header/Footer/Watermark dialog box.*

Creating a Header

If you plan to display the same header on every page, choose the **Header A** option. The Header A dialog box is displayed in Figure 21.3.

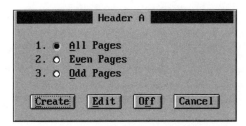

Figure 21.3 *The Header A dialog box.*

To specify the pages that you want the headers to appear:

1.   Type **1** to place the header on every page.

2.   Type **C** or click on the **Create** button. An editing screen is displayed, as in Figure 21.4.

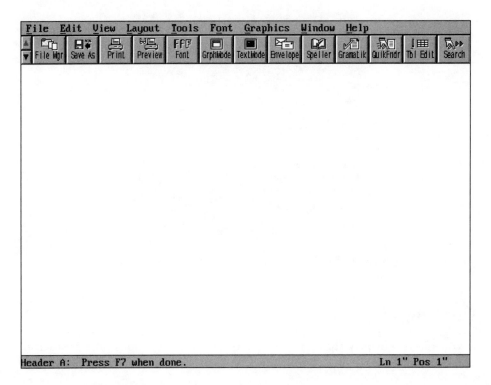

Figure 21.4 *The header editing screen.*

Although most headers only contain (and should only contain) one line of text, WordPerfect lets you place as many lines of text in your headers as you desire. In addition, you can choose different font sizes, attributes, or even include graphics. If you want your header text to be right, left, or center justified, follow the steps discussed in Chapter 14. Type in the following header text:

```
Teach Yourself WordPerfect 6.0
```

1. Select the header text and use center justify
2. Open the File menu and choose **Exit**.
3. You return you to your document. The header text does not appear on your screen.

To display the header, print your document or select the File menu **Print Preview** option.

Assigning Different Headers to Odd and Even Pages

In the previous example, you used Header A on every page of your document. To display a different header on odd and even pages, determine the header you want to display on even pages and assign it to Header A. When it displays the Header A dialog box, previously shown in Figure 21.3, select **Even Pages**. After you create the even page header, repeat this process, assigning the odd page header to Header B.

Creating a Footer

The steps to create a document footer are almost identical to those you just performed to create a header. To create a footer that contains the text in Chapter 2:

1. Open the Layout menu and choose **Header/Footer/Watermark**.
2. When the Header/Footer/Watermark dialog box is displayed, select the desired footer (A or B).
3. Select the **Odd**, **Even**, or **All pages** option.
4. Select **Create** and type in the text you desire.
5. Open the File menu **Exit** option or press **F7**.

Controlling the Spacing around Headers and Footers

By default, WordPerfect places your document text no closer than 0.167 inches to your header or footer. If you need to change this spacing:

1. Open the Layout menu and choose **Header/Footer/Watermark**.
2. Select **Header** or **Footer** and then type **3** or click on the space box.
3. Type in the amount of space you desire and press **Enter**.

Understanding Watermarks

A *watermark* is a drawing, logo, or large text that you display shaded behind a document's text. If you are working on a draft document, for example, you might place the letters DRAFT as a watermark that appears behind your text. You might include a graphic of your company's logo shaded behind a letter or report cover page. To better understand how you might use a watermark:

1. Open the File menu and choose the letter (AIRGIZMO.LTR) you created in Chapter 2.
2. Open the Layout menu and choose **Header/Footer/Watermark**.
3. Select **Watermark A**. WordPerfect displays a dialog box asking you which pages you want the watermark to appear on.
4. Select **All** and then choose **Create**.
5. A screen is displayed in which you can create the watermark.

In this case, place a graphic of hot air balloons as a watermark:

1. Open the Graphics menu and choose **Retrieve Graphic Image**.
2. Type in the path name **\WP60\GRAPHICS\HOTAIR.WPG** and press **Enter**.
3. WordPerfect inserts the graphic in the watermark.

4. Select **Exit**.

5. When you return to your document, select the File menu **Print** option to print your document, showing the watermark.

WordPerfect treats watermarks just as it does headers and footers, allowing you to assign a different watermark to odd and even pages.

Editing or Turning Off a Header, Footer, or Watermark

Just as there are times when you change the contents of your document, there are times when you want to edit or turn off the display of an existing header, footer, or watermark. To perform an edit operation:

1. Open the Layout menu and choose **Header/Footer/Watermark**.

2. Select the item you want to Edit.

3. Type **E** or click on the **Edit** button.

4. WordPerfect displays the current item in an editing screen.

5. Perform the changes you desire and select the File menu **Exit** option.

To turn off a header, footer, or watermark:

1. Open the Layout menu and choose **Header/Footer/Watermark**.

2. Select the item you want to turn off.

3. Type **F** or click on the **Off** button.

Summary

As the size of your document increases, you may want to display specific text, such as the document title or creation date at the top or bottom of each page. Headers and footers provide an easy way to display such information on every page or on even and odd pages. Creating a header or footer in WordPerfect, is very much like creating a document. You can specify one or more lines of text, right, left, or center justify the text, and use the fonts you desire. In addition, you can even include small graphics.

A *watermark* is a graphic or text that appears shaded behind your document text. Common uses of watermarks include company logos, document security classifications, and so on. Like a header or footer, you can display watermarks on every page or on even or odd pages.

New Terms

- ◆ **Footer.** Text or a small graphic that appears at the bottom of your document pages, immediately above the bottom margin.

- ◆ **Header.** Text or a small graphic that appears at the top of your document pages, immediately below the top margin.

- ◆ **Watermark.** A drawing, logo, or large text that is displayed shaded behind a document's text.

Chapter 22

Basic Text Formatting

In this chapter you:

- ◆ Understand hard and soft returns
- ◆ Insert and delete page breaks
- ◆ Control line spacing
- ◆ Turn line numbering on and off
- ◆ Set document margins
- ◆ Specify the paragraph separation distance
- ◆ Create a hanging indent
- ◆ Understand hyphenation and hyphenation zones

Using Hard and Soft Returns

As you learned in Chapter 2, when you type in WordPerfect, you only press the Enter key at the end of paragraphs or short lines. When your text reaches the right margin, it automatically wraps your text to the start of the next line. When WordPerfect wraps your text it places a hidden code in your document called a *soft return*. When you press **Enter**, WordPerfect places a hard return in your document. To better understand hard and soft returns type:

> Albert Einstein was born in Germany in 1879. In 1905, Einstein received his Ph.D. in physics. During his lifetime, Einstein wrote four major papers, the most important of which was his theory of relativity.
>
> In 1922, Einstein received the Nobel Prize for Physics. Einstein's work in relativity remains one of the most important contributions to the field of physics.

When you press **Enter** to separate the two paragraphs, WordPerfect places a second hard return in your document. Figure 22.1 illustrates the use of hard and soft returns.

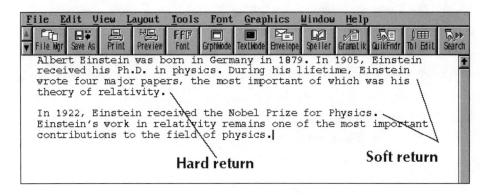

Figure 22.1 The use of hard and soft returns.

Because WordPerfect inserts soft returns to wrap text, it won't let you delete them. If you place the cursor in front of the word *received* on line two and press the **Backspace** key, it combines the words *Einstein* and *received,* wrapping both words, as in Figure 22.2.

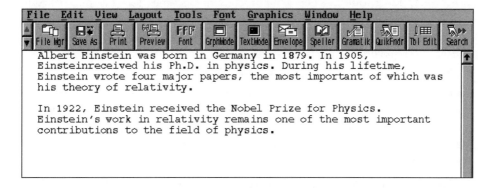

Figure 22.2 WordPerfect does not let you remove soft returns.

In this case, press the **Spacebar** to separate the words. WordPerfect moves the word *Einstein* back up one line, restoring the original text wrapping. Next, place the cursor in front of the word *In* at the start of paragraph two. When you press **Backspace**, it deletes the hard return you previously created by pressing **Enter**. As WordPerfect removes the hard return, it moves your text up one line. Press **Backspace** a second time, It removes the second hard return, combining the two paragraphs into one, as in Figure 22.3.

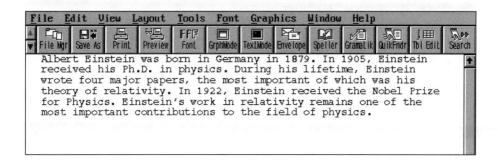

Figure 22.3 Removing hard returns from your document.

As you work with WordPerfect, remember that you can use Backspace or Del to remove hard return characters.

Understanding Page Breaks

As you may have found, when your document becomes long, it automatically breaks your text, moving it to the next page. When WordPerfect moves text to the start of a new page in this way, it places a hidden code in your document called a *soft page break*.

When you type a long document, there may be times when WordPerfect breaks text at the bottom of a page, at the start of a paragraph, or passage you want to keep together. To help you control document formatting, WordPerfect lets you insert your own hard page breaks by pressing **Ctrl-Enter**. When you press **Ctrl-Enter**, creating a hard page break, WordPerfect displays double lines in your document.

To better understand hard page breaks, close the Einstein document using the File menu **Close** option. Do not save the document. Next, type the following text:

```
Page 1 Stuff
Page 2 Stuff
Page 3 Last Stuff
```

Place the cursor at the start of the text *Page 2 Stuff* and press **Ctrl-Enter**. WordPerfect separates the first two lines of text with a double underline. Repeat this processing, pressing **Ctrl-Enter** in front of the text.

Select the File menu **Print/Fax** option and print the document. Each line of text is printed on its own page.

Place the cursor at the start of the line *Page 3 Last Stuff* and press **Backspace**. The double underlines are removed from between the last two lines of text. When you pressed **Backspace**, it deleted the hard page break you previously inserted. If you select the File menu **Print/Fax** option, it prints the text on two pages. Place the cursor in front of the text *Page 2 Stuff* and press **Backspace**. The underlines are removed. If you print the text, all three lines are printed on the same page. As you work with larger documents, there may be times when you want to control where the pages break. Press **Ctrl-Enter** to insert a hard page break.

Controlling Line Spacing

All of the documents you have created thus far have single spaced text. When you create reports or other large documents, you may need to use 1 1/2 or double spacing. WordPerfect assigns line spacing from the current cursor position forward in your document. If you want to change the line spacing for your entire document, move the cursor to the top of your document and change the line spacing. To change the line spacing for a specific section of text, select the text using a block operation and then apply the desired line spacing to the block. To better understand line spacing type the following text:

> Martin Luther King, Jr. was a Baptist minister when he began his pursuit of civil rights in 1955. Although his work lasted nearly 14 years, King is best known for the 1963 "March on Washington" and his words:
>
> "I have a dream that one day this nation will rise up and live out true meaning of this creed-We hold these truths to be self evident: that all mean are created equal..."

1. Place the cursor in front of the words *"I have a dream.*

2. To double space the quote, select the Layout menu and choose **Line**. The Line Format dialog box is displayed in Figure 22.4.

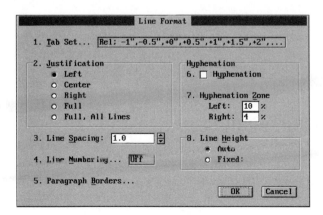

Figure 22.4 *The Line Format dialog box.*

3. Type **3** or click on the **Line Spacing** option.

4. Type in the value **2.0** and press **Enter**.

The double spaced quote is displayed in Figure 22.5.

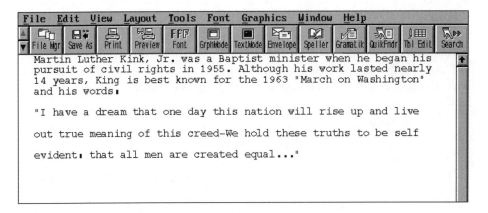

Figure 22.5 *Using single and double spaced lines.*

The Line Format dialog box Line Spacing option lets you select the desired line spacing in multiples of a single spaced line. If you wanted to use 1 1/2 line spacing, for example, you would type in the value 1.5.

 Once you specify a line setting, WordPerfect assigns the line spacing for the remainder of your document or until you change the spacing once again.

N O T E

In the case of Martin Luther King's quote, if you want to resume single spaced lines after the quote, select the Line Format dialog box and type in the value **1.0** in the **Line Spacing** option.

Turning Line Numbering On and Off

If you are creating a draft copy of a document, there may be times when you want to turn on line numbering. In this way, if you make specific changes to the document you can reference a page and line number. For example, you may need to delete line 5 from page 3. WordPerfect turns line numbering on and off from the current cursor position. If you want to number your entire document, move the cursor to the start of your document before assigning the line numbers. To turn line numbers on and off in your document, select the Layout menu and choose **Line**. The dialog box's **Line Numbering** option lets you turn line numbering on and off.

Controlling Your Document Margins

By default, WordPerfect places a one inch margin around your document. Depending on your needs, there may be times when you want to change the margin settings. To change the top, bottom, left or right margin, open the Layout menu and choose **Margins**. The Margin Format dialog box is displayed in Figure 22.6.

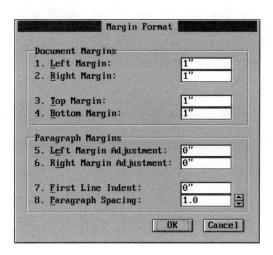

Figure 22.6 *The Margin Format dialog box.*

To change a specific margin in your document, type the number that corresponds with the desired margin or click on the **Margin** option. Next, type in the desired setting.

The Margin Format dialog box contains two parts, one labeled Document Margins and one Paragraph Margins. The Document Margin settings control the margins for your entire document. There may be times when you want to change the margins for one or more paragraphs that appear in your document. To change the paragraph's margins, select the paragraph using a block operation. Use the Margin Format dialog box's **Paragraph Margins** to change the margins for only the selected paragraphs leaving the rest of your document unchanged.

Controlling Paragraph Spacing

By default, WordPerfect separates paragraphs using a single line. In other words, if you press **Enter** to generate a hard return (which marks the end of a paragraph), it advances the cursor to the start of the next line. If you normally double space between paragraphs, you can use the Margin Format dialog box **Paragraph Spacing** option to specify the desired spacing. The option's value is a multiple of a single spaced line. If you want to double space between paragraphs, set the value to 2.0:

Creating a Hanging Indent

A *hanging indent* describes an indentation that causes the first line of paragraph to project further left than the paragraph's remaining lines as shown here:

```
The best executive is the one who has sense enough to
        pick good men to do what he wants done, and
        self-restraint enough to keep from meddling
        with them while they do it.
```

To create a hanging indent, use the Margin Format dialog box **First Line Indent** option.

In the case of the previous text, a hanging indent of 1/2 inch was used. To create a half inch hanging indent, you need to indent the first line 0.5 inches to the left or -0.5.

Understanding Hyphenation

As you know, when your text reaches the right margin, it wraps the text to the next line. When you use full justification, there may be times when a long word does not fit at the end of the line, but wrapping the word causes WordPerfect to place too many spaces in the sentence, as in Figure 22.7.

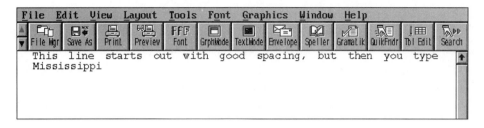

Figure 22.7 *An example of large spaces to enable full justification.*

To help you correct problem words, you can hyphenate the word, as in Figure 22.8.

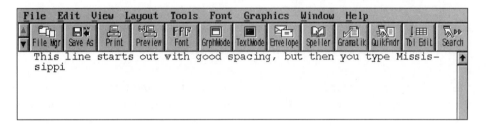

Figure 22.8 *Correcting spacing with hyphenation.*

In this case, the problem was solved by manually hyphenating the word. If you type the hyphen character (-), WordPerfect automatically inserts a hard hyphen. Unfortunately, if you later delete the word, your manual hyphenation remains, as in Figure 22.9.

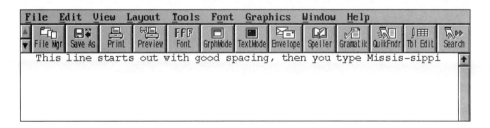

Figure 22.9 *An example of a hard hyphen remaining in a word.*

To avoid such situations, you can place soft hyphens in a word by pressing **Ctrl** when you type the hyphen. When you use a soft hyphen, WordPerfect automatically removes the hyphen when it is no longer needed.

To simplify hyphenation operations, you can automatically hyphenate your document. To select automatic hyphenation, choose the Layout menu **Line** option. The Hyphenation check box lets you turn automatic hyphenation on and off.

WordPerfect uses hyphenation zones to determine when to apply automatic hyphenation. The hyphenation zone is the percentage of the line in which hyphenation can occur.

If you have a document that uses many large words, you may want to increase the hyphenation zone.

Completing the Online Tutorial

In Chapter 9 you learned how to use WordPerfect's online tutorial. You are now ready to complete the tutorial. Select the Help menu and choose **Tutorial**. Within the tutorial perform lessons 3 (Formatting text) and 4 (Finishing up). If you have time, you might want to quickly review lessons 1 and 2.

Recording While You Were Out Messages

If you are tired of returning to a desk that is cluttered with pink While You Were Out messages, you may want to use the companion disk's While You Were Out document. As shown in Figure 22.10, the document lets you place four such messages on the same page.

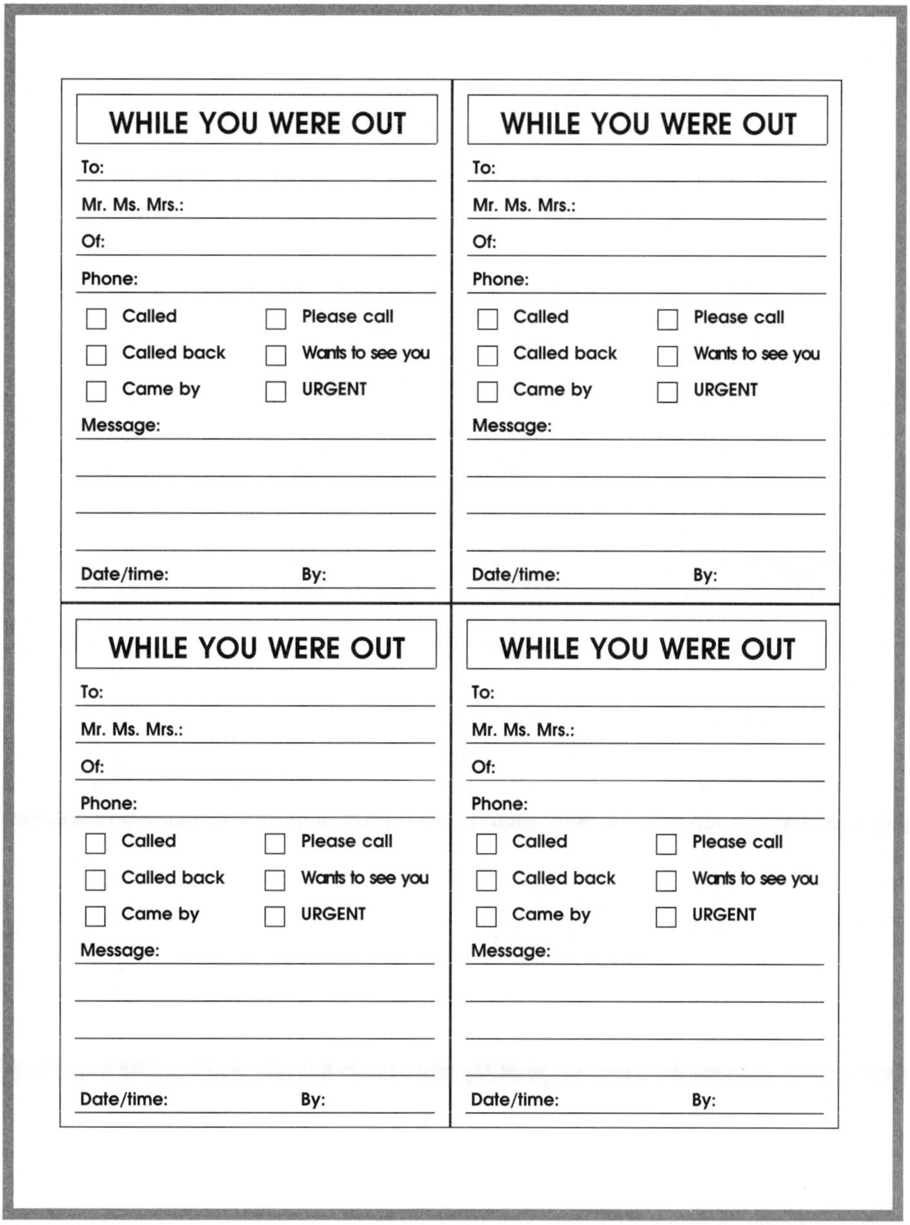

WHILE YOU WERE OUT

To: _____

Mr. Ms. Mrs.: _____

Of: _____

Phone: _____

☐ Called   ☐ Please call

☐ Called back   ☐ Wants to see you

☐ Came by   ☐ URGENT

Message: _____

_____

_____

_____

Date/time: _____ By: _____

WHILE YOU WERE OUT

To: _____

Mr. Ms. Mrs.: _____

Of: _____

Phone: _____

☐ Called   ☐ Please call

☐ Called back   ☐ Wants to see you

☐ Came by   ☐ URGENT

Message: _____

_____

_____

_____

Date/time: _____ By: _____

WHILE YOU WERE OUT

To: _____

Mr. Ms. Mrs.: _____

Of: _____

Phone: _____

☐ Called   ☐ Please call

☐ Called back   ☐ Wants to see you

☐ Came by   ☐ URGENT

Message: _____

_____

_____

_____

Date/time: _____ By: _____

WHILE YOU WERE OUT

To: _____

Mr. Ms. Mrs.: _____

Of: _____

Phone: _____

☐ Called   ☐ Please call

☐ Called back   ☐ Wants to see you

☐ Came by   ☐ URGENT

Message: _____

_____

_____

_____

Date/time: _____ By: _____

Figure 22.10 *The companion disk While You Were Out document.*

To use the While You Were Out document:

1. Open the File menu and select **Open**.
2. Type in the filename **OUTMSGS.DOC**.
3. Type in your message.
4. Save the document to your hard disk as WHILEOUT.DOCU using the File menu **Save As** option.

When you need to record one or more While You Were Out messages for another office member, you can open this document, type in the messages, and then save the document to a file that corresponds to the user name. When the user returns, you can print the document, combining their messages on one page.

Summary

As you type documents, WordPerfect places soft returns at the end of each line to wrap text. When you press Enter at the end of a line (or paragraph), WordPerfect places a hard return in your document. Using the Del or Backspace key, you can delete hard return characters. To combine two paragraphs, for example, you would remove the hard return character that separates them. In a similar way, when a document reaches the end of page, WordPerfect inserts a soft page break in a document to start text on the next page. Depending on the document's contents, there may be times when you want to control where WordPerfect breaks a page by pressing Ctrl-Enter to insert a hard page break. WordPerfect lets you control line spacing and numbering. When you perform line operations, WordPerfect applies the operation from the current point in the documentation forward. Lastly, WordPerfect's Layout menu Margin option lets you control your document margins as well as the margins of selected paragraphs. Using the Margin option you can quickly define a hanging indent.

New Terms

◆ **Hanging Indent.** A paragraph whose first line extends further left of the lines that follow.

◆ **Hard page break.** A character code created when you press Ctrl-Enter that directs WordPerfect to place the text that follows at the start of the next page.

◆ **Hard return.** A character code created when you press the Enter key that performs a carriage return linefeed operation.

◆ **Hyphenation zone.** The portion of the line in which WordPerfect's automatic hyphenation operations can insert a hyphen.

◆ **Soft page break.** A character code placed in your document automatically to define the end of the current page and to move text to the start of the next page.

◆ **Soft return.** A character code placed in your document that automatically wraps text at the right margin.

Chapter 23

Creating a Bulleted List

In this chapter you:

- ◆ Create a bulleted list
- ◆ Use WordPerfect's special characters

Understanding Bulleted Lists

When you create documents there may be times when you need to create a list of items:

- ◆ Tasks workers must perform.
- ◆ Key points emerging from a meeting.
- ◆ Important points that you want the reader to focus.
- ◆ And much, much more.

When you place a list of items in a document, placing a character (called the bullet) in front of lists helps the reader distinguish between list items. Note how the following list is less effective:

Tasks workers must perform.

Key points emerging from a meeting.

Important points that you want the reader to focus.

And much, much more.

Creating a Bulleted List

To better understand how to create a bulleted list:

1. Select the File menu and choose **New**.
2. Type in the following text:

```
WordPerfect 6.0 provides the following key features:
    A WYSIWYG user interface
    Drag and drop move and copy operations
    An online help facility with a tutorial and coaches
    A button bar that simplifies common operations
    Built-in FAX support
```

3. Place the cursor in front of the words A WYSIWYG.
4. Open the Font menu, shown in Figure 23.1.

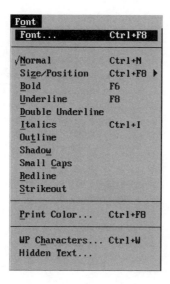

Figure 23.1 *The Font menu.*

5. Select the **WP Characters** option. The WordPerfect Characters dialog box is displayed in Figure 23.2.

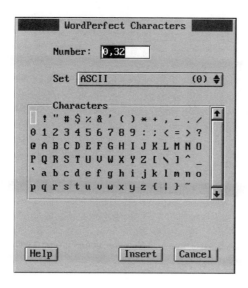

Figure 23.2 *The WordPerfect Characters dialog box.*

6. Press **Tab** to select the **Set** option and press **Enter**, or click on the option. A list of available character sets is displayed in Figure 23.3.

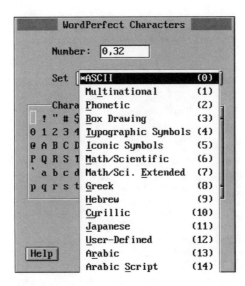

Figure 23.3 *Displaying the available character sets.*

7. Type **4** or click on the **Typographic Symbols** option. The Typographic Symbols set displayed in Figure 23.4.

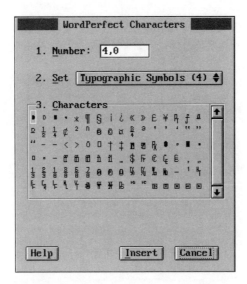

Figure 23.4 *The Typographic Symbols set.*

8. Highlight the box character that appears at the start of the fourth row of characters.

9. Press **Esc** and type **I** or click on the **Insert** button. WordPerfect displays the box character in front of the list item.

10. Press the **Spacebar** twice to put two spaces between the box and the text.

11. Repeat this process for the remaining list items.

Understanding WordPerfect Characters

In the previous section, you selected the typographic symbols to insert a box character as the bullet in a bulleted list. WordPerfect provides several different character sets to help users type characters using the Greek, Hebrew, Cyrillic, Japanese, or Arabic character sets. In addition, it provides symbols that you can use in mathematical expressions. Admittedly, not every user needs these character sets, however, there are several characters in the WordPerfect's Iconic Symbols character set that you can use to give your letters and memos personality:

1. Open the Fonts menu and choose **WP Characters**.

2. When the WordPerfect Characters dialog box is displayed, select the **Iconic Symbols** character set. The symbols are displayed in Figure 23.5.

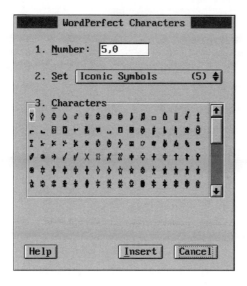

Figure 23.5 *The Iconic Symbols set.*

3. Highlight the character that appears at the center of the first row (actually nine characters from the right) and select **Insert**. WordPerfect inserts a happy face character in your document. Depending on the purpose of your letter or memo, you may want to use such a character as the bullet in a bulleted list, or at the end of a sentence. Experiment with the characters provided in the iconic symbols character set. You may find several symbols that you like to use in your documents.

Using the Bullet Coach

In Chapter 18 you learned that WordPerfect's online help facility provides a set of Coaches that walk you through specific operations. Once such coach is the Bullet Coach. To use the Bullet Coach:

1. Open the Help menu and choose **Coaches**.
2. In the Coaches dialog box, highlight Bullet Coach and press **Enter** or double click on the option.
3. Follow the instructions that appear on your screen.

Summary

To help the user distinguish entries that appear in lists in a document, you may want to precede each entry with a special symbol called a bullet. The advantage of using bullets include:

- ♦ Draws the user's attention to the list.
- ♦ Distinguishes list elements.
- ♦ Breaks up the appearance of your text.

To help you create more interesting bullets, you can select one of the alternate character sets. You don't have to restrict your use of WordPerfect's alternative character sets to bullets. If you need to generate characters in a foreign character set or if you need to enter a mathematical symbol, WordPerfect provides a character set to meet your needs.

New Terms

◆ **Bullet.** A character that precedes each item in a list for the purpose of drawing the reader's attention to distinct list entries.

◆ **Character Set.** A collection of symbols you can display in a document. WordPerfect provides character sets for several foreign alphabets as well as iconic, mathematical, and box drawing symbols.

Formatting
a Page of Text

In this chapter you:

- ◆ Assign page numbers to your document
- ◆ Learn how to center pages
- ◆ Learn how to force a page to an even or odd page number
- ◆ Select a paper size and type
- ◆ Learn how to print labels
- ◆ Subdivide a page
- ◆ Turn off headers, footers, watermarks, or page numbers
- ◆ Delay formatting codes
- ◆ Create a page border

Understanding Page Formatting

In Chapter 22 you learned how to perform basic text formatting operations. WordPerfect makes many common formatting operations available at the page level. For example, to assign page numbers to your document, you must do so at the page level. If you want to print mailing labels you have to do it at the page formatting level. To get started with the Page formatting capabilities, open the Layout menu and choose **Page**. The Page Format dialog box is displayed in Figure 24.1.

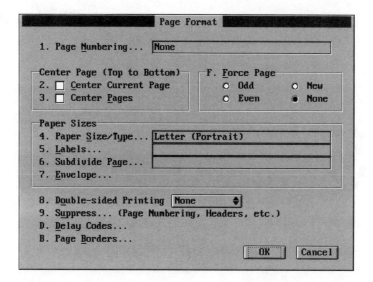

Figure 24.1 *The Page Format dialog box.*

From in the Page Format dialog box, you can perform considerable document formatting.

Assigning Page Numbers to Your Document

Page numbers are assigned from the current document position forward. If you want to number each document page:

1. Move the cursor to the start of your document before assigning page numbers.

2. Open the Page Format dialog box **Page Numbering** option. The Page Numbering dialog box is displayed in Figure 24.2.

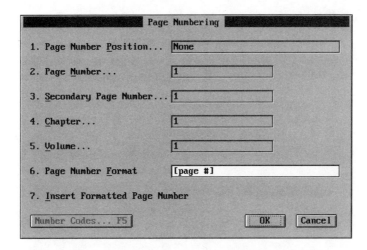

Figure 24.2 *The Page Numbering dialog box.*

Positioning the Page Number

You can display the page number in several different locations. To specify the location, type **P** or click on the **Page Number Position** option. The Page Number Position dialog box is displayed Figure 24.3.

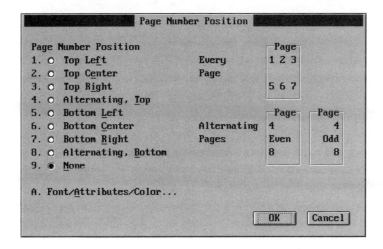

Figure 24.3 *The Page Number Position dialog box.*

Using the possible page number positions as your guide, type the number that corresponds to the desired position, or click on the position button.

Specifying the Starting Page Number and Number Type

By default, WordPerfect begins its page numbering with page 1. If you are creating a multi-chapter document, however, you may want WordPerfect to begin numbering at a different number. For example, Chapter 2 might start on page 23. To assign the starting page number:

1. Type **N** or click on the **Page Number** option. The Set Page Number dialog box is displayed in Figure 24.4.

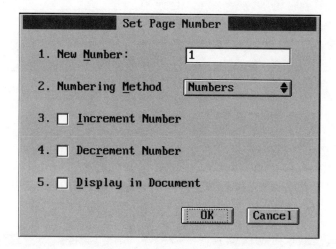

Figure 24.4 *The Set Page Number dialog box.*

2. To assign a starting line number, type **N** or click on the **New Number** box.

3. Type in the page number you desire.

WordPerfect lets you use numbers, Roman numerals, or even letters of the alphabet as page numbers. To select the page number type, type **M** or click on the **Numbering Method** button.

The Set Page Number dialog box lets you direct the increment or decrement page numbers. In addition, you can direct it to display page numbers in your document. By default, page numbers only appear when you print your document.

Assigning Secondary Page Numbers

There are times when you print or fax a document and you only want to print or send specific pages. To make such operations easier, WordPerfect lets you assign secondary page numbers to parts of your document. For example, you want to print 10 pages beginning at page 17. Rather than having to remember that you want to print pages 17 through 27, you can assign the secondary page numbers 1 through 10 to the pages. Later, when you want to print or fax the pages, you can refer to the secondary page numbers. The process of assigning a secondary page number is identical to that you just performed to assign standard page numbers.

Using Chapter and Volume Numbers

Depending on your document, there may be times when you want to assign pages to a chapter or volume. Select the Page Numbering dialog box **Chapter** or **Volume** options.

Changing the Page Number's Appearance

By default, WordPerfect displays the page number. In some cases, you may want to precede the page number with a word, such as *Page 14*. To control a page number's appearance, select the Page Numbering dialog box **Page Number Format** option. Type in the text you desire and select **OK**.

Centering a Page

In Chapter 13 you learned how to center justify text, placing the text between the pages left and right margins. In a similar way, you can center text between the top and bottom margin. Select the Page Format dialog box **Center Page** options. When you center a page of text, WordPerfect automatically centers the text as it prints.

Controlling Paper Sizes

By default, WordPerfect prints your documents on letter sized 8 1/2 by 11 paper. If your printer is capable of printing on different sized paper, such as legal paper, or if you want WordPerfect to print your documents in landscape as opposed to portrait mode, open the Page Format dialog box **Paper Size/Type** option. The Paper Size/Type dialog box is displayed in Figure 24.5.

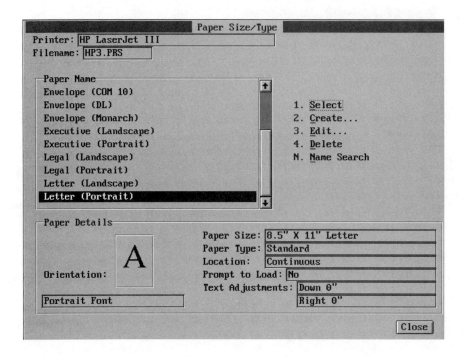

Figure 24.5 *The Paper Size/Type dialog box.*

From in Paper Name list, you can quickly select a commonly used paper size. The list includes entries for portrait and landscape mode. The lower half of the dialog box describes the details about the selected paper. If you need to change one of the details, highlight the paper in the Paper Name list and choose **Edit**. The Edit Paper Size/Type dialog box is displayed in Figure 24.6.

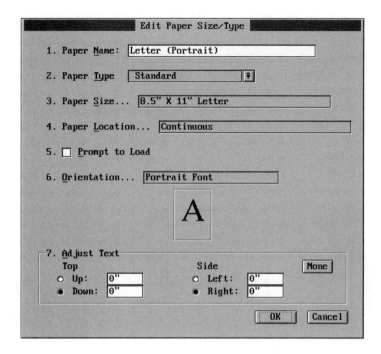

Figure 24.6 *The Edit Paper Size/Type dialog box.*

In this dialog box you can change the print location from which the paper is fed, direct it to prompt you to load the specific paper in the printer, or perform text positioning adjustments.

Printing Labels

If you have a printer capable of printing labels, WordPerfect makes it very easy to print mailing lists. In the Page Format dialog box:

1. Type **L** or click on the **Labels** option. The Label File dialog box is displayed.

2. Highlight the Predefined Labels and choose **Select**. The Labels dialog box is displayed in Figure 24.7.

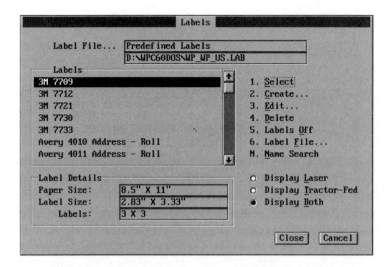

Figure 24.7 The Labels dialog box.

3. Using the Arrow keys or mouse, you can scroll through the label names listed in the Labels list.

4. Highlight a label name, The label details are displayed, such as label size and spread in the Label Details dialog box.

5. Select the label size that matches your labels and type **1** or click on the **Select** option.

6. You return to the Page Format dialog box.

7. Select **OK**. WordPerfect then displays a column that corresponds to the label width.

8. Type in the information you want to place on the label.

If the label supports five lines of text and you only have three, you can press **Enter** following your last line of text or you can press **Ctrl-Enter** to create a page break. The next label is selected. The best way to view how many labels you have used is to open the View menu and choose **Page**. WordPerfect displays your document with the correct number of label columns.

Subdividing Your Page

Depending on your document, there may be times when you want WordPerfect to divide a physical page (a piece of paper) into several smaller pages. For example, if you are printing raffle tickets or you are trying to use WordPerfect to counterfeit twenty-dollar bills. A logical page in this case would correspond to a raffle ticket or a dollar bill. Because you can fit several of these items on a sheet of paper, you may want to subdivide your page. To do so, open the Page Format dialog box **Subdivide Page** option. The Subdivide Page dialog box, displayed in Figure 24.8, asks you to specify the number of rows and columns in each logical page.

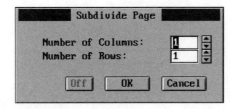

Figure 24.8 *The Subdivide Page dialog box.*

Type in the number of rows and columns you desire and select **OK**.

Printing Envelopes

To type in a mailing and return address you want to print on an envelope, open Page Format and select **Envelope**. Chapter 28 discusses in detail the steps you must perform to print envelopes.

Double-Sided Printing

If your printer supports double-sided printing you can print documents on both sides. Open the Page Format dialog box **Double-Sided Printing** option. When you select this option, WordPerfect displays the list of binding options.

If you are binding your document along the top or bottom, select the **Short Edge** option. If you are binding the document along the right or left side, select the **Long Edge** option.

Suppressing Page Numbers, Headers, and Footers

There may be times when you want to turn off headers, footers, page numbers, or watermarks on the current page. To do so:

1. Open the Page Format dialog box and select **Suppress (This Page Only)**. The Suppress (This Page Only) dialog box is displayed in Figure 24.9.

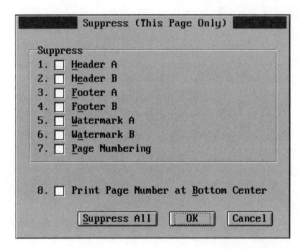

Figure 24.9 The Suppress (This Page Only) dialog box.

2. Select the options that you want to suppress and then choose **OK**.

Delaying Code Placement

By default, WordPerfect (when auto code placement is enabled) moves many formatting codes to the top of the current page, regardless of the cursor's position when you entered the code. If you don't want the codes to affect the current page, you can have them placed on a later page. Moving codes to a later page in this way is called *delaying a code*. To delay codes:

1. Open the Page Format dialog box and select **Delay Codes**.

2. Type in the number of pages you want to wait before applying the codes and select **OK**.

3. A dialog box is displayed where you can place the codes you want to delay.

4. Enter the codes and press **F7**.

Creating a Page Border or Filling the Page

WordPerfect lets you display a frame that appears at your page margins. In addition, you can display your text on a shaded background. To add such a border to your document, select the Page Format dialog box **Page Border** option. The Create Page Border dialog box is displayed in Figure 24.10.

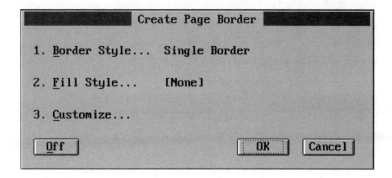

Figure 24.10 *The Create Page Border dialog box.*

Creating a Page Border

To place a border around your page:

1. Type **1** or click on the Border Style dialog box. The Border Styles dialog box is displayed in Figure 24.11,

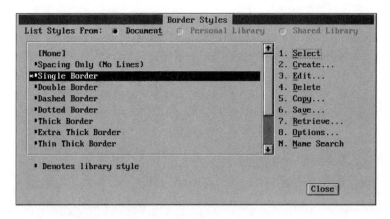

Figure 24.11 *The Border Styles dialog box.*

2. Highlight the border style you desire.

3. Type **1** or click on the **Select** dialog box.

Filling Your Page Background

By default, WordPerfect prints your document text on a white page. Depending on the effect you want, you may want to display the text on a shaded background. When you select page shading, it displays the shaded background in the rectangular region defined by your document's margins. To assign background shading:

1. Type **2** or click on the **Fill Style** option. The Fill Styles dialog box is displayed in Figure 24.12.

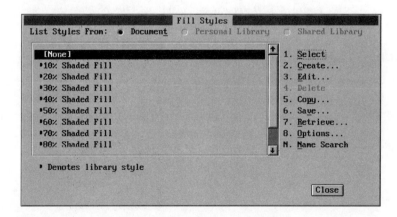

Figure 24.12 *The Fill Styles dialog box.*

2. Highlight the fill percentage you desire. The lower the percentage, the lighter the fill.

3. Type **1** or click on the **Select** option.

Creating a Custom Border, Fill Style, or Drop Shadow

In addition to letting you choose one of its custom borders or fill styles, WordPerfect lets you create a custom border, that may, for example, only frame two sides of the page. You can display a drop shadow along one or more edges of the page. To perform a custom operations type **3** or click on the **Customize** option. The Customize Page Border dialog box is displayed in Figure 24.13.

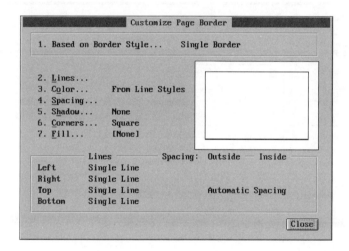

Figure 24.13 *The Customize Page Border dialog box.*

Creating a Document Packing List

If you work for a company that ships merchandise to a customer, you can use the Packing List document provided on the companion disk. As shown in Figure 24.14, the document lets you type in the ship to address, purchase order information, and ordering information.

Company Name
Company Slogan
9999 North Main Street
Anytown, USA 98765-4321
(702) 555-1212
(702) 555-1212 (Fax)

PACKING LIST

Ship To: Bill To:

P. O. Number	Order Number	Shipping Date	Ship Via	Shipping Weight	Number of Boxes	Packed By

Quantity Ordered	Quantity Shipped	Description

Figure 24.14 *The companion disk Packing List document.*

To use the packing list document:

1. Select **Open** from the File menu. Type in the filename **PACKLIST.DOC**.
2. Edit the document to customize the form for your company.
3. Select the File menu **Save** option to save your changes.

When you need to send out a packing list, open PACKING.DOC and type in the corresponding information. Select the File menu **Save As** option to save the document to a meaningfully named file. Use the File menu **Print/Fax** option to print the document.

Summary

WordPerfect provides several formatting options through the Layout menu Page option. Using WordPerfect's Page Format dialog box you can assign page numbers to your document, center text on the page, place a border around each page, add a drop shadow along the outer page edge, and even print labels.

New Terms

*   ◆ **Delaying a code.** Directions not to place a formatting code (when auto code placement is enabled) on the current page, but rather, to place the code on the page that follows.
*   ◆ **Logical page.** A portion of the page you want to treat as a fixed-size page.
*   ◆ **Page formatting.** Operations that affect the appearance of one or more pages in your documents.
*   ◆ **Physical page.** The page of paper on which you are printing.

Chapter 25

Using Document Formatting Techniques

In this chapter you:

- ◆ Learn how to specify a document's initial codes
- ◆ Specify a document's initial font
- ◆ Control your document's redlining
- ◆ Control your document's display pitch
- ◆ Select WordPerfect's character map
- ◆ Control the baseline placement

273

Understanding Document Formatting

WordPerfect's document formatting techniques let you specify options that control your document's initial codes, font, display pitch, character map and baseline placement. If several of these terms are new to you, don't worry, this chapter explains their use. To perform document formatting operations, open the Layout menu and choose **Document**. The Document Format dialog box is displayed in Figure 25.1.

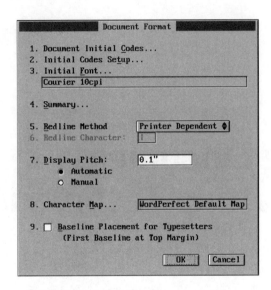

Figure 25.1 *The Document Format dialog box.*

Changing the Document's Initial Codes

Chapter 38 discusses WordPerfect's internal (hidden) formatting codes in detail. WordPerfect places hidden codes in your document text. These codes may turn a font attribute such as bolding on or off, or it may change the document's margins. Each time you open a document, WordPerfect places some formatting codes at the start of the document. The Document Format dialog box

Document Initial Codes option lets you edit the formatting codes that appear at the start of your document. When you select this option, WordPerfect displays the Document Initial Codes dialog box shown Figure 25.2.

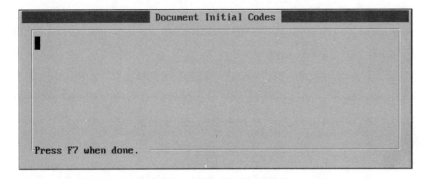

Figure 25.2 *The Document Initial Codes dialog box.*

Document codes appear in between left and right brackets [Code]. Using the Arrow keys, you can highlight a formatting code and press **Del** or **Backspace** to delete the code. You can insert other codes by selecting the menu option or pressing the shortcut key that enables the code. For example, if you want to enable italic text at the start of your document, you select the Font menu and choose **Italic**. WordPerfect inserts the [Italc On] code in the initial codes dialog box. After you have placed the codes you desire in the box, press **F7**.

Defining the Initial Codes

Depending on your preferences, you may want to use these formatting codes to select specific margins, choose a particular font, or even turn on page numbering. The Document Format dialog box Initial Codes Setup option lets you specify the formatting codes. To place codes at the start of a document you create:

1. Select the **Initial Codes Setup** option, it displays the Initial Codes Setup dialog box, shown in Figure 25.3.

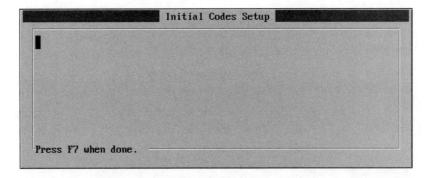

Figure 25.3 *The Initial Codes Setup dialog box.*

2. Highlight an existing code.

3. To delete a code, press **Del** or **Backspace**.

4. To add formatting code, select the menu options or press the shortcut keys for the desired formatting option. For example, if you want to automatically place page numbers on every page, you can open the Layout menu and choose **Page**, assigning the page number.

 Changes you make in the Initial Codes Setup dialog box, affect every document you create in the future. Make sure you fully understand the formatting options you include before you place codes in this dialog box.

Selecting the Initial Font

Each time you create a document, WordPerfect begins with the same font. Use the Document Format dialog box **Initial Font** option, to select the font for each document you create. To change the initial document font, type **3** or click on the **Initial Font** option. The Initial Font dialog box is displayed in Figure 25.4.

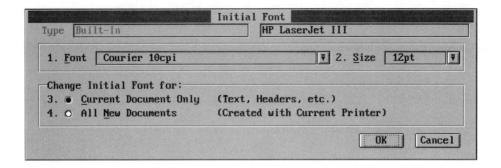

Figure 25.4 *The Initial Font dialog box.*

To select a font:

1. Type **1** or click on the **Font** option. A list of available fonts is displayed.
2. To change the default font size, type **2** or click on the **Size** option.

Changing the Document's Summary

In Chapter 10 you learned how to use WordPerfect's document summary information. The Document Format option **Summary** lets you access the summary information. Selecting the Summary option is identical to selecting the File menu Summary option.

Controlling Redlining

Redlining is an editing technique that marks out document text an editor wants to delete.

~~This text has been redlined.~~

The advantage of using redlining is that you can read and approve the editor's changes before the document text is actually removed. To help you find redlined text in a large document, WordPerfect normally displays a character such as the vertical bar (|) in the margin next to the line containing the edit.

The Document Format dialog box **Redline Method** option lets you control how redlined text appears in your document. When you select the option, a list of options is displayed

In a similar way, the **Redline Character** option lets you specify the character WordPerfect displays in the margin to indicate redlined text.

Controlling Display Pitch

Pitch defines the spacing that occurs between characters. If characters in your document window overlap or do not fit, you can change the pitch used to display the document on your screen. WordPerfect only changes your document's screen appearance, it does not change the format of a printed page. To change your document's display pitch:

1. Type **7** or click on the **Display Pitch** option.
2. Type in the spacing value you desire.
3. Select Manual.

Changing the Character Map

If you are using a language module that contains characters for a non-Roman language, such as Greek, Japanese, or Hebrew, you can reduce your document size when typing by opening the Document Format dialog box **Character Map** option. You can select the current language from the **Character Map** dialog box. Highlight the language and choose **Select**. Your selection only affects the current document.

Controlling a Document's Baseline Placement

A document's *baseline* is the invisible reference line on which the bottom of most characters (except those like y and g) sit. If you are preparing your document for typesetting, you can place the document's first baseline even with the top margin on your page:

1. Type **9** or click on the **Baseline Placement for Typesetters** option.
2. Place an **X** in the check box.

Summary

Each time you create a document, WordPerfect places hidden formatting codes at the start of the document. These codes control the document's margins, justification, fonts, and so on. Using the Layout menu Document option, you can select the Document Format dialog box. In this dialog box you can control the codes WordPerfect places not only in the current document, but every document you create.

New Terms

◆ **Document baseline.** The invisible reference line on which the bottom of most characters (except those like y and g) sit.

◆ **Formatting code.** A hidden code WordPerfect places in your document to control formatting. For example, to display a word in italics, the word is grouped between two formatting codes, one that turns italics on, and one that turns italics off: [Italc On]Word[Italc Off].

◆ **Initial formatting code.** A formatting code automatically placed at the start of new documents.

◆ **Pitch.** The spacing that occurs between characters.

◆ **Redlining.** An editing technique that lets editors mark the text they want to cut. The text is not removed from the document until after the change has been approved.

Chapter **26**

Working with Styles

In this chapter you:

- ◆ Understand how styles make document formatting easier
- ◆ Create your own style
- ◆ Apply styles to text
- ◆ Edit a style and the corresponding text

Understanding Styles

When you create a large document, such as a school report or even a computer book, many parts of your document have the same formatting attributes while some are different. For example, if you look at the paragraphs of this book, you find that every paragraph uses the same font, margins, line spacing and so on. The chapter heads (the titles that appear before paragraphs–such as, Understanding Styles) use the same formatting. One way to achieve formatting throughout your document is to select each section, one piece at a time, applying fonts, justification, and so on. A better way to achieve consistent formatting, is to apply styles to different parts of your document.

A *style* is a name assigned to a set of formatting attributes (such as margins, fonts, justification, and so on). In this chapter, we use a chapter title style, a style for paragraph text, a notes style that displays messages in italics and so on. The advantage of using styles is that you define the style only one time, specifying the font, margins, justification, and so on. When you want to use the style, you apply the style to selected text. Because the formatting attributes are contained in the style itself, you reduce the possibility of forgetting an attribute, such as the font size when you are later formatting your text. More importantly, if you later change the style definition, the text to which you have assigned the style is immediately updated.

Once you have worked with styles on one or two documents, you may find that you want to create and use them for all your documents, large or small. Styles are a very powerful formatting tool that makes formatting your document very easy.

Using Styles

WordPerfect provides a few predefined styles that you can use to get started. To better understand how styles work, open the File menu and choose **New**. Type in the following text:

```
My Life Story
```

```
This is the abridged reader's digest version of my
life story—at least my life to this point.

The Early Years

I was born in Seattle, Washington. In grade school I
learned to shoot a basketball.

The Middle Years

By the time I moved to Phoenix for high school, I
could shoot the basketball really well.

The College Years

Basketball got me to college, which introduced me to
computers. 11 years of college later—I don't shoot
the basketball quite as well, but I really understand
computers.
```

As you can see, the text has a title, three heads, and some text. For the title, use an extra large bold font and center the text. Use a large bold font for each of the heads. Make the story text appear in italics. Following is a list of the three styles needed to complete the document's formatting.

- **StortTitle**—Extra large bold font, centered text.
- **StoryHead**—Large bold font, left justified text.
- **StoryText**—Normal font size, but italic.

Creating a Style

To create a style:

1. Open the Layout menu and choose **Styles**. The Style List dialog box is displayed in Figure 26.1.

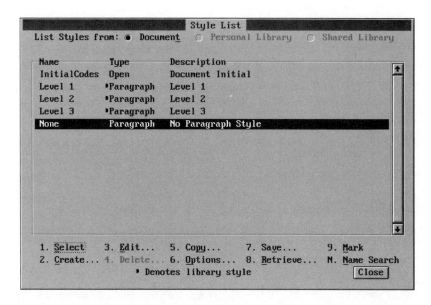

Figure 26.1 The Style List dialog box.

2. Type **2** or click on the **Create** option. WordPerfect displays the Create Style dialog box shown in Figure 26.2.

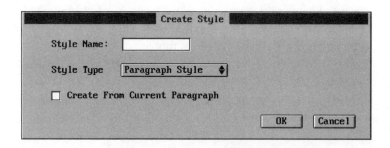

Figure 26.2 The Create Style dialog box.

3. Type in the style name **StoryTitle** and press **Tab**.

4. In the Style Type option select **Paragraph Style**.

5. Choose **OK**. The Edit Style dialog box is displayed, as in Figure 26.3.

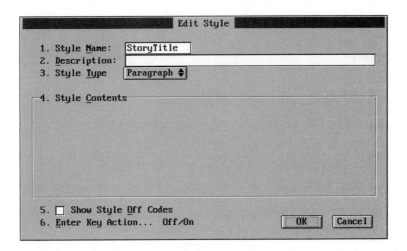

Figure 26.3 *The Edit Style dialog box.*

6. Type **4** or click on the **Style Contents** option.

7. Press **Ctrl-F8** to assign a Font. The Font dialog box is displayed.

8. Choose **Bold** attribute and **Extra Large**.

9. If your printer supports multiple fonts, choose a font that gives an interesting appearance.

10. Choose **OK**.

11. Press **Shift-F8** to assign the style's formatting (center the title). The Format dialog box is displayed in Figure 26.4.

Figure 26.4 *The Format dialog box.*

12. Type **1** or click on the **Line** option.

13. The Line Format dialog box is displayed. In the Justification field select **Center**.

14. Choose **OK**.

15. Select **Close** in the Format dialog box.

16. Press **F7** when the Edit Style dialog box returns.

17. Select **OK** to return to the style list.

18. Select **Create** to define the styles StoryHead and StoryText.

19. When all three styles have been defined close the Style List dialog box.

20. Select the story's title.

21. Open the Layout menu and choose **Styles**.

22. Highlight the StoryTitle style and choose **Select**. The story's title is centered, displaying it in a bold, extra large font.

23. Using the Style List dialog box, choose the **StoryHead** style. WordPerfect displays the head using a large bold font.

24. Assign the StoryHead style to the remaining heads.

25. Select a paragraph of story text. Using the Style List dialog box, apply the **StoryText** style.

26. Repeat this process for all of the text.

The story is displayed in Figure 26.5.

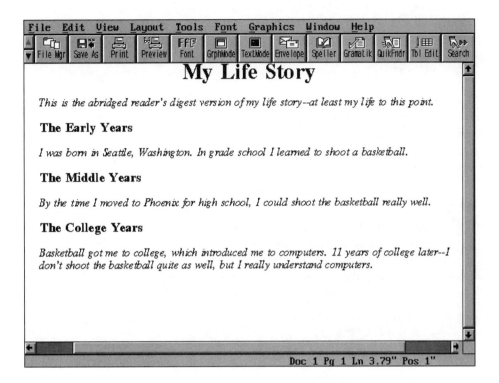

Figure 26.5 *The story with style applied.*

As you can see, creating and applying your own styles is very easy.

Changing a Style

Assume that after you apply a style, you don't like how text appears in your document. For example, in the case of the StoryText style, the italics may make your story hard to read. To change a style:

1. Open the Layout menu and choose **Styles**.
2. When the Edit Style list is displayed select the **StoryText** style and choose **Edit**. The Edit Style dialog box is displayed.

3. Type **4** or click on the **Style Contents** option.

4. Highlight the **[Italc On]** field and press **Del**, turning off the style's italics.

5. Press **F7**.

When the dialog boxes close you return to your document. WordPerfect automatically updates all of the text to which you have assigned the StoryText style, removing the italics. As your documents become more complex, you may want touse styles on a regular basis. Take some time now to experiment with the styles you just created.

Assigning a Style to a Button Bar. If you work with styles on a regular basis, you may want to assign the Style List dialog box to your button bar. In that way, when you need to apply a style, you can click on the button and quickly select the style you need. Follow the steps presented in Chapter 20 to assign the dialog box to your button bar.

Creating a Fax Log Sheet

If you work in an office where the Fax machine is always in use and where management insists the machine is being misused–causing high phone bills, you may want to use the companion disk Fax Log sheet, displayed in Figure 26.6.

Company Name
Company Slogan
9999 North Main Street
Anytown, USA 98765-4321
(702) 555-1212
(702) 555-1212 (Fax)

FAX LOG

–: Fill out for each fax sent.

Date	Time	Fax Number Called	Business/Person Called	Pages	Caller

Figure 26.6 *The companion disk Fax Log sheet.*

The document lets you record the date and time of each fax, the number and business called, the number of pages sent, and the person sending the fax. One of the simplest ways to use this form is to print a copy, placing it next to the fax machine. However, if you want to track your faxes in the document, you can type in the specifics, using the Arrow keys to move from one field to the next. To use the fax log sheet document:

1. Select the File menu **Open** option and type in the filename **FAXLOG.DOC**.
2. Edit the form to customize it for your company.
3. Use the **Save** option to save your changes.
4. To print a copy of the document, select the **Print/Fax** option.

Summary

A style is a name assigned to a set of related formatting options. When you create large documents, styles simplify formatting operations and insure consistency. WordPerfect lets you create your own styles. A style can be as simple as a font attribute, or it can contain margins, justification, leading, and much more. To use a style you select the target text and apply the style from WordPerfect's Style List dialog box. WordPerfect makes its very easy to create, edit, and apply your own styles.

New Terms

◆ **Applying a style.** The process of using a style to format selected text.
◆ **Style.** A name assigned to a collection of related formatting options.

Chapter 27

Importing, Exporting, and Password Protecting

In this chapter you:

- ◆ Learn how to export your document in a form usable by a word processor other than WordPerfect

- ◆ Learn how to import documents created by a word processor other than WordPerfect

- ◆ Learn how to password protect your files

Understanding Export and Import Operations

If you work in an office with people who use a word processor other than WordPerfect 6.0, you may eventually have to exchange documents with them. For example, your company is putting together its annual report and you have been asked to write the status report for your section. You are using WordPerfect 6.0 to create your report, but the person who is consolidating the different reports into one is using a different word processor, such as Microsoft Word, or even WordPerfect 5.1. Unfortunately, different word processors store documents on disk using unique file formats. In order for the user's word processor to be able to use your WordPerfect 6.0 document, you must export the document to disk in a file format the target word processor understands.

Another example is if you are working with another user who is giving you a document file that was created by a different word processor, and it is still in that word processor's file format. Depending on which word processor the person used to create the document, you may be able to import the document into WordPerfect. The process of exporting and importing document files, therefore, is really the process of converting a document from one word processor's format (such as WordPerfect 6.0) to that of another (Microsoft Word).

Exporting a Document File

When you *export* a document file, you store the document in a different word processor's file format. To better understand the process of exporting a file:

1. Open the File menu and select **New**.
2. Type the following text:

    ```
    This document will be stored in Word 5.5 format
    on disk.
    ```

3. Open the File menu and choose **Save As**. The Save Document dialog box is displayed, as in Figure 27.1.

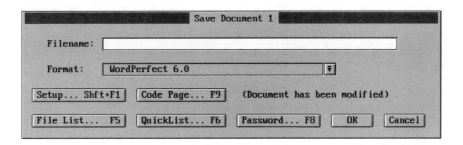

Figure 27.1 The Save dialog box.

4. Type in the filename **WORDTEST.DOC** and press **Tab**. The Format box is highlighted.

5. Type **R** or click on the **Format** option. A list of available file formats is displayed, as in Figure 27.2.

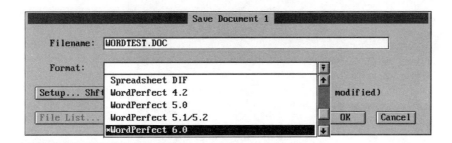

Figure 27.2 Displaying available export file formats.

6. Highlight **MS Word 5.5** and press **Enter**.

7. When the Save dialog box is displayed, press **Enter** to choose **OK** and Save the file on disk in Microsoft Word 5.5 format.

8. Open the File menu and select **Close**.

Importing a File

Importing is the process of opening and using a file that was created by a word processor other than WordPerfect. You do not have to do anything special when you import a file. You simply open the file using the File menu **Open** option. As

WordPerfect examines the file's contents, it recognizes that the file was not created by WordPerfect. As such, it displays a dialog box asking you to specify the word processor that created the file. In most cases, WordPerfect recognizes the source word processor from examining the file's format. In that case, the name of the source word processor is highlighted in the dialog box.

To better understand the process of importing a file:

1. Open the File menu and choose **Open**.

2. Type in the filename **WORDTEST.DOC**, which you just created (in Microsoft Word 5.5 format). The different file format is recognized and WordPerfect displays the File Format dialog box, shown in Figure 27.3.

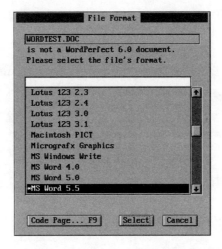

Figure 27.3 *The File Format dialog box.*

3. If the correct source word processor is highlighted, press **Enter**. Otherwise highlight the correct word processor and choose **Select**.

Password Protecting a File

If you work in an office where other users have access to your computer or files, you can prevent users from viewing or editing your files by assigning a *password* to the file. Before a user can access a password protected file, the user must type in the correct password. To help you reduce the chance of forgetting a password, you probably want to use the same password for each file you create, or come up with a unique system that helps you remember the password. For example, you might use the letters of the filename spelled backwards for a password. In this way, every file has a unique password, and it is easy for you to remember the password you assigned to each.

To assign a password to your file:

1.   Open the File menu and select the **Save As** option.

2.   Type in the desired filename if you have not previously done so.

3.   Press **F8** or click on the **Password** button. The Password dialog box is displayed in Figure 27.4.

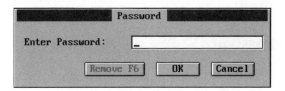

Figure 27.4 *The Password dialog box.*

4.   Passwords can contain twenty-three characters. For passwords, WordPerfect does not recognize the difference between uppercase and lowercase letters.

5.   Type in the password you desire and press **Enter**.

6.   It asks you to retype the password to insure you typed it correctly. Do so and press **Enter**.

Later when you use the File menu **Open** option to access the file, WordPerfect displays a dialog box prompting you for the password. Type in the password and press **OK**. If the password typed is not correct, WordPerfect displays the dialog box shown in Figure 27.5, stating the file is password protected and cannot be opened.

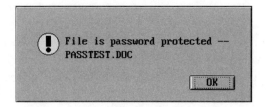

Figure 27.5 *The password protection dialog box.*

 Make sure you assign document passwords that you can readily recall. If you forget a document password, you're out of luck. Even WARNING WordPerfect's technical support cannot help you recover the document.

Removing a Password

If you decide you no longer need to password protect the current document, open the File menu and choose **Save As**. WordPerfect displays the **Save** dialog box. Press **F8** or click on the **Password** button. The password dialog box is displayed. Select **Remove**.

Summary

If you exchange files with users who work with word processors other than WordPerfect 6.0, you may need to export your documents. You need to use a file format the user's word processor understands or you may need to import a file created by a different word processor. Exporting and importing files is nothing more than converting a document from one word processor's format to another. WordPerfect supports the file formats for most popular word processors. If you work in a place where other users have access to your files, you may want to password protect your documents.

New Terms

◆ **Exporting.** The process of writing a document file to disk in the format of another word processor.

◆ **Importing.** The process of reading a document file created and stored on disk in the format of a different word processor.

◆ **Password protection.** The process of assigning a document a secret word that must be typed in before WordPerfect opens a document file.

Chapter **28**

Using WordPerfect to Address Envelopes

In this chapter you:

◆ Use WordPerfect to address envelopes

◆ Assign Postal Numeric Encoding Technique (POSTNET) symbols to an envelope

◆ Customize the Envelope dialog box

299

WordPerfect's Envelope Capabilities

If you are using a printer that lets you print on envelopes, WordPerfect makes it very easy for you to quickly type in a mailing and return address. To address an envelope using WordPerfect, place one or more envelopes into your printer's envelope feeder. Next, choose **Envelope** from the Layout menu. The Envelope dialog box is displayed Figure 28.1.

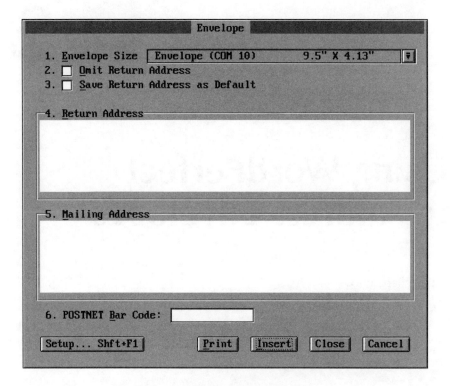

Figure 28.1 *The Envelope dialog box.*

To select the envelope size, type **1** or click on the **Envelope Size** option. WordPerfect displays the list of supported envelope sizes. Highlight envelope size you want and press **Enter**, or click on the size.

To type in the return address you want on the envelope, type **4** or click on the **Return Address** option. Type in the return address and press **F7**. Because you are likely to use the same return address for each letter you create, WordPerfect lets you select the current return address as the default for all letters you create by selecting the **Save Return Address as Default** check box.

If there are times when you don't want the default return address to appear on a letter, select the **Omit Return Address** check box.

To type in the mailing address, type **5** or click on the **Mailing Address** option. Type in each line of the address and then press **F7**.

A POSTNET (Postal Numeric Encoding Technique) bar code contains bar code symbols for the destination zip code. By placing a POSTNET bar code on your envelopes, the Post Office can sort and route your letter faster. The POSTNET bar code appears directly above the mailing address, as shown in Figure 28.2.

MIS:Press
115 West 18th Street
New York, NY 10011

Figure 28.2 *A POSTNET bar code and envelope.*

To print the envelope, type **P** or click on the **Print** button.

If you are displaying WordPerfect's button bar, select the envelope dialog box.

N O T E

Placing a Graphic in Your Return Address

In Chapter 32 you learned how to place a WordPerfect graphic in your document, sizing the graphic as required. If you have a company logo stored on disk as a WordPerfect graphic, you can place the logo on your envelope, as shown in Figure 28.3.

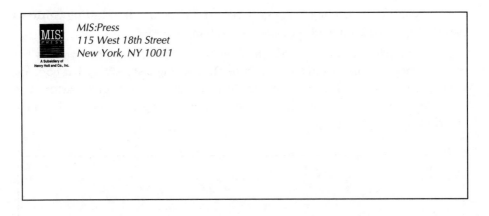

Figure 28.3 Placing a graphic in a return address.

Customizing the Envelope Dialog Box

If the Envelope dialog box does not display the envelope size you normally use, create your own envelope type by using the **Setup** option.

When you select **Setup**, The Envelope Setup dialog box is displayed in Figure 28.4.

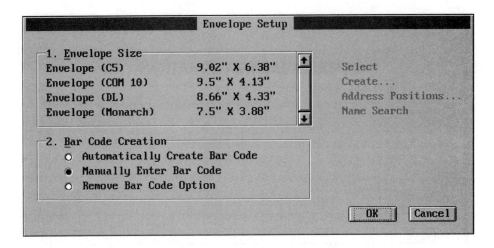

Figure 28.4 *The Envelope Setup dialog box.*

In the Setup dialog box, you can control the use of the POSTNET option and you can change or create envelope sizes and layouts.

Documenting Important Personal Information

Everyone has important personal information others may need in an event of an emergency. To help you organize this information, the companion disk that accompanies this book provides a Personal Information form, as displayed in Figure 28.5.

PERSONAL INFORMATION

IDENTIFICATION

Name:	Date of Birth:
SSN:	Place of Birth:
Home Phone:	Business Phone:
Home Address:	Business Address:

EMERGENCY CONTACTS

Contact	Name	Relationship	Work Phone	Home Phone
Spouse				
Parent				
Parent				
Friend				
Bus. Associate				
Other				

EMERGENCY INSTRUCTIONS

MEDICAL INFORMATION AND INSTRUCTIONS

ADDITIONAL INFORMATION

Type	Company	Address	Phone
Health Insurance			
Location of Will			
Life Insurance Policy			
Safety Deposit Box			
Other			

Figure 28.5 The companion disk Personal Information form.

To open the document containing the personal information form:

1. Select **Open** from the File menu.

2. Type in the filename **PERSINFO.DOC** and press **Enter**.

3. When the form is displayed, type in the information for each field. Use your Arrow keys to move from one field to the next.

4. Select the File menu **Print/Fax** option to print your personal information.

5. Use the File menu **Save** option to save your changes.

Summary

If you are using a printer that supports envelopes, WordPerfect lets you quickly address and print an envelope. WordPerfect provides support for several common envelope sizes. If necessary, you can create your own custom envelope sizes. Because WordPerfect treats an envelope like a standard document, you can place a graphic in your return address, such as a company logo.

New Terms

◆ **POSTNET bar code.** A machine-readable bar code-representation of a zip code the post office uses to sort and route letters. POSTNET is an abbreviation for *Postal Numeric Encoding Technique.*

Working with
Footnotes and Endnotes

In this chapter you:

- ◆ Create a footnote
- ◆ Edit a footnote
- ◆ Delete a footnote
- ◆ Change the footnote style
- ◆ Create an endnote
- ◆ Understand the difference between footnotes and endnotes

Using Footnotes and Endnotes

If you are creating a document for school, you will probably be required to use footnotes or endnotes to document the source of your information. The fundamental difference between a footnote and endnote is location. Footnotes appear at the bottom of your page, whereas endnotes appear at the end of a chapter or the end of the document. Because most users find endnotes much easier, most instructors let you use endnotes. As you learn in this chapter, however, WordPerfect makes both footnotes and endnotes easy to use.

Assigning a Footnote

To better understand the process of creating a footnote, select the File menu and choose **New**. Next, type in the following text:

> The 1960's were the Kennedy era. The United States found hope and change in youth. The nation looked within to find solutions to its problems, while dreaming of a day when man would walk on the moon. John Kennedy, himself, provides insight into the nation's mood in his words, "And so my fellow Americans: ask not, what your country can do for you- ask what you can do for your country."

To properly document Kennedy's quote, you need to include a footnote in the passage. To assign a footnote, open the Layout menu and choose **Footnote**. WordPerfect cascades the Footnote menu, displayed in Figure 29.1.

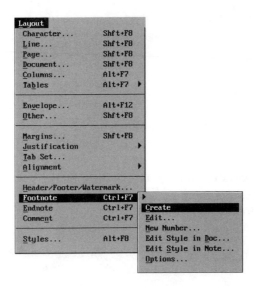

Figure 29.1 *Cascading the Footnote menu.*

Select **Create**. WordPerfect opens a document window in which you can type your footnote, placing the small number 1 in the upper-right corner. Type the following text:

John F. Kennedy, Inaugural Address, January 20, 1961.

After you type in the footnote, press **F7**. WordPerfect returns to your document, showing the footnote number immediately after your text, as shown in Figure 29.2.

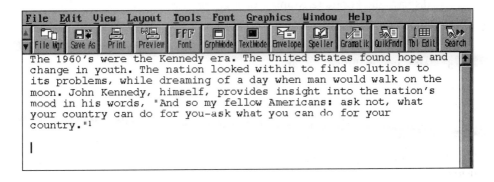

Figure 29.2 *A footnote number following your text.*

Select **Print/Fax** from the File menu to print your document. The footnote is displayed at the bottom of your page. Continue typing your document, adding the following text:

```
Kennedy's influence reached far beyond the borders of
the United States. In June of 1963, five months before
his death, Kennedy's charm rang out through Berlin
when he spoke the four words "Ich bin ein Berliner."
```

As before, select **Footnote** form the Layout menu and choose **Create**. This time, WordPerfect displays the footnote editing screen, displaying the footnote number 2. Type in the following text and press **F7**:

```
John Kennedy, Address at City Hall, West Berlin,
Germany, June 26, 1963.
```

As you can see, WordPerfect automatically keeps track of your footnote numbering. Use the **Print/Fax** option to print your document. WordPerfect displays both footnotes at the bottom of your page. As you can see, WordPerfect makes footnoting your document very easy.

Editing a Footnote

As you proofread your document, you may find that you need to make changes to one or more footnotes. To edit a footnote:

1. Select **Footnote** from the Layout menu and choose **Edit**. WordPerfect displays the Footnote Number dialog box.

2. Type in the number of the footnote you need to edit. The corresponding footnote is displayed in an editing screen.

3. After you make your changes, press **F7**.

Removing a Footnote

Normally, you won't remove a footnote in your document, but you may remove the corresponding the text so the footnote is no longer required. For example, using the Kennedy document, select and delete the following text:

Removing a Footnote

Normally, you won't remove a footnote in your document, but you may remove the corresponding the text so the footnote is no longer required. For example, using the Kennedy document, select and delete the following text:

```
John Kennedy, himself, provides insight into the
nation's mood in his words, "And so my fellow
Americans: ask not, what your country can do for you-
ask what you can do for your country."¹
```

When you delete the text (which also deletes footnote number 1), WordPerfect automatically renumbers the remaining footnotes throughout your document.

Renumbering Footnotes

If you are creating a multi-chapter document, there may be times when you want to continue your footnote numbers from one chapter to the next. By default, however, WordPerfect starts each document's footnote at 1. To change the footnote numbers, select **Footnote** from the Layout menu and choose **New Number**. The Set Footnote Number dialog box is displayed in Figure 29.3.

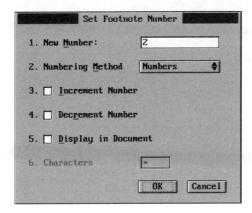

Figure 29.3 The Set Footnote Number dialog box.

In this dialog box you can assign a footnote number and specify whether you want WordPerfect to increment or decrement successive footnote numbers. After

In this dialog box you can assign a footnote number and specify whether you want WordPerfect to increment or decrement successive footnote numbers. After you make your selections, choose **OK**.

Controlling Footnote Appearance

WordPerfect, by default, uses a superscript font attribute and a smaller font size to display footnote numbers in your document. To change the way WordPerfect displays footnote numbers:

1. Select **Footnote** from the Layout menu and choose **Edit Style in Doc**. The Footnote Style in Document dialog box is displayed, as in Figure 29.4.

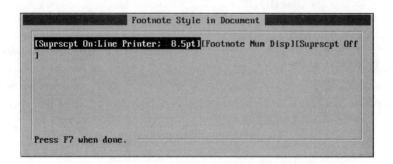

Figure 29.4 The Footnote Style in Document dialog box.

2. Using your Arrow keys, position the cursor in the dialog box. As you select different menu options, such as Bold or Italics, WordPerfect inserts the corresponding formatting codes. (Chapter 38 discuses WordPerfect's formatting codes in detail.)

In a similar way, WordPerfect lets you control how the footnote number appears n the footnotes at the bottom of your page. To change the style of your footnotes:

1. Select **Footnote** from the Layout menu and choose **Edit Style in Note**.

2. WordPerfect displays the Footnote Style in Note dialog box, in which you can specify the footnote's formatting.

Other Footnote Options

If you use a considerable number of footnotes, the bottom of your page can become quite crowded. To help you control your page appearance, WordPerfect lets you specify the amount of space between your document text and footnotes, how much of a footnote must remain on the current page, the line used to separate multiple footnotes, and so on. To control such footnote options, select **Footnote** and choose **Options**. WordPerfect displays the Footnote Options dialog box, as shown in Figure 29.5.

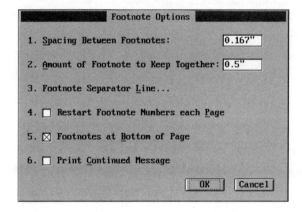

Figure 29.5 *The Footnote Options dialog box.*

Select the options you desire and select **OK**.

Working with Endnotes

If you are still working with the Kennedy document, type in the following text:

Like a prophet of his own destiny, Kennedy's life may
be best defined by his own words: "For without belit-
tling the courage with which men have died, we should
not forget those acts of courage with which
men...have lived...A man does what he must-in spite
of the personal consequences, in spite of all obsta-
cles and dangers and pressures-and that is the basis
of all human mortality."

1. Open the Layout menu and choose **Endnote**. WordPerfect cascades the
    Endnote menu.

2. Select **Create**.

3. An editing screen in which you can type the endnote is displayed.

4. Type the following text and press **F7**:

    John Kennedy, Profiles in Courage, 1956.

5. WordPerfect returns you to your document. Print your document. As
    you will find, WordPerfect places your endnote on its own page at the
    end of your document.

If you examine the Endnote menu, you will find that most of the menu options
are identical to those found in the Footnote menu.

Maintaining a Log of Your Long Distance Calls

If you work in an office where the long distance phone bill is getting out of
hand, you may want to track your own long distance phone calls using the companion disk Long Distance Telephone Call Log, shown in Figure 29.6.

Company Name
Company Slogan
9999 North Main Street
Anytown, USA 98765-4321
(702) 555-1212
(702) 555-1212 (Fax)

LONG-DISTANCE TELEPHONE CALL LOG

–: Fill out for each long distance telephone call.

Date	Time	Number Called	Business/Person Called	Caller

Figure 29.6 *The companion disk Long Distance Telephone Call Log.*

To use the Long Distance Telephone Call Log:

1. Select **Open** from the File menu. Type in the filename **PHONELOG.DOC**.
2. Edit the form to customize it for your company.
3. Use the File menu **Save** option to save your changes.

To track your phone calls, you have two choices. First you can print a copy of the document, placing it next to your phone so you can hand-write information. Second, you can edit the document adding entries as required. If you choose to edit the document, use your Arrow keys to move the cursor from one box to the next.

Summary

When you create reports for school or academic journals, you must document your sources of information. The two most common ways of performing such documentation are footnotes and endnotes. The primary difference between footnotes and endnotes is placement. Footnotes appear at the bottom of your page while endnotes appear at the end of your document. Whether you choose to use footnotes or endnotes, WordPerfect makes both very easy to use.

New Terms

- **Endnote.** A text reference that is displayed on a separate page at the end of your document.
- **Footnote.** A text reference that is displayed at the bottom of the page on which the reference occurs.

Chapter 30

Getting Started with Macros

In this chapter you:

- ◆ Record your own macros
- ◆ Add macros to WordPerfect's button bar
- ◆ Playback WordPerfect's predefined macros

Understanding Macros

WordPerfect performs most operations using one or two menu selections. As your document formatting becomes more complex, there may be times when the operations you perform require many steps. To help you simplify such operations, WordPerfect lets you record the keystrokes (menu selections and shortcut keys) as well as mouse operations into a file called a *macro*. A macro, therefore, is essentially a collection of keystrokes that perform a specific task. When you need to perform the task, you can *play back* the macro. WordPerfect responds to the macro's contents just as if you had pressed the same keys or clicked your mouse on the same objects.

Recording a Simple Macro

To better understand how macros work, record a macro that places your return address at the current document location:

1. Open the Tools menu and choose **Macro**. WordPerfect cascades the menu shown in Figure 30.1.

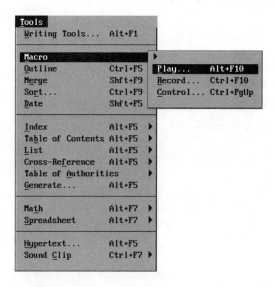

Figure 30.1 *Cascading the Macro menu.*

2. Select **Record**. WordPerfect displays the Record Macro dialog box displayed in Figure 30.2.

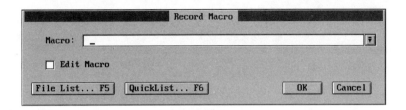

Figure 30.2 *The Record Macro dialog box.*

3. Type in the macro name, **RETURNAD** (for return address) and press **Enter**. WordPerfect begins recording each keystroke and mouse operation that you perform. Note that a message is displayed in the status bar reminding you that you are recording a macro.

4. In this case, type in the following return address, or use your own:

```
MIS: Press
115 West 18th Street
New York, New York 10011
```

5. Open the Tools menu and choose **Macro**.

6. When WordPerfect cascades the menu, select **Stop**.

Using a macro is called *playing back* the macro. To try out your new RETURNAD macro:

1. Open the File menu and choose **New**.

2. When WordPerfect displays the new document, open the Tools menu and choose **Macro**.

3. In the cascaded Macro menu, select **Play**. WordPerfect displays the Play Macro dialog box as shown in Figure 30.3.

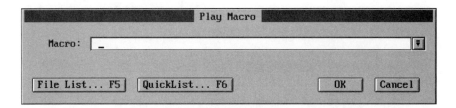

Figure 30.3 *The Play Macro dialog box.*

4. Type in the macro name **RETURNAD** and press **Enter**. WordPerfect immediately inserts your return address into the document. Macros let you easily record keystrokes.

As you know, each time you select Print/Fax, WordPerfect displays the Print/Fax dialog box. To print your document, you must select the Print option in the dialog box–an often unnecessary second step. To simplify print operations, record a macro named PRINTIT that automatically performs these two steps for you:

1. Open the Tools menu and choose **Macro**.

2. When WordPerfect cascades the Macro menu, choose **Record** and type **PRINTIT** and press **Enter**.

3. Select the File menu and choose **Print/Fax**. The Print/Fax dialog box is displayed.

4. Select **Print**.

5. Open the Tools menu, select **Macro**, and choose **Stop**.

To playback the PRINTIT macro:

1. Select the Macro and choose **Play**.

2. When WordPerfect displays the Play Macro dialog box, type in **PRINTIT** and press **Enter**.

Assigning a Macro to the Button Bar

In Chapter 20 you learned that WordPerfect lets you customize the button bar to make your common operations easily accessible. When you record macros that you use on a regular basis, you can place the macros in the button bar. For

you use on a regular basis, you can place the macros in the button bar. For example, to place the PRINTIT macro you just recorded in the button bar:

1. Open the View menu and choose **Button Bar Setup**. WordPerfect cascades the menu shown in Figure 30.4.

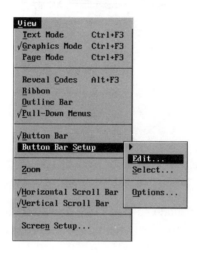

Figure 30.4 Cascading the Button Bar Setup menu.

2. Choose the **Edit** option. WordPerfect displays the Edit Button Bar dialog box shown in Figure 30.5.

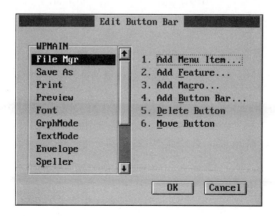

Figure 30.5 The Edit Button Bar dialog box.

3. Type **3** or click on the **Add Macro** option. The Macro Button List dialog box is displayed in Figure 30.6.

Figure 30.6 *The Macro Button List dialog box.*

The Macro Button List contains all of the WordPerfect macro files contained on your disk. WordPerfect provides several of its own macros. Using your Arrow keys or mouse, highlight the PRINTIT macro and choose **Select**. WordPerfect adds the macro to your button bar list. Select **OK** to exit the Edit Button Bar dialog box. If you look at the last button in your button bar, you will find the PRINTIT macro button.

To move the button, follow the steps presented in Chapter 20. The tape recorder that appears within the PRINTIT icon indicates that the button corresponds to a macro (the tape stands for recorded keystrokes and operations).

Checking Out WordPerfect's Predefined Macros

When you install WordPerfect, the installation program preloads several macros on to your disk. The easiest way to play back the macro is to display them in the button bar. To help you do so, WordPerfect predefines a Macro button bar. To display the macro button bar:

1. Open the View menu and choose **Button Bar Setup**.
2. Choose **Select** from the cascading menu. WordPerfect displays the Select Button Bar dialog box shown in Figure 30.7.

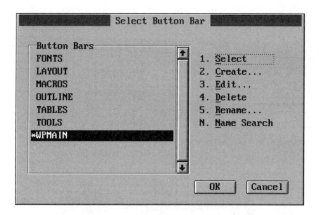

Figure 30.7 *The Select Button Bar dialog box.*

3. Using your mouse or Arrow keys, highlight the MACROS option and choose **Select**. The buttons are displayed in Figure 30.8.

Figure 30.8 *The Macro button bar.*

WordPerfect's predefined macros are:

◆ **Mod_atrb** replaces one font attribute with another.

◆ **Initcaps** assigns an uppercase letter to each word in the selected text.

◆ **Pleading** creates a style, named Pleading to number the lines of a document similar to that used by legal documents.

◆ **SpaceTab** converts each tab within your document to a specified number of space characters.

◆ **Calc** is an on-screen calculator.

◆ **Bullet** inserts a bullet.

◆ **Memo** lets you quickly create a memo, fax, or letter.

◆ **Editcode** edits the formatting code at the current cursor position.

◆ **Glossary** lets you build a glossary of definitions.

◆ **Notecvt** converts footnotes to endnotes, and endnotes to footnote.

◆ **Allfonts** displays samples of the available fonts.

Using the On-Screen Calculator

In the simplest sense, a macro is a collection of keystrokes, menu choices, and mouse operations. To help you build more powerful macros, WordPerfect provides a set of macro commands. These commands are similar to the instructions programmers use to create programs. To help you understand how powerful your macros can become, click on the button bar labeled **Calc** (or play back the Calc macro using the Macro menu Play option). WordPerfect displays an on screen calculator, shown in Figure 30.9.

Figure 30.9 *The Calc macro's on-screen calculator.*

1. Using a mouse, click on the calculator buttons you want WordPerfect to select. If you don't have a mouse, press the key that appears underlined in each button.

2. To multiply 55 times 3, for example, type **55** on your keyboard, type the asterisk key (* for multiplication), type **3**, then type the equal sign (**=**).

3. The calculator displays 165 in its window.

4. To remove the calculator from your screen, press **Esc** or click on **Close**.

Displaying the Available Fonts

To help you better understand the fonts you have available to use, play back the Allfonts macro. The macro creates a document that contains samples of the available fonts, as in Figure 30.10.

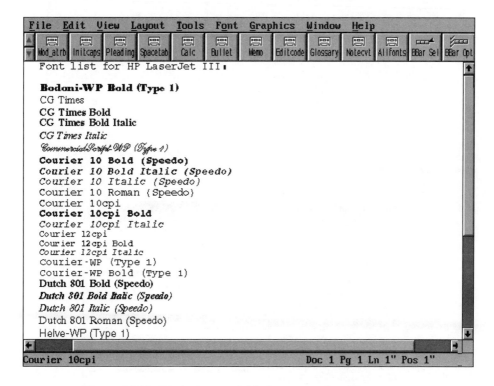

Figure 30.10 *Displaying available fonts using the Allfonts macro.*

Creating a Memo, Letter, or Fax Cover Sheet

If you need to create a memo, letter, or fax cover sheet, play back the Memo macro. The macro begins by displaying a dialog box that asks you the document type.

In this case, select the **Memo** option. WordPerfect displays the Create a Memo dialog box, as shown in Figure 30.11.

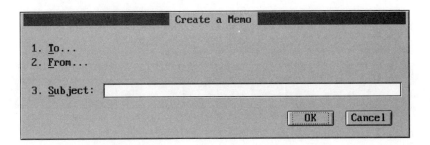

Figure 30.11 The Create a Memo dialog box.

Type **1** or click on the **To** option. The macro displays the Add Entry dialog box, as shown in Figure 30.12.

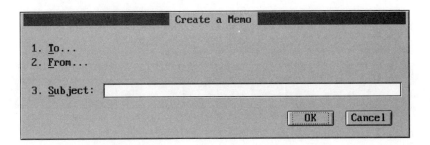

Figure 30.12 The Add Entry dialog box.

When you address a memo, fax, or letter, the macro records the information you type in a file. If you later want to send a second letter or memo to the same person, the macro lets you quickly select the individual. Type in the information for each option:

1. Press the **Tab** key to move from one entry to the next. When you are done, select **OK**.

2. When the macro redisplays the Create a Memo dialog box, type **2** or click on the **From** option.

3. The macro again displays the Add Entry dialog box. Type in the same information about yourself. The macro remembers the information in the future.

4. When the macro returns to the Create a Memo dialog box, type **3** or click on the **Subject** option.

5. Type in a one line description of the memo's contents and press **Enter**.

6. Select **OK** to continue. The macro then inserts the memo information at the start of your document, as in Figure 30.13.

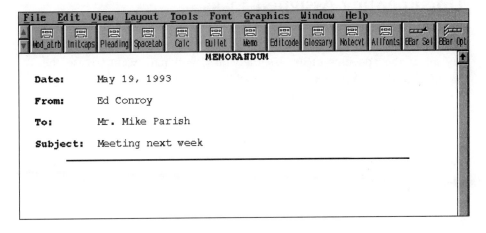

Figure 30.13 *Building a memo header.*

As you send memos, letters, and faxes to different people, the macro will remember the names you enter, letting you select them later.

How to Create Your Own Macro Programs

As you have seen, WordPerfect provides commands that let you build powerful macros. To view the commands used to create one of the predefined macros:

1. Open the Tools menu and choose **Macro**. From the cascaded Macro menu, choose **Record**.

2. When WordPerfect displays the Record dialog box, type in the macro name, but do not press Enter.

3. Press the **Tab** key to select the **Edit Macro**. Press the S**pacebar** to place an X in the check box.

4. Select **OK**.

WordPerfect displays the macro commands on your screen. Use Print/Fax to print a copy of the commands. Use Close to close the document when you are done viewing its contents.

Documenting Assigned Tasks

If you work in an office and find that your employees have trouble remembering all of the specifics of an assigned task, you may want to use the Task Assignment Form provided on this book's companion disk. As shown in Figure 30.14, the document lets you describe the task, set completion dates, as well as define milestones.

Company Name
Company Slogan
9999 North Main Street
Anytown, USA 98765-4321
(702) 555-1212
(702) 555-1212 (Fax)

TASK ASSIGNMENT FORM

GENERAL DESCRIPTION OF ASSIGNMENT

TASKS TO BE ACCOMPLISHED/ITEMS TO BE DELIVERED

Due Date	Task/Deliverable Description

MILESTONES TO BE MET

Due Date	Milestone Description

The above describes the assignment to be performed.

_____   _____
Assigner's Signature   Date

I agree to perform the above assignment.

_____   _____
Agreement Signature   Date

Figure 30.14 The companion disk Task Assignment Form.

To use the task assignment form:

1. Select the File menu and choose **Open**. Type in the filename **TASK.DOC**.
2. Edit the form to customize it for your company.
3. Use the File menu **Save** option to save your changes.

When you need to describe a task, use the File menu **Open** option to open the document. Type in the description of the task, using your Arrow keys to move from one line to the next. When the form is complete, use **Save As** to save the form to a file on disk whose name meaningfully describes the task.

Summary

WordPerfect macros let you automate common or difficult tasks. In the simplest sense, a macro is a file that contains the keystrokes, menu selections, and mouse operations you would normally perform to complete a task. The process of creating a macro is called *recording*. When you want to use the macro, you play back its contents. As the complexity of the operations you want to automate increases, you can use WordPerfect's macro commands to program your own applications!

New Terms

◆ **Macro.** A collection of keystrokes, menu selections, mouse operations, and WordPerfect commands that automates a specific task.

◆ **Macro command.** A predefined command you can place within a macro file that you are editing to perform a specific operation.

◆ **Macro playback.** The process of using a macro.

◆ **Macro recording.** The process of placing the keystrokes, menu selections, and mouse operations you want to automate into a macro file.

Chapter 31

Getting Started with WordPerfect Tables

In this chapter you:

- ◆ Create a simple text table
- ◆ Size and delete table columns
- ◆ Apply formulas to a table cell
- ◆ Calculate formulas
- ◆ Join table columns
- ◆ Change the lines that surround a cell

Getting Started with WordPerfect Tables

As you create different reports using WordPerfect, you will find that tables provide a compact way of presenting a considerable amount of information. To help you create tables in your documents, WordPerfect provides a table editor. Your tables can contain text entries, numbers, or both. WordPerfect provides very powerful table editing capabilities. If you are listing your company's expenses in a table, for example, you can direct WordPerfect to calculate totals, averages, and so on. In fact, several of the forms provided on this book's companion disk make extensive use of WordPerfect's table capabilities to calculate total expenses, sales tax on a purchase order, and so on. When you create a table in WordPerfect, you need to first know the numbers of rows and columns. Rows go down your pages while columns go from left to right, as shown in Figure 31.1.

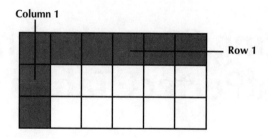

Figure 31.1 *Identifying table rows and columns.*

To use WordPerfect's table editor, open the Layout menu and choose **Tables**. WordPerfect cascades the menu, as shown in Figure 31.2.

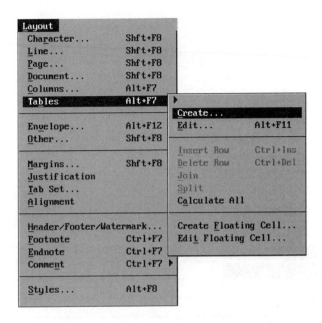

Figure 31.2 *Cascading the Tables menu.*

Creating a Simple Table

The following table contains four rows of entries. Each row contains three columns.

Equipment	Cost	Purchased From
Computer	$1500	Computer World
Fax machine	$800	Office Land
Copier	$650	Office Land

To create this table, select **Create** from the Tables menu. WordPerfect may display a dialog box asking you if you want to create a table or parallel columns. Select the table option. WordPerfect then displays the Create Table dialog box, as shown in Figure 31.3.

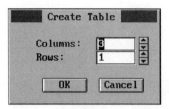

Figure 31.3 *The Create Table dialog box.*

In the Columns option, type in the number of columns—which in this case is three. In the Rows option, type in the number of rows, which is four. Select **OK**. WordPerfect displays the table in the table editor, as shown in Figure 31.4.

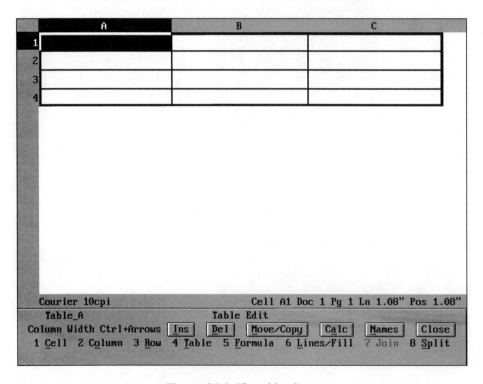

Figure 31.4 *The table editor.*

WordPerfect refers to each table entry as a *cell*. The table editor lets you add, delete, and size cells. You can also change the line type that surrounds each cell or shade a cell. For now, because the box size looks pretty close to what you need, select the **Close** option. WordPerfect displays the table in your document. Type in the text previously shown, using your Arrow keys to advance the cursor from one cell to the next. Your table should resemble Figure 31.5.

Equipment	Cost	Purchased From
Computer	$1500	Computer World
Fax machine	$800	Office Land
Copier	$650	Office Land

Figure 31.5 *Editing a table's contents.*

Use the File menu **Print/Fax** option to print your document. In this case, the table contains text and numeric entries. As discussed, your tables can contain only text, numbers, or as shown in this case, both.

Sizing a Table

If you examine the table you just created, you may decide that the column containing the cost amounts is too large. Using the table editor, you can quickly reduce the column's width. Open the Layout menu and choose **Tables**. When WordPerfect cascades the Tables menu, choose **Edit**. WordPerfect displays the table editor. Using your Arrow keys, highlight one of the cells in the center column. Next, hold down the **Ctrl** key and press the **Left Arrow** key. Each time you press the **Left Arrow** key, WordPerfect reduces the column's width. Repeat this process until the column is considerable thinner, as in Figure 31.6.

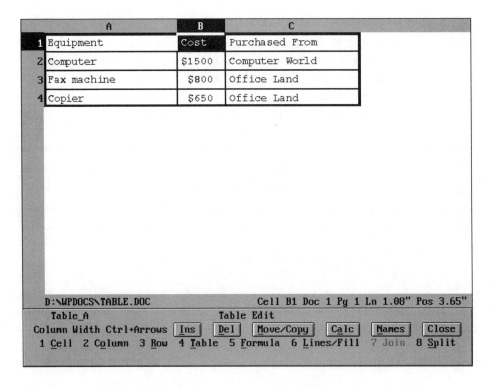

Figure 31.6 *Reducing a column's width.*

Following are the Ctrl-key combinations to size a column or row.

♦ **Ctrl-Left Arrow** reduces a column's width.

♦ **Ctrl-Right Arrow** increases a column's width.

When you are done sizing the column, you can select **Close** to return to your document.

Understanding Cell Names

Every cell in a table has a unique name. If you examine your table in the table editor, you will find that WordPerfect labels cell columns using letters of the alphabet and cell rows using numbers.

As you perform different table operations, you may need to refer to specific cell names.

Assigning Table Attributes

Depending on the contents of your table, you may want to assign different attributes, such as bolding or italics as shown here.

Equipment	Cost	Purchased From
Computer	$1500	Computer World
Fax machine	$800	Office Land
Copier	$650	Office Land

WordPerfect's table editor lets you assign such attributes to the entire table, a row, column, or even just a cell. To assign an attribute:

1. Select the table editor.

2. Using your Arrow keys, highlight a cell in the desired row or column. In this case, move the cursor to the first column.

3. Type **2** or click on the table editor **Column** option. WordPerfect displays the Column Format dialog box, shown in Figure 31.7.

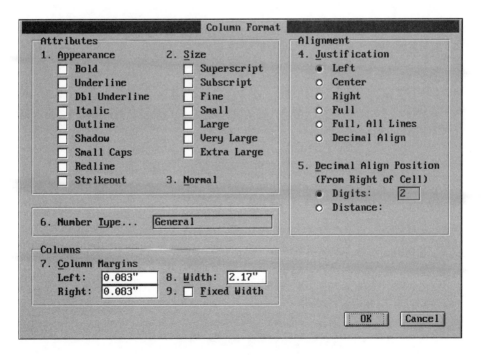

Figure 31.7 *The Column Format dialog box.*

4. Type **1** and select the **Bold** attribute. As you can see, the Column Format dialog box lets you control a column's fonts, justification in the cell, number of digits that follow the decimal point in numeric values (normally 2 for currency values), and the column margin and width.

5. After you assign the bold font attribute, select **OK**.

6. Place the cursor in the third column and use the Column Format dialog box to assign the italic attribute.

WordPerfect lets you assign attributes at the column, row, table, and even the cell level. To perform an operation on a specific row, column, or cell, highlight the desired object and select the corresponding table editor option.

Adding and Deleting Rows and Columns

Over time, the size of your table may change. Using the table editor, you can quickly add or delete rows or columns. Assume for example, you want to add a total field to the table as shown here:

Equipment	Cost	Purchased From
Computer	$1500	Computer World
Fax machine	$800	Office Land
Copier	$650	Office Land
Total	$2950	

In this case, you will be adding a row that contains two columns:

1. Select the table editor.

2. Move the cursor to the last entry in the first column (Copier).

3. Type **I** or click on the **Insert** option. The Insert dialog box is displayed in Figure 31.8.

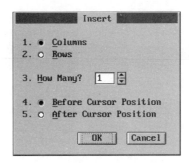

Figure 31.8 *The Insert dialog box.*

4. Select the **Row** options and choose one row.

5. Type **5** or click on the **After Cursor Position** option.

6. Choose **OK**. WordPerfect inserts a row with three columns, as shown in Figure 31.9.

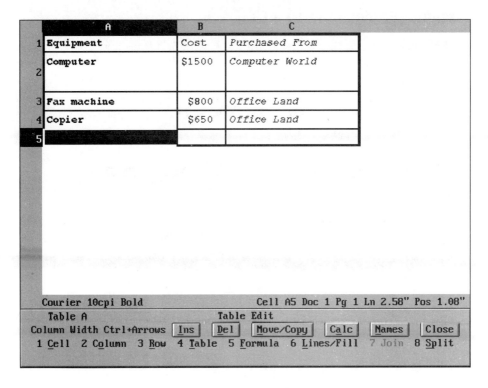

Figure 31.9 *Inserting a row of table columns.*

If you look at the previous table, however, you really only want two columns. Deleting the last cell, however, is not as easy as you might guess. The table editor does not let you delete a cell. However, using the **Join** option, you can combine two cells into one.

Joining Two Cells

A join operation lets you combine two cells into one. In this case, use your Arrow keys to highlight cell B5. Drag your mouse from cell B5 to cell C5. WordPerfect highlights both cells. Type **7** or click on **Join**. A dialog box asking you if you want to join the cells is displayed. Select **Yes**. WordPerfect makes the two cells one.

In this case, you can probably add up the equipment costs to determine your total. However, by assigning a formula to cell B5, you can direct WordPerfect to perform the calculation for you.

Assigning a Formula to a Cell

To help you create tables whose entries are numeric values and possibly based on the totals or averages of the listed values, WordPerfect lets you place formulas in cell tables. In the case of the previous table, you can direct WordPerfect to automatically total the costs listed in column B to create a total. To do so, move the cursor to cell B5. Type **5** or click on **Formula**. The Table Formula dialog box is displayed in Figure 31.10.

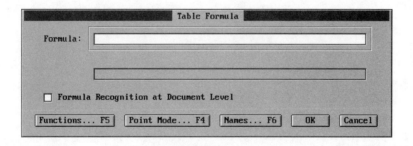

Figure 31.10 *The Table Formula dialog box.*

In this case, type in the following formula to direct WordPerfect to add the contents of cells B2, B3, and B4:

```
B2 + B3 + B4
```

WordPerfect displays the total (2950) in the cell.

WordPerfect provides several built-in functions you can use within your formulas. To display the available functions, select **Functions** in the Table Formula dialog box.

In this case, WordPerfect does not precede the amount with a dollar sign. To direct WordPerfect to display the amount in currency format, highlight the cell and select **Cell**. WordPerfect displays the Cell Format dialog box. Type **6** or click on the **Number Type**. WordPerfect displays the Number Type Formats dialog box, shown in Figure 31.11.

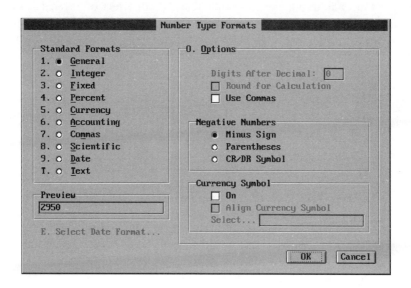

Figure 31.11 *The Number Type Formats dialog box.*

Type **5** or click on **Currency**. Go to the Options field and choose **0** digits after the decimal and then remove the X from the Use Commas field. Select **OK**. WordPerfect displays the amount in the currency format.

Close the table editor and return to your document editing screen. Add the text **Total** to cell A5. Your table should be similar to Figure 31.12.

Equipment	Cost	Purchased From
Computer	$1500	Computer World
Fax machine	$800	Office Land
Copier	$650	Office Land
Total	$2950	

Figure 31.12 *The finished table.*

Assume, however, you find the computer only cost $1250 as opposed to $1500. Edit the table to change the amount. When you change the cost value, you will find that the total amount does not change. WordPerfect only recalculates table formulas when you tell it to do so. To update the total, select **Tables** from the Layout menu and choose **Calculate All**. WordPerfect automatically updates the table.

 If you plan to use tables that contain formulas on a regular basis, place a Table menu **Calculate All** option on your button bar. For instructions on creating a button bar button, see Chapter 20.

Customizing the Table Lines, Border, and Shading

In the table that you just created, the outside border used double lines and cells were separated using single lines. WordPerfect's table editor lets you control the borders and shading at the cell, row, column, or table level. To change the border or shading, select the table editor. If you want to change the lines or shading for a specific cell or group of cells, drag your mouse to select the desired cells, otherwise, your changes affect the entire table. Type **6** or click on **Lines/Fill**. The Table Lines dialog box is displayed in Figure 31.13.

Figure 31.13 *The Table Lines dialog box.*

The options in the Table Lines dialog box change the lines that are at the top, left, right, or bottom of the selected object. You can also select the desired fill pattern. In the case of the previous table, use your mouse to select the top row of the table by dragging it across the columns. Next, in the Table Lines dialog box, choose **Fill**. WordPerfect displays the Fill Style and Color dialog box. Type **1** or click on **Fill Style**. The Fill Styles dialog box is displayed in Figure 31.14.

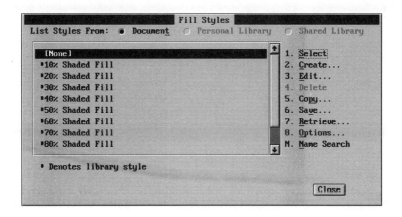

Figure 31.14 *The Fill Styles dialog box.*

Highlight the **20% Shaded Fill** option and choose **Select**. WordPerfect returns you to the Fill Style and Color dialog box. Select **OK**. WordPerfect returns you to the Table Lines dialog box. Select **Close**. When you exit the table editor, your table should look like Figure 31.15.

Equipment	Cost	Purchased From
Computer	$1250	Computer World
Fax machine	$800	Office Land
Copier	$650	Office Land
Total	$2700	

Figure 31.15 *Shading a table row.*

Working with a Table Document

If you travel on business, you may have to keep track of your expenses so you can be reimbursed or so you can deduct the expenses from your taxes. To help you track your expenses, the companion disk provides the Expense Report document shown in Figure 31.16.

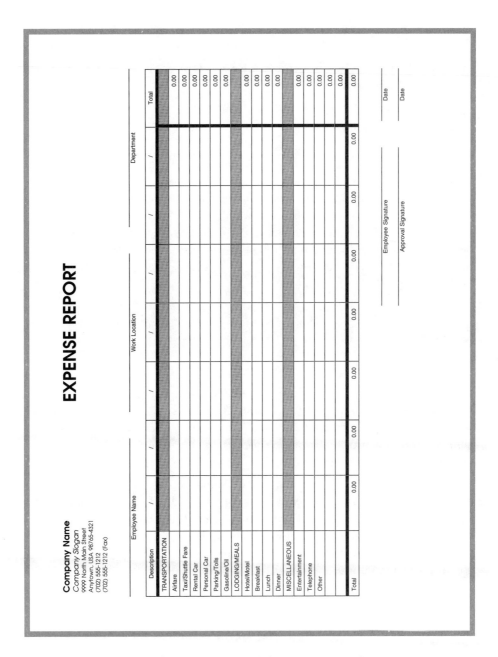

Figure 31.16 *The companion disk Expense Report document.*

To use the expense report document:

1. Select the File menu and choose **Open**. Type in the filename **EXPENSE.DOC**.
2. Edit the form to customize it for your company.
3. Use the File menu **Save** option to save your changes.

When you need to track your expense reports, open the document and type in your expenses. As you can see, the document provides several different expense totals. After you type in the amounts you want WordPerfect to total, select **Table** from the Layout menu and choose **Calculate All**. Each time you change an amount in the table, you need to use the Calculate All option to generate the new totals. Save the document to a file on disk whose name describes the week the expenses were incurred (such as MAY1-8.DOC) or the trip name (SALESMTG.DOC).

Summary

To help you quickly create tables in your document, WordPerfect provides a powerful table editor. When you create a table, you must tell the table editor the number of rows and columns you desire. Table rows go up and down the page while columns move from left to right. WordPerfect refers to each entry in the table as a cell. Each cell as a unique name that corresponds to the cells column (a letter of the alphabet) and row number, such as B1 or C3.

To help you perform calculations on table entries, WordPerfect lets you assign formulas to table cells. When you want WordPerfect to perform the formula (calculate the cell's result), you must select **Calculate All** from the Table menu. WordPerfect does not automatically update a formula's result each time you change a table entry. To help you improve your table appearance, the table editor lets you customize the boxes and lines that surround a cell, row, column, or even the table itself. In addition, you can shade different cells to help draw the reader's attention. In Chapter 32 you will learn how to place graphic images into your documents, such as logos or other pictures.

New Terms

- ◆ **Cell.** A table entry.
- ◆ **Row.** Table entries that appear from left to right.
- ◆ **Column.** Table entries that appear up and down.
- ◆ **Table.** A collection of one or more rows and columns.

Working with Graphic Images

In this chapter you:

- ◆ Retrieve WordPerfect's graphics into your document
- ◆ Move and size graphics
- ◆ Customize graphic image settings

Retrieving a WordPerfect Graphic File

When you install WordPerfect 6.0, the installation places several different image files that have the WP (WordPerfect Graphic) extension in the directory \WP60\GRAPHICS. Figure 32.1 illustrates two WordPerfect graphic images.

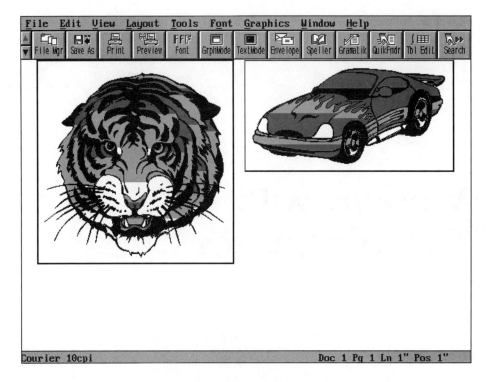

Figure 32.1 *The graphic images.*

To better understand how you can use WordPerfect graphics images in your documents:

1. Select **New** from the File menu.
2. Open the Graphics menu, shown in Figure 32.2.

Figure 32.2 *The Graphics menu.*

3. Select **Retrieve Image**. WordPerfect displays the Retrieve Image File dialog box, as shown in Figure 32.3.

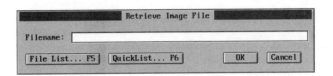

Figure 32.3 *The Retrieve Image File dialog box.*

4. Press **F5** or click on **File List**.

5. WordPerfect may display the Select List dialog box highlighting WordPerfect's GRAPHICS directory. If so, press **Enter** or click on **OK**. WordPerfect displays a list of the image files contained in the GRAPHICS directory, as shown in Figure 32.4.

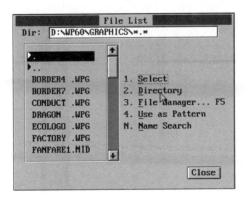

Figure 32.4 *A list of the image files.*

6. Using your Arrow keys, highlight the file JEEP.WPG and press **Enter**. WordPerfect retrieves a graphic of a jeep, as shown in Figure 32.5.

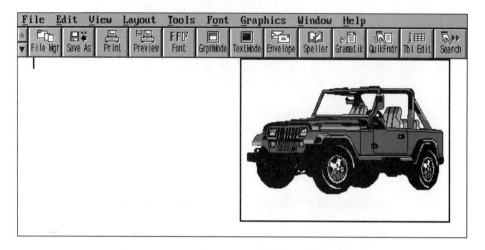

Figure 32.5 *Insert the jeep image into your document.*

Moving and Sizing a Graphic Image

After you retrieve an image into your document, you may need to move the graphic to a specific location. To move a graphic image, point your mouse at the image. Hold down the mouse button and drag the image to the desired location. Using this technique, move the jeep image around your document.

In a similar way, you may need to change the size of an image so that it better fits in your document. To size a graphic, click on the image. WordPerfect highlights the image displaying size boxes at different points of the image, as in Figure 32.6.

Figure 32.6 *A selected image.*

Aim your mouse at one of the size boxes and hold down the mouse button and the **Shift** key. To decrease the image size, push the size box toward the center of the image. To increase the image size, pull the size box away from the document's center. If you drag one of the size boxes that appear at the corner of an image, WordPerfect changes the image's height and width at the same time.

Deleting, Copying, and Cutting a Graphic Image

Just as there are times when you need to edit your document's text, there may be times when you need to remove a graphic image. To delete a graphics image, click on the image to select it. Press the **Del** key. WordPerfect displays a dialog box asking you if you want to delete the image Select **Yes** to delete the image.

In Chapter 11 you learned how to use WordPerfect's Edit menu to cut and paste text from one document location to another or to copy text throughout your document. Unfortunately, in WordPerfect, such operations only apply to text. You cannot use the Edit menu to cut and paste graphic images.

Working with Graphic Settings

If you look at all of the graphic images in this book, you will find that they have figure captions that explain their contents. WordPerfect lets you add captions to your graphics. In addition, WordPerfect lets you change or remove the frame that surrounds the graphic, attach the graphic to different elements on a page, and even edit the graphics image. To better understand how to perform these operations, open the File menu and choose **New**. Next, use **Retrieve Image** from the Graphics menu file to retrieve the graphic GRIZZLY.WPG. WordPerfect displays a graphic of a Grizzly bear on your screen. Using your mouse, double click on the graphic. WordPerfect displays the Edit Graphics Box dialog box, shown in Figure 32.7

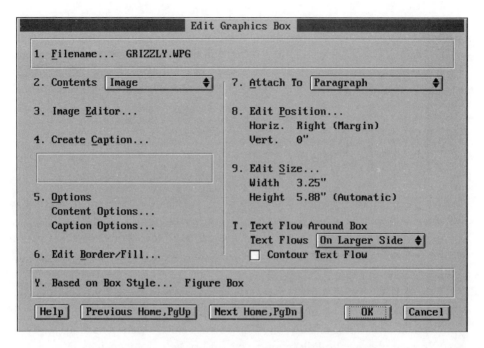

Figure 32.7 *The Edit Graphics Box dialog box..*

Editing the Graphics Image

WordPerfect lets you edit an image, changing its height, width, position, rotation, and more. To edit an image, type **3** or click on **Image Editor**. WordPerfect displays the image editing screen, shown in Figure 32.8.

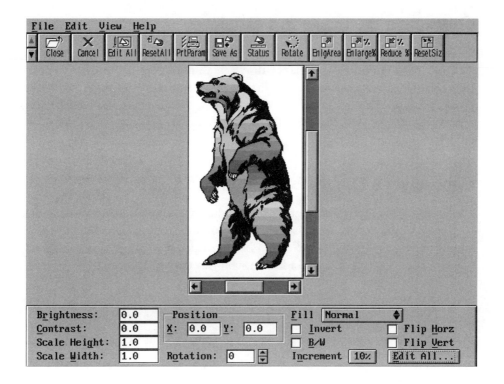

Figure 32.8 *The image editor.*

Assigning a Graphic Caption

To assign a caption to a graphic in your document:

1. Type **4** or click on **Edit Caption**. WordPerfect displays a small editing window in which you can type the desired caption.

2. After you are done typing, press **F7**.

3. To control where WordPerfect displays the caption, type **5** or click on **Options**.

4. Select **Captions Options**. WordPerfect displays a dialog box whose entries let you position and size the caption.

Controlling the Image Box Display

To simplify graphic image positioning, WordPerfect treats images as a rectangular box. By default, WordPerfect draws a thin border around the image. Depending on your document, you may want to remove or change the border. To do so, type **6** or click on **Edit Border/Fill**. WordPerfect displays a dialog box whose entries let you select the border frame and select a fill shadow for the white region in the box.

Controlling a Graphic's Position and Size

The easiest way to position a graphic is to drag the graphic using your mouse. Likewise, as previously discussed, using your mouse you can quickly size a graphic. The Edit Graphics Box dialog box provides several options that let you position and size a graphic. In addition, you can control how text and graphics intermix. By default, WordPerfect moves text to the left or right side of the graphic depending on which side has more room. Using the **Text Flows** option, however, you can flow text around or even through the graphic.

As you begin using graphics more frequently in your documents, you may want the ability to edit many of these options.

Putting a Graphic Image to Use

The companion disk that accompanies this book contains a custom letterhead similar to that shown in Figure 32.9.

Company Name
Company Slogan
9999 North Main Street
Anytown, USA 98765-4321
(702) 555-1212
(702) 555-1212 (Fax)

Figure 32.9 *The companion disk custom letterhead.*

As you can see, the letterhead contains a graphic image. The form uses the image file MTNCLIMB.WPG. To use the custom letterhead:

1. Select the File menu and choose **Open**.
2. In the Open dialog box, type in the document name **LETTERHD.DOC**, and press **Enter**.
3. Edit the document to customize it for your company.
4. Use the File menu **Save** option to save your changes.

When WordPerfect loads the letterhead, edit the text to insert your name, address, and phone numbers. Use the File menu **Save As** option to save the file to your hard disk with the filename MYLETTER.DOC. When you later want to create a letter using your letterhead.

1. Open the File menu and choose **Retrieve**.
2. In the Retrieve Document dialog box, type in the filename **LETTERHD.DOC**.
3. Position the cursor beneath the letterhead and type in the desired text.
4. Use the File menu **Save As** option to save the document to a file on disk.

Using the techniques discussed in this chapter you can size, delete, or assign a different graphic to the custom letterhead.

Summary

To improve the appearance of your documents, WordPerfect provides several graphics images. After you retrieve an image into your file, you can quickly size or move the image using your mouse. If your document contains text, WordPerfect (by default) positions the text to the left or right of the graphic, depending on which side has more space. However, using the Edit Graphics Dialog box, you can control not only text wrapping, but an image's size, position, framing, caption and more.

New Terms

- ◆ **WordPerfect graphics image.** A graphics image you can insert into a WordPerfect document. WordPerfect provides several graphics images files in the GRAPHICS directory.

- ◆ **Size box.** A small box WordPerfect displays on the corners and sides of a selected graphic image you can drag using your mouse, with the **Shift** key, to size the image.

Chapter **33**

Creating Boxes and Lines

In this chapter you:

◆ Draw lines in your document

◆ Place borders around pages and paragraphs

◆ Create and edit graphic boxes

◆ Create and edit graphic lines

Using WordPerfect's Line Drawing Capabilities

As you create documents, there may be times when you want to place a line between text. For example assume that you want to draw attention to the following quote:

```
    With regard to excellence, it is not enough
     to know, but we must try to have and use it.
                      Aristotle
```

One way to draw the reader's attention to the quote is to place lines above and below the text as shown here:

```
    _____


    With regard to excellence, it is not enough
     to know, but we must try to have and use it.


                      Aristotle


    _____
```

WordPerfect makes it very easy for you to draw such lines. To get started:

1. Open the File menu and choose **New**.
2. Open the Layout menu, choose **Justification** and select **Center**.
3. Press **Enter** twice. Type in the following text:

```
    With regard to excellence, it is not enough
     to know, but we must try to have and use it.

                      Aristotle
```

4. Select the text using a block operation and then apply Italics from the Font menu. WordPerfect displays the selected text using italics.

5. Move the cursor to the two lines above the quote.

6. Open the Graphics menu and choose **Line Draw**. WordPerfect displays the Line Draw dialog box at the bottom of your screen, shown in Figure 33.1.

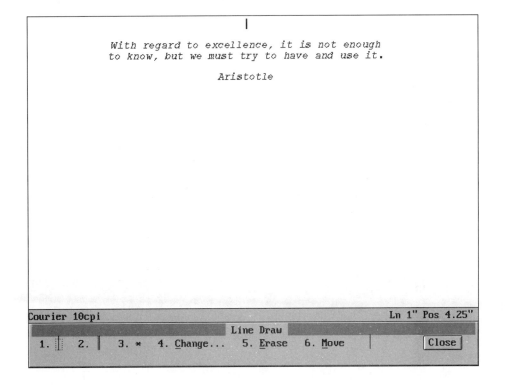

Figure 33.1 *The Line Draw dialog box.*

The Line Draw dialog box lets you select the character you want to use to draw the line–single line, a double line, or an asterisk.

1. Type **1** or click on the single-line character.

2. Press your **Right Arrow** twenty times key to draw the line.

3. Select **Close**.

4. Move the cursor two lines below *Aristotle's* name.

5. Open the Graphics menu a second time, again choosing **Line Draw**.

6. Using these same techniques, draw a line beneath the quote. Your screen should look like Figure 33.2.

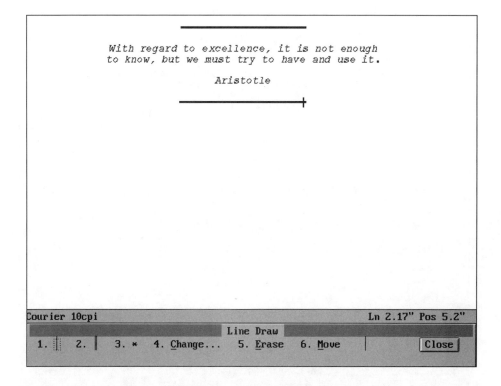

```
                With regard to excellence, it is not enough
                to know, but we must try to have and use it.

                            Aristotle

                ────────────────────────────────────┼


Courier 10cpi                                      Ln 2.17" Pos 5.2"
                            Line Draw
  1. ▓    2. ▓    3. *    4. Change...   5. Erase   6. Move   │   [Close]
```

Figure 33.2 *Drawing lines above and below text.*

If you draw and line and then decide that you no longer want the line within your document, you can delete the line characters using the **Del** or **Backspace** key. In the previous example, you used the **Right Arrow** key to draw the line. When the Draw Dialog box is visible, WordPerfect draws the line in the same direction as the arrow key you press. If you press the **Up Arrow** or **Down Arrow** keys, WordPerfect draws vertical lines. If you press the **Right Arrow** or **Left Arrow** keys, WordPerfect draws a horizontal line.

Taking Advantage of Borders

Depending on your documents, there may be times when you want to place a border around a paragraph, the current page, or even the current column. To place a border in your document:

1. Move the cursor to the location at which you want the border to start. Open to Graphics menu and choose **Borders**. WordPerfect cascades the menu, as shown in Figure 33.3.

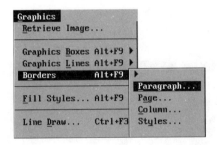

Figure 33.3 *The Cascading Borders menu.*

2. Select the **Paragraph**, **Page**, or **Column** option as needed. WordPerfect displays a dialog box that lets you control the border's appearance.

3. To better understand the process of assigning a border, open the File menu and choose **New**. Next, type in the following text:

        In any moment of decision, the best thing you can
        do is the right thing, the next best thing is the
        wrong thing, and the worst thing you can do is
        nothing. — Theodore Roosevelt

4. Place the cursor at the start of the paragraph, immediately before the word *In.*

5. Open the Graphics menu and choose **Borders**. When WordPerfect cascades the menu, select **Paragraph**. WordPerfect displays the Create Paragraph Border dialog box shown in Figure 33.4.

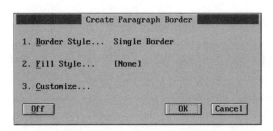

Figure 33.4 *The Create Paragraph Border.*

6. Type **1** or click on the **Border Style** option. WordPerfect displays the Border Styles dialog box that lets you select the desired border type, as shown in Figure 33.5.

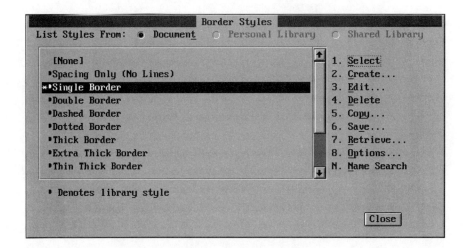

Figure 33.5 *The Border Styles dialog box.*

7. Using your Arrow keys or mouse, highlight the desired border style and choose **Select**. In this case, select **Thick Border**. WordPerfect returns to the Create Paragraph Border dialog box.

8. Select **Fill Styles**. The Fill Styles dialog box is displayed in Figure 33.6, from which you can select the shading to use in the border.

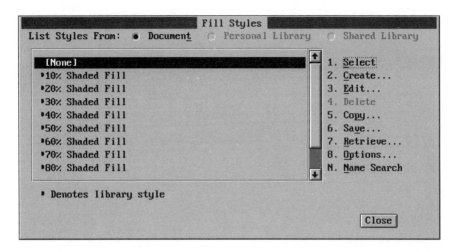

Figure 33.6 *The Fill Styles dialog box.*

9. Using your Arrow keys or mouse, highlight the desired shading (the lower the percentage, the lighter the shading) and choose **Select**. In this case, highlight **20% Shaded Fill**. WordPerfect returns to the Create Paragraph Border dialog box.

10. Select **OK**.

Working with a Graphics Box

In Chapter 32 you learned how to retrieve graphics images into your document. When you place an image in your document, WordPerfect stores the image in a box. By double clicking on the box, WordPerfect displays the Edit Graphics dialog box in which you can change the box size, border, shading, and many other options. If you aren't using a mouse, you can edit a graphic image's box by selecting the Graphics menu and choosing **Graphics Boxes**. WordPerfect cascades the menu. Choose **Edit**. The Select Box To Edit dialog box is displayed in Figure 33.7.

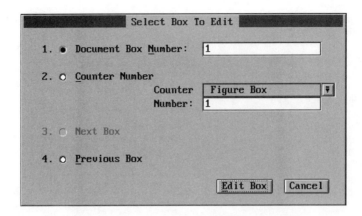

Figure 33.7 *The Select Box To Edit dialog box.*

Type in the number of the box and press **Enter**. WordPerfect displays the Edit Graphics Box dialog box.

Controlling Box Numbering

By default, WordPerfect assigns incrementing numbers to the boxes you place in your documents. Depending on your document, you may want WordPerfect to display the box numbers as letters or roman numerals, in either uppercase or lowercase. Likewise, you may want WordPerfect to decrement the box numbers instead of incrementing them. To control WordPerfect's box numbering;

1. Open the Graphics menu select **Graphics Boxes** and choose **Numbering**. The Counters dialog box is displayed in Figure 33.8.

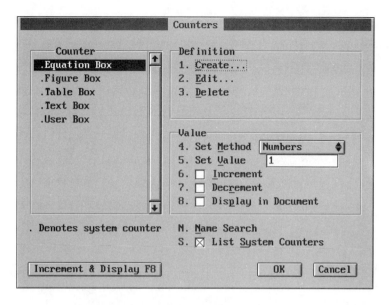

Figure 33.8 *The Counters dialog box.*

2. Highlight the box type you desire.

3. Select **Set Method**. WordPerfect displays the box number options you can use.

4. After you make your selections, choose **OK**.

Working with a Graphics Line

Earlier in this chapter you used WordPerfect's line drawing characters to create lines in your documents. WordPerfect also lets you create graphics lines for which you specify the line's location, size, orientation (vertical or horizontal), and style. To create a graphics line, select the Graphics menu and choose **Graphics Lines**. WordPerfect cascades the menu. Select **Create**. WordPerfect displays the Create Graphics Line dialog box, as shown in Figure 33.9.

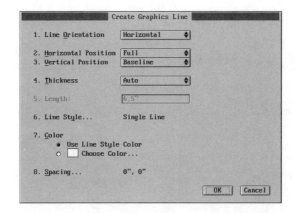

Figure 33.9 *The Create Graphics Line dialog box.*

Line Orientation lets you select a horizontal or vertical line. **Horizontal Position** lets you specify the lines justification. If you select **Set**, WordPerfect lets you type in the location of the line's left edge, relative to the edge of the page. In a similar way, **Vertical Position** specifies the line's starting location from the top of the page. **Thickness** lets you select automatic thickness or manual set the thickness to the option you desire.

If you are creating a line other than a line that is fully justified, the **Length** field lets you control the line's length. For fully justified lines, the line extends from margin to margin. **Line Style** lets you control the line's appearance. When you select this option. The Line Styles dialog box is displayed in Figure 33.10.

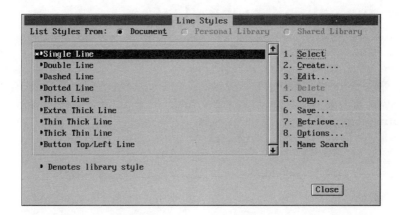

Figure 33.10 *The Line Styles dialog box.*

The **Color** option in the Create Graphics Line dialog box lets you specify whether you want WordPerfect to use the color that corresponds to the selected line style, or if you want to assign your own color.

If you select the **Choose Color** option, WordPerfect displays a dialog box from which you can select the desired style.

Spacing lets you control the amount of space WordPerfect places above and below the line. If you select this option, WordPerfect displays a dialog box asking you to enter the desired spacing.

Editing a Graphics Line

If you place a graphics line in your document and decide you want to change the line in some way, double click your mouse on the line. WordPerfect displays the Edit Graphics Line dialog box where you can make your changes. If you are not using a mouse, open the Graphics menu and choose **Graphics Lines**. When WordPerfect cascades the menu, choose **Edit**. WordPerfect displays a dialog box asking you to specify the desired line number. Type in the line number and press **Enter**. WordPerfect displays the Edit Graphics Lines dialog box.

If your document has more than one graphics line, you can use the **Previous** and **Next** buttons to quickly display the line specifics for the line that immediately precedes or follows the current line.

Creating a Customer Invoice

If you work in an office that sells merchandise and invoices customers, you may want to take advantage of the companion disk invoice document. As shown in Figure 33.11, the Invoice form lets you type in shipping information, the invoice date and number, the purchase order number and terms. In addition, you can type in each item sold, the quantity, description, and price.

Company Name
Company Slogan
9999 North Main Street
Anytown, USA 98765-4321
(702) 555-1212
(702) 555-1212 (Fax)

INVOICE

Sold to: Ship to:

Date	Invoice Number	P. O. Number	Terms	Contact

Item	Quan	Units	Description	Price	Total
					0.00
					0.00
					0.00
					0.00
					0.00
					0.00
					0.00
					0.00
					0.00
					0.00
					0.00
					0.00
					0.00
					0.00
					0.00
					0.00
					0.00
					0.00
					0.00
					0.00
					0.00
					0.00
					0.00
			Sub-Total		0.00
			Sales Tax (7%)		0.00
			Shipping & Handling		
			Total Due		0.00

Figure 33.11 *The companion disk Invoice form.*

To use the invoice form:

1. Select **Open** from the File menu. Type in the filename **INVOICE.DOC**.
2. Select **Open** from the File menu. Type in the filename **INVOICE.DOC**.
3. Use the File menu **Save** option to save your changes.

You want to edit the invoice document to assign your company name, slogan, address, phone numbers, and possibly the sales tax amount. Save your changes to a document file on disk. When you later need to create an invoice, open the document, type in the corresponding fields (using the Arrow keys to move from one field to the next). The form contains a column for totals. If you select **Tables** from the Layout menu and then choose **Calculate All**, WordPerfect automatically calculates the totals for you.

Summary

To draw the readers attention to specific text in your document, you can place lines, boxes, or even shaded borders around your text. WordPerfect provides two ways to draw lines. First, you can use WordPerfect's line drawing characters and your Arrow keys. Using this technique, you can draw a vertical or horizontal line that bends to create an L shape. Second, WordPerfect lets you create a graphics line for which you specify a starting location and size. WordPerfect predefines several different graphics line styles such as dotted or double lines. When you place image files or equations (see Chapter 41) in your document, WordPerfect places them in boxes. Depending on your document's contents, you may need to change the box's size, shading, border, or other elements. By using lines, borders, and boxes in your documents, you can improve your document's appearance.

Chapter 34

Controlling Document Tabs

In this chapter you:

- ◆ Display the tab ruler
- ◆ Clear and set tab stops
- ◆ Understand left, right, center, and decimal tabs
- ◆ Use dot leaders before tabs

Understanding Tab Stops

Each time you press the **Tab** key, WordPerfect advances the cursor to a location called a tab stop. By default, WordPerfect places tab stops every half inch. Depending on your document, there may be times when you want to change the tab stop locations. To do so, open the Layout menu and choose **Tab Set**. WordPerfect displays its Tab Set dialog box, as shown in Figure 34.1.

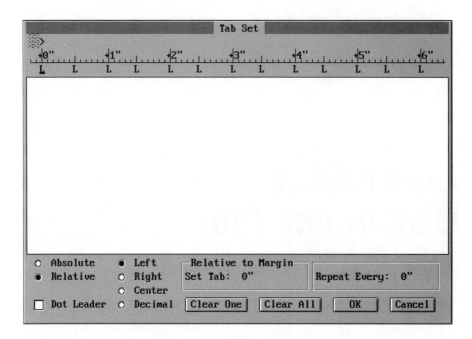

Figure 34.1 *The Tab Set dialog box.*

The Tab Set dialog box lets you clear, set, or change the type of a Tab stop. If you look at the top of the dialog box, you will find a *ruler* that shows location of each tab stop.

The uppercase letters that appear in the tab ruler correspond to WordPerfect's tab stops. WordPerfect lets you set or clear tab stops at specific locations.

Understanding Tab Stop Types

WordPerfect supports four types of tabs: left, right, center, and decimal tabs, as described in Table 34.1.

Table 34.1 *The tab stop types.*

Tab Type	Ruler Letter	Purpose
Left	L	Left justifies text at the tab stop.
Right	R	Right justifies text at the tab stop.
Center	C	Center justifies text at the tab stop.
Decimal	D	Aligns the decimal point in numbers at the tab stop.

Figure 34.2 illustrates the use of each tab stop type. Note the tab stop letter in the ruler and how WordPerfect aligns text in a document.

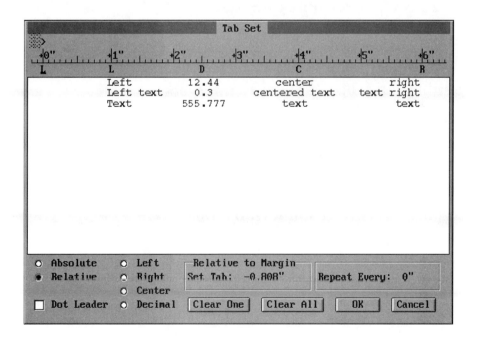

Figure 34.2 *Using the different tab stop types.*

Setting a Tab Stop

To set a tab stop, you must select the position in the tab ruler where you want to place the tab stop. Using your keyboard's **Right Arrow** and **Left Arrow** keys, you can move the ruler's position indicator. If you are using a mouse, click the mouse at the desired location. Next, indicate the type of tab stop you desire. To specify a tab stop, type the letter **L**, **R**, **C**, or **D** or click on the desired type using your mouse.

You can also direct WordPerfect to place a tab stop at a specific location by typing **S** or on the **Set Tab** option. WordPerfect prompts you for the desired location. Type in the location you desire and press **Enter**.

Clearing One or More Tab Stops

If you are creating a table, for example, there may be times when you want to remove one or more existing tab stops. To clear a specific tab stop:

1. Move the tab stop position indicator to the desire tab stop.
2. Type **O** or click on the **Clear One** option.
3. If you want to remove all of the existing tab stops, type **A** or click on the **Clear All** option.

Setting Tab Stops at Specific Intervals

There may be times when you want to place tab stops at a specific interval, such as every inch or inch and a half. To do so, clear the existing tab stops. Next, type **P** or click on the **Repeat Every** option. WordPerfect prompts you for the tab stop interval you desire. Type in the interval you desire and press **Enter**.

Relative Versus Absolute Tab Stops

By default, WordPerfect positions tab stops relative to the left margin. If you change a document's margins, the relative spacing between your tab stops does not change. Depending on your document, there may be times when you want WordPerfect to position tab stops at absolute positions on your page (regardless of the margin settings). You must choose **Absolute** or **Relative** tab stop positioning for your entire document.

Understanding Dot Leaders

Normally, when you press the **Tab** key, WordPerfect advances the cursor to the next tab stop, leaving white space between the cursor's previous and new location. There may be times, however, when you want WordPerfect to place periods (dots) between the cursor's previous position and the tab stop. For example, assume you are creating a table of contents for your document, you might use *dot leaders* as shown here:

```
Chapter 1 Getting Started with WordPerfect ......1
Chapter 2 Creating Your First Document ........20
Chapter 3 Editing a Document .................35
Chapter 4 Printing Your Document .............46
```

To create a table like this, place a right justified tab stop at the location and turn on WordPerfect's dot leaders.

Creating a Travel Itinerary

If you travel for business or pleasure, you probably know how frustrating it can be to arrive at your hotel, airline, or rental car company and have a problem. To help you better organize your trips, the companion disk that accompanies this book provides a Travel Itinerary form, as shown in Figure 34.3.

Company Name
Company Slogan
9999 North Main Street
Anytown, USA 98765-4321
(702) 555-1212
(702) 555-1212 (Fax)

TRAVEL ITINERARY

Traveler: _____

AIRLINE

Date	Airline/flight	From	To	Depart	Arrive	Notes

RENTAL CAR

Date	Days	City	Company	Price	Phone	Confirmation

ACCOMODATIONS

Date	Nights	Establishment Name and Address	Price	Phone	Confirmation

NOTES

_____

Figure 34.3 *The companion disk Travel Itinerary form.*

Using the travel itinerary form you can record your flight numbers, times, airlines, confirmation numbers, as well as your rental car and hotel information. You won't be left guessing at the counter because you have the rate you were quoted and a confirmation number. To use the travel itinerary document:

1. Select **Open** from the File menu and type the filename **TVLITIN.DOC**.
2. Edit the form to customize it for your company.
3. Use the File menu **Save** option to save your changes.

Using the **Print/Fax** option, you can print a copy of the document and hand write your the information. A better alternative, however, is to open the document, type in your travel information and then save the document to a filename that corresponds to your trip, then use **Print/Fax** to print your typed document. As you edit the document, use your Arrow keys to move from one section of the document to another.

Summary

A tab stop specifies a location to which WordPerfect advances the cursor when you press the **Tab** key. By default, WordPerfect places tab stops at every half inch. Depending on your document, you may want to add or remove (*clear*) tab stops. WordPerfect supports four types of tab stops. The most common, a left tab stop, directs WordPerfect to left justify the text you type at the tab stop. In a similar way, WordPerfect's right and center tab stops direct WordPerfect to right and center justify text, respectively, around a tab stop. Lastly, a decimal tab stop directs WordPerfect to align the decimal point that may appear in numbers on the tab stop.

New Terms

◆ **Decimal tab stop.** A tab stop at which WordPerfect aligns the decimal point that appears in a numeric value.

◆ **Dot leaders.** The display of periods (dots) from the cursor's previous location up to the next tab stop.

◆ **Tab stop.** A location along the document's current line to which WordPerfect advances the cursor when you press the **Tab** key.

Chapter 35

Using the Ribbon Bar

In this chapter you:

- ◆ Turn on the display of the ribbon bar
- ◆ Use the ribbon bar to control the screen display
- ◆ Use the ribbon bar to assign styles
- ◆ Use the ribbon bar to select the number of columns
- ◆ Use the ribbon bar to justify text
- ◆ Use the ribbon to select a font and font size

Turning on the Ribbon Bar

As you have learned, WordPerfect's button bar makes common operations a mouse click away. In a similar way, WordPerfect provides a *ribbon bar* that simplifies many formatting operations. To turn on the ribbon bar display, open the View menu and choose **Ribbon**. The ribbon bar beneath the menu bar is displayed in Figure 35.1.

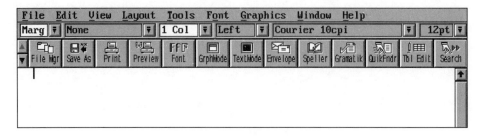

Figure 35.1 *The ribbon bar displayed beneath the menu bar.*

Using the ribbon bar, you can quickly select different text formatting options.

Changing Your Document's Display Size

By default, WordPerfect displays your document from the left to right margin. Depending on your document's contents, there may be times when you want WordPerfect to *zoom in* or *zoom out* of a specific part of your document, or to display an entire page. To quickly change your document's display size, click on the left ribbon bar option. WordPerfect lists available display sizes.

Assigning a Style

In Chapter 26 you learned how to apply styles in your document. If you want to select a specific style or apply a style to selected text, click on the ribbon bar's style box. WordPerfect displays a list of available styles.

Controlling the Number of Columns

In Chapter 36 you learn that WordPerfect lets you use up to twenty four columns in your documents. WordPerfect starts your columns at the current cursor position. To change columns, select the ribbon bar's column box. WordPerfect displays a list of available columns.

Controlling Justification

In Chapter 13 you learned how to left, right, center, and fully justify text. To select the current justification or justify selected text, click on the ribbon bar's justification box. WordPerfect displays a list of available justifications.

Selecting a Font and Font Size

In Chapter 8 you learned how select the current font or apply a font to selected text. To quickly select a font using the ribbon bar, click on the font box. WordPerfect displays a list of available fonts.

Also in Chapter 8, you learned how to choose a font size. To choose a font size using the ribbon bar, click on the font size box. WordPerfect displays a list of available font sizes.

Creating a Meeting Review

If you work in an office and attend meetings, you may find that weekly meetings alway seem to focus on the same topics. If you are frustrated because things don't seem to get done, start recording information on the Meeting Review Form provided in this book's companion disk. As shown in Figure 35.2, the Meeting Review Form lets you record the meeting's attendees, topics, decisions, and most importantly, the assigned tasking.

Company Name
Company Slogan
9999 North Main Street
Anytown, USA 98765-4321
(702) 555-1212
(702) 555-1212 (Fax)

MEETING REVIEW
FORM

GENERAL INFORMATION

Date/Time:	Location:	Purpose:
Attendees:		

DISCUSSION SUBJECTS

❏ _____
❏ _____
❏ _____
❏ _____
❏ _____
❏ _____
❏ _____
❏ _____

DECISIONS AND RESULTS

❏ _____
❏ _____
❏ _____
❏ _____

TASK ASSIGNMENTS

Due Date	Assigned To	Task Description

_____
Signed

Figure 35.2 *The companion disk Meeting Review Form.*

To use the Meeting Review Form:

1. Select **Open** from the File menu. Type in the filename **MEETING.DOC**.
2. Edit the form to customize it for your company.
3. Use the File menu **Save** option to save your changes.

When you need to record information about a meeting, open the MEETRVU.DOC document file, type in the meeting specifics, then save the document to a file whose name corresponds to the meeting, such as BUDGET.MTG, or EMPLOYEE.MTG.

Summary

If you are using a mouse, you can quickly perform common document formatting by displaying and using WordPerfect's ribbon bar. The ribbon bar contains options that let you change the document's display size, assign styles, change the number of columns, select or assign justification, or control fonts. If you spend considerable time formatting your documents, enable the display of WordPerfect's ribbon bar.

New Terms

◆   **Ribbon bar.** A bar of formatting options displayed immediately beneath the menu bar, which you can quickly select using your mouse.

Chapter 36

Working with Multiple Columns

In this chapter you:

- ◆ Use two and three columns in a document
- ◆ Create and use parallel columns
- ◆ Understand column block protecting

Working with Multiple Columns

So far, all of the documents you have created have used only a single column of text. If you create a newsletter, magazine, or other similar document, you may use two or more columns. To help you better understand WordPerfect's column capabilities, this book's companion disk provides the document INDEPEND.DOC that contains the start of the declaration of independence. To load and use the document:

1. Select **Open** from the File menu.

2. Type in the document filename **INDEPEND.DOC** and press **Enter**. WordPerfect loads and displays the document, as shown in Figure 36.1.

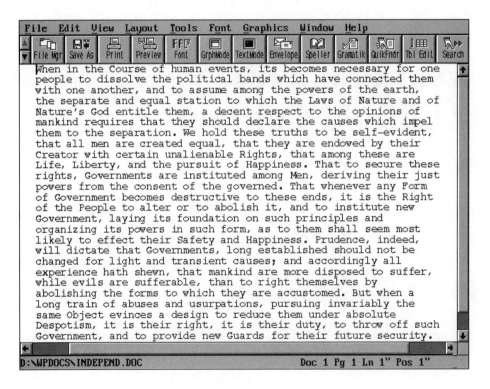

Figure 36.1 *Displaying the document file INDEPEND.DOC.*

WordPerfect supports two column types: *newspaper* and *parallel* columns. When you want to display columns of text where the text flows from the end of one column to the start of the next, use newspaper columns. Figure 36.2, for example, displays the document INDEPEND.DOC using two newspaper columns.

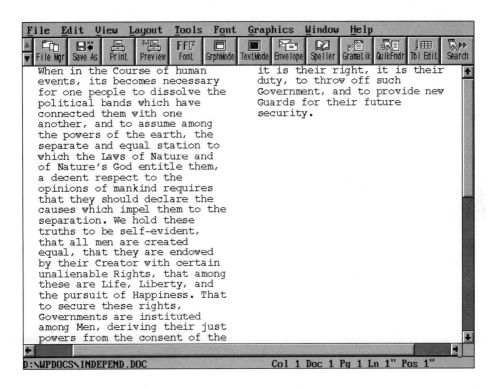

Figure 36.2 Newspaper columns.

When you want to create table-like entries, you can use WordPerfect's parallel columns. Figure 36.3, for example, displays parallel column entries.

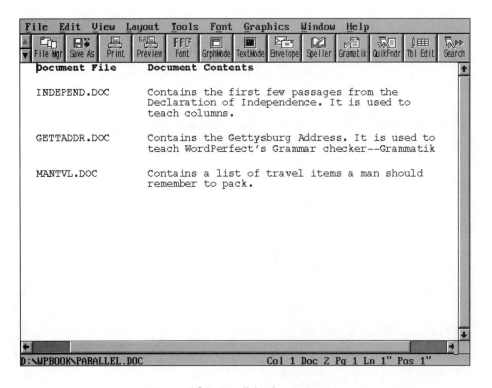

Figure 36.3 Parallel column entries.

When you assign columns, WordPerfect begins the columns at the current cursor position. If you want your entire document to be multi-column, place the cursor at the start of your document and then assign the columns. If you want the columns to begin at some other document position, place the cursor at the desired location and then create the columns.

Using Newspaper Columns

Newspaper columns flow text from the end of one column to the start of the next:

1. Place your cursor at the start of the document INDEPEND.DOC.

2. Open the Layout menu and choose **Columns**. The Text Columns dialog box is displayed in Figure 36.4.

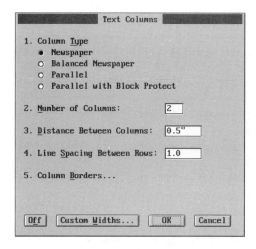

Figure 36.4 *The Text Columns dialog box.*

3. The Text Columns dialog box lets you specify the type, number, and spacing between your columns. Select the **Newspaper** option and choose **OK**. WordPerfect formats your document using one long column and one short one, as shown in Figure 36.5.

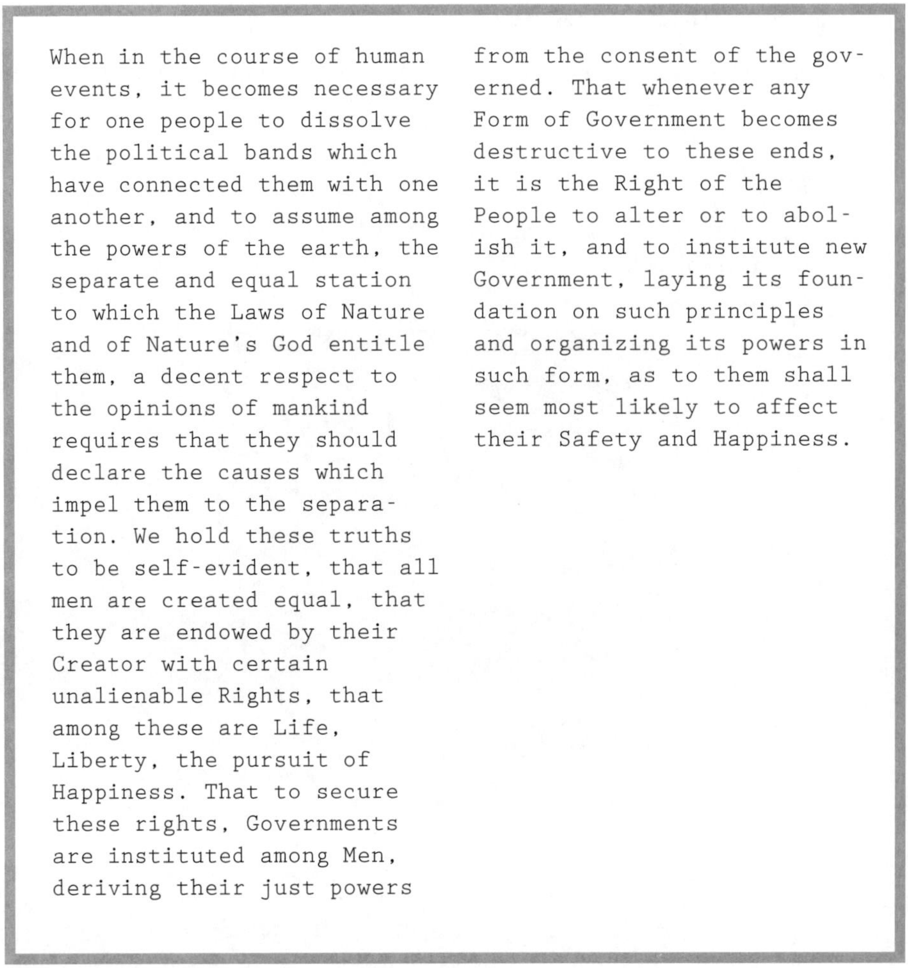

When in the course of human
events, it becomes necessary
for one people to dissolve
the political bands which
have connected them with one
another, and to assume among
the powers of the earth, the
separate and equal station
to which the Laws of Nature
and of Nature's God entitle
them, a decent respect to
the opinions of mankind
requires that they should
declare the causes which
impel them to the separa-
tion. We hold these truths
to be self-evident, that all
men are created equal, that
they are endowed by their
Creator with certain
unalienable Rights, that
among these are Life,
Liberty, the pursuit of
Happiness. That to secure
these rights, Governments
are instituted among Men,
deriving their just powers

from the consent of the governed. That whenever any
Form of Government becomes
destructive to these ends,
it is the Right of the
People to alter or to abolish it, and to institute new
Government, laying its foundation on such principles
and organizing its powers in
such form, as to them shall
seem most likely to affect
their Safety and Happiness.

Figure 36.5 Newspaper columns.

4. Select the Layout menu and again choose **Columns**.

5. Select the **Balanced Newspaper** option, which directs WordPerfect to display the same amount of text in each column.

6. Type **2** or click on the **Number of Columns** option. Type in the value **3** to create three columns and choose **OK**. WordPerfect displays the document's text using three balanced columns, as shown in Figure 36.6. WordPerfect lets you use up to twenty four columns.

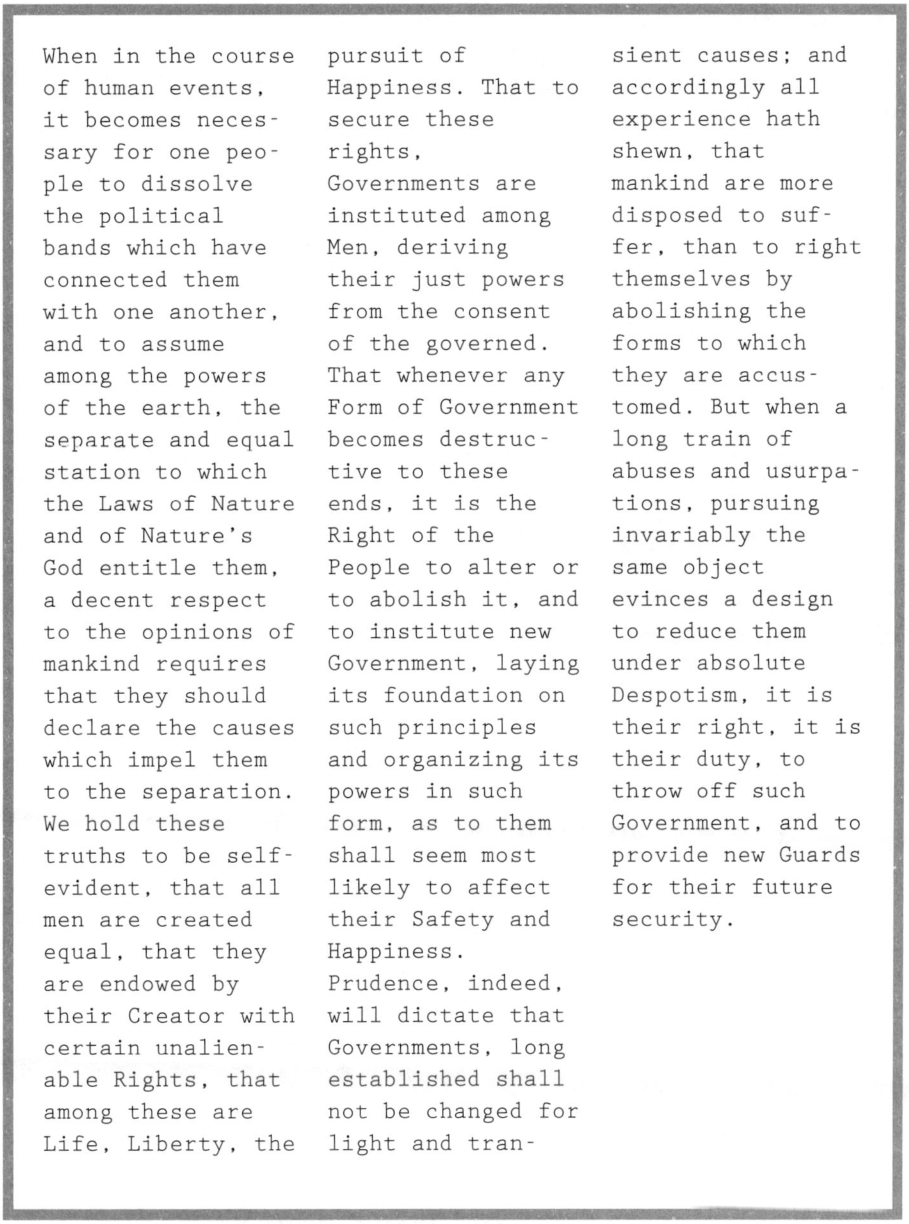

When in the course of human events, it becomes necessary for one people to dissolve the political bands which have connected them with one another, and to assume among the powers of the earth, the separate and equal station to which the Laws of Nature and of Nature's God entitle them, a decent respect to the opinions of mankind requires that they should declare the causes which impel them to the separation. We hold these truths to be self-evident, that all men are created equal, that they are endowed by their Creator with certain unalienable Rights, that among these are Life, Liberty, the pursuit of Happiness. That to secure these rights, Governments are instituted among Men, deriving their just powers from the consent of the governed. That whenever any Form of Government becomes destructive to these ends, it is the Right of the People to alter or to abolish it, and to institute new Government, laying its foundation on such principles and organizing its powers in such form, as to them shall seem most likely to affect their Safety and Happiness. Prudence, indeed, will dictate that Governments, long established shall not be changed for light and transient causes; and accordingly all experience hath shewn, that mankind are more disposed to suffer, than to right themselves by abolishing the forms to which they are accustomed. But when a long train of abuses and usurpations, pursuing invariably the same object evinces a design to reduce them under absolute Despotism, it is their right, it is their duty, to throw off such Government, and to provide new Guards for their future security.

Figure 36.6 *Three balanced newspaper columns.*

Turning the Display of Columns Off

Should you decide you don't want to use columns, WordPerfect lets you quickly turn the columns back off by selecting the **Off** option that appears in the Text Columns dialog box. To turn off columns:

1. Position the cursor at the point where you want the column use to stop.
2. Open the Layout menu and choose **Columns**.
3. In the Text Columns dialog box, type **F** or click on the **Off** button.

By turning column use on and off throughout your document, you can control how and where columns are used. Use the File menu **Close** option to close the document INDEPEND.DOC. Do not save your changes to the document file.

Understanding Parallel Columns

Parallel columns allow you to create table-like columns of text. To better understand how parallel columns work:

1. Type in the following text. Note the use of the *hard page break* (created by pressing **Ctrl-Enter**) to separate column entries.

```
Document File Ctrl-Enter

Document Contents Ctrl-Enter

INDEPEND.DOC Ctrl-Enter

Contains the first few passages from the
Declaration of Independence. It is used to teach
columns. Ctrl-Enter

GETTADDR.DOC Ctrl-Enter

Contains the Gettysburg Address. It is used to
teach WordPerfect's grammar checker-Grammatik.
Ctrl-Enter
```

```
MANTVL.DOC Ctrl-Enter
```

```
Contains a list of travel items a man should remem-
ber to pack. Ctrl-Enter
```

Your screen looks similar to Figure 36.7.

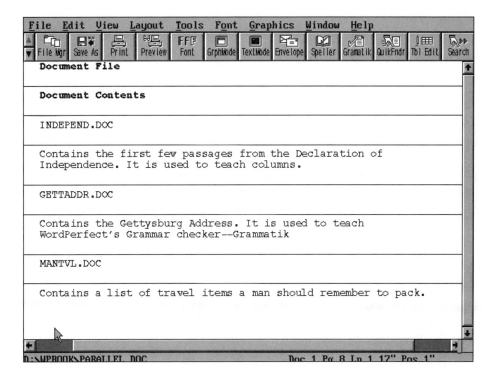

Figure 36.7 *Text for parallel column use.*

2. Move the cursor to the start of the document.

3. Open Layout menu and choose **Columns**.

4. When WordPerfect displays the Text Columns dialog box, select the **Parallel** option and choose **OK**. WordPerfect displays your text as a two-column table.

Understanding Parallel Columns with Block Protect

Depending on the contents of your parallel column entries, there may be times when WordPerfect cannot fit all information on the current page. In such cases, It simply continues the text, using the column format, on the page that follows. If you don't want to break a column entry in this way, you can block protect the columns, directing WordPerfect to move the entire entry to the start of the next page if the entire entry does not fit on the current page. The Text Columns dialog box provides an option, **Parallel with Block Protect**, to let you protect your column entries in this way.

Customizing Your Columns

To improve the appearance of your documents that use columns, WordPerfect lets you control each column's width, the spacing between columns, and the distance between entries when you use parallel columns. In addition, WordPerfect lets you place a border around your columns and optionally shade the columns background. Open Layout menu and choose **Columns**. WordPerfect displays the Text Column dialog box.

To control the amount of space WordPerfect uses to separate columns, type **3** or click on the **Distance Between Columns** option. Type in the amount of separation you desire.

If you are using parallel columns, you can control the amount of space WordPerfect places between successive entries. Type **4** or click on the **Line Spacing Between Rows** option.

Depending on your document, you may want to use different column widths. To change the width of a column, type **6** or click on the **Column Widths** option. Next, highlight the desired column and press **Enter** or double click on the column. WordPerfect displays a dialog box in which you can specify the column's width.

Most documents simply use the separation space to distinguish columns. If you want to frame columns or place a line between columns, or if you want to shade the background behind the column text, type **5** or click on the **Columns Borders** option. The Create Column Border dialog box is displayed in Figure 36.8.

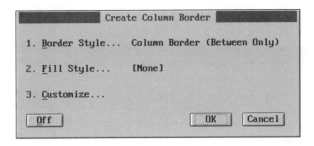

Figure 36.8 *The Create Column Border dialog box.*

Framing Your Columns

To frame your columns, select **Border Style**. WordPerfect displays the Border Styles dialog box, as shown in Figure 36.9.

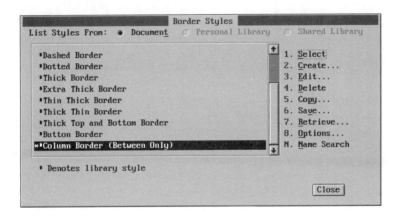

Figure 36.9 *The Border Styles dialog box.*

Select the border style you desire and choose **Select**. If you later decide you don't want to frame your columns, choose **None** as the border style.

Filling the Column Background Area

To shade the background area behind your columns, select **Fill Style** in the Create Column Border dialog box. The Fill Styles dialog box is displayed in Figure 36.10.

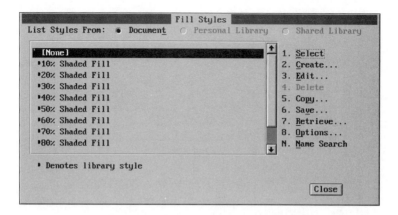

Figure 36.10 *The Fill Styles dialog box.*

Select the fill percentage you desire. The lower the percentage, the lighter the shading. If you later decide you want to turn off shading, select **None**.

Creating a Company Credit Application

If you sell merchandise or services, you may want your customers to complete a Credit Application. To help you do so, the companion disk that accompanies this book provides the document file CREDIT.DOC, shown in Figure 36.11.

Company Name
Company Slogan
9999 North Main Street
Anytown, USA 98765-4321
(702) 555-1212
(702) 555-1212 (Fax)

CREDIT APPLICATION

Provide information about your company:

Company Name:	Main Phone:
Address:	Type of Business: □ Partnership □ Sole Proprietorship □ Corporation, State of Incorporation:
Years in Business:	Type of Product or Service:
Annual Net Sales $:	
Number of Employees:	Dun & Bradstreet Number:

List Principal Owners, Partners, or Officers:

Name	Title	Phone

List Your Company's Major Bank Accounts:

Bank	Address	Account	Phone

List References for Other Companies That Have Extended You Credit:

Company	Address	Contact	Phone

Attach a Current Balance Sheet.

I certify that the above is true and correct to the best of my knowledge.

_____   _____
Signature   Title

_____   _____
Print Name   Date

Figure 36.11 *The Credit Application provided in CREDIT.DOC.*

To use the credit application form:

1. Select **Open** from the File menu, type **CREDIT.DOC**, and press **Enter**.
2. Edit the form to customize it for your company.
3. Use the File menu **Save** option to save your changes.

When you want to complete a credit application on a customer, print the document and complete it by hand, or open the document file, type in the customer information and, save the information to a new file on disk.

Summary

WordPerfect lets you use from two to twenty-four columns in your documents. WordPerfect supports two types of columns. Newspaper columns allow the text to flow from the end of one column to the start of the next. Parallel columns, on the other hand, let you create tables. When you use parallel columns, you must place a page break (created by pressing **Ctrl-Enter**) between each column entry. To improve your column appearance, WordPerfect lets you place borders around your columns or shade the columns text background.

New Terms

◆ **Block protected column.** A parallel column for which WordPerfect moves an entire the entire entry to the next page if it cannot display all of the information on the current page.

◆ **Newspaper columns.** Columns that allow text to flow from the end of one column to the start of the next.

◆ **Parallel columns.** Columns used to display entries in a table-like format.

Chapter 37

Performing Mail Merge Operations

In this chapter you:

◆   Create a small mailing list

◆   Print a boilerplate letter using the mailing list entries

Understanding Merge Operations

If you work in an office, there may be times when you generate the same letter several times for a group of people. For example, you might send each of your customers a letter announcing a new product. One way to send the letter is to simply create a form letter of which you print several copies. However, because the form letter does not contain names, addresses, and so on, it loses the familiarity you want your customers to feel as they read the letter. As a solution, WordPerfect lets you create a *boilerplate* document that contains your letter's text. In addition, the boilerplate contains codes that direct WordPerfect to place into the document such information as a name and address that you have stored in a second *merge file*. When you perform a merge operation, WordPerfect takes entries, one at a time, from the merge file and places them into the boilerplate document. WordPerfect then prints the document, repeating this process for the next entry. To perform a merge operation, therefore, you must have two documents, one containing the boilerplate and one containing your mailing list (the merge file).

Creating the Merge File

The best way to understand merge files is to think of a mailing list. Assume, for example, that you want to mail letters to the following people:

```
Bill Smith
1282 Main St.
Phoenix, Arizona 85035

Tom Davis
1234 First Avenue
Las Vegas, Nevada 89117

Julie Adams
1929 May Drive
Seattle, Washington 98188
```

The individual entries within the mailing list are called *records*. In this case, the mailing list has three records. Each record is made up of fields. In this case, there are three fields, one for the name, address, and city, state, and zip code. When you create a merge file, you must tell WordPerfect where each record begins and ends, as well as the location of each field in the records. To get started:

1. Select **New** from the File menu and type in the following text. Note that the text adds a fourth field that we call *first name*.

    ```
    Bill Smith
    1282 Main St.
    Phoenix, Arizona 85035
    Bill

    Tom Davis
    1234 First Avenue
    Las Vegas, Nevada 89117
    Tom

    Julie Adams
    1929 May Drive
    Seattle, Washington 98188
    Julie
    ```

2. Use the File menu **Save As** option to save the document to the file MAILLIST.DOC. As discussed, you now need to tell WordPerfect where each field and record begins and ends.

3. Place the cursor at the end of the first line that contains the name *Bill Smith*.

4. Open the Tools menu and select Merge. WordPerfect cascades the menu shown in Figure 37.1.

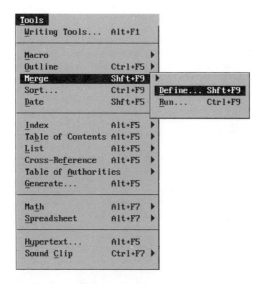

Figure 37.1 *The cascading Merge menu.*

5. Select **Define**. The Merge Codes dialog box is displayed in Figure 37.2.

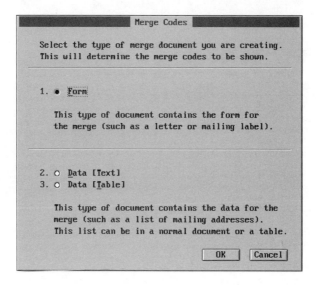

Figure 37.2 *The Merge Codes dialog box.*

The Merge Codes dialog box lets you tell WordPerfect whether you are working with the template file (that contains the letter text–WordPerfect calls it the *Form*), or if you are working with the data.

6. In this case, type **2** or click on the **Data [Text]** option. WordPerfect displays the Merge Codes (Text Data File) dialog box, shown in Figure 37.3.

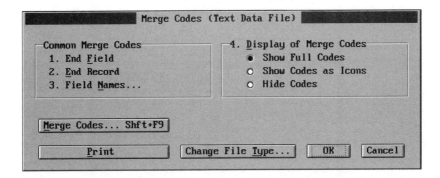

Figure 37.3 *The Merge Codes (Text Data File) dialog box.*

To create your mailing list:

1. Select the Common Merge Code. Type **1** or click on **End Field**. WordPerfect inserts an End Field code in your document.

2. Delete the blank line inserted after the code.

3. Perform these same steps to place the End Field code at the end of the first three lines in the document.

4. The first record's last entry is the line containing the name Bill. Use the Merge Codes dialog box to place an End Record code after the name.

WordPerfect uses the double lines to separate records.

Depending on the number of records in your mailing list, traversing menus and dialog boxes to assign the End Field and End Record codes can be quite time consuming. As a quick shortcut, follow the steps presented in Chapter 20 to place the Merge Codes dialog box in your button bar. Then, by clicking on the button, you can quickly insert the fields.

Repeat these steps to define the fields and records for each entry in your mailing list, as shown in Figure 37.4.

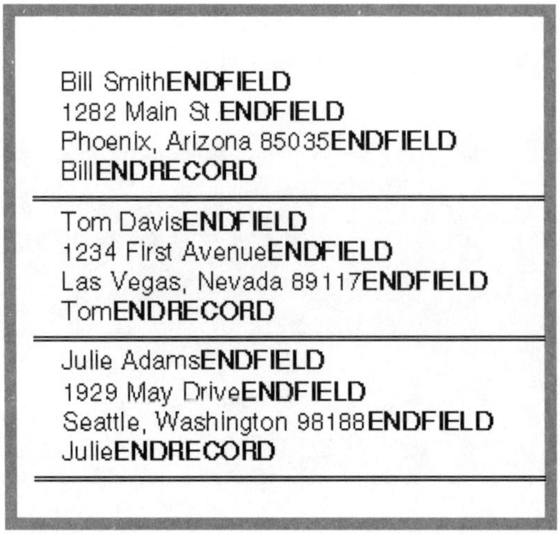

Bill Smith**ENDFIELD**
1282 Main St.**ENDFIELD**
Phoenix, Arizona 85035**ENDFIELD**
Bill**ENDRECORD**

Tom Davis**ENDFIELD**
1234 First Avenue**ENDFIELD**
Las Vegas, Nevada 89117**ENDFIELD**
Tom**ENDRECORD**

Julie Adams**ENDFIELD**
1929 May Drive**ENDFIELD**
Seattle, Washington 98188**ENDFIELD**
Julie**ENDRECORD**

Figure 37.4 Assigning record and field settings.

Naming Your Fields

After you assign the Field End and Record End codes throughout your document, you need to tell WordPerfect the names by which you want to refer to each field. In this case, use the following field names:

```
FullName
Address
CityStateZip
FirstName
```

1. In the Merge Codes (Text Data File) dialog box, type **3** or click on **Field Names**. WordPerfect displays the Field Names dialog box, as shown in Figure 37.5.

Figure 37.5 *The Field Names dialog box.*

2. Type in the field name **FullName**, and press **Enter**.

3. Repeat this process for the field names **Address**, **CityStateZip**, and **FirstName**.

4. Select **OK**. WordPerfect places a FIELDNAMES entry at the start of your document:

    ```
    FIELDNAMES(FULLNAME;ADDRESS;CITYSTATEZIP;FIRST-
    NAME)ENDRECORD
    ```

5. Use the File menu **Save** option to save your mailing list document.

Creating the Boilerplate Document

Use the File menu **New** option to create a new document. In this case, create a simple letter that includes the address, the person's name, and a short message similar to the following:

```
Bill Smith
1282 Main St.
Phoenix, Arizona 85035
```

```
Dear Bill,

I am really glad you had a chance to come to the
party. Hope to see you at our party again next year.
Please call me if you have any questions about our
products.

Ted
```

To create the letter, use field names for the items shown here in italics:

```
Bill Smith
1282 Main St.
Phoenix, Arizona 85035

Dear Bill,

I am really glad you had a chance to come to the
party. Hope to see you at our party again next year.
Please call me if you have any questions about our
products.

Ted
```

Later, WordPerfect automatically pulls the correct names and addresses from your mailing list file. To place the field references in your document:

1. Open the Tools menu and choose **Merge**, then **Define**. WordPerfect displays the Merge Codes dialog box.

2. Select **Form** and choose **OK**. WordPerfect displays the Merge Codes (Form File) dialog box shown in Figure 37.6.

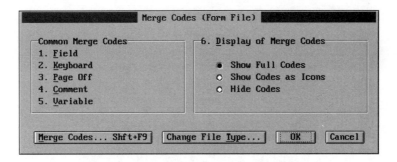

Figure 37.6 *The Merge Codes (Form File) dialog box.*

3. Type **1** or click on **Field**. The Parameter Entry dialog box is displayed in Figure 37.7.

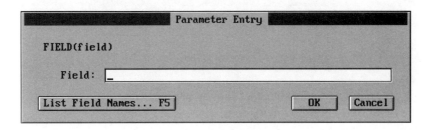

Figure 37.7 *The Parameter Entry dialog box.*

4. Press **F5** or click on the **List Field Names** button. WordPerfect displays the Select Data File For Field Names dialog box shown in Figure 37.8.

Figure 37.8 *The Select Data File For Field Names dialog box.*

5. Type in the filename **MAILLIST.DOC** that you just created. The List Field Names dialog box is displayed in Figure 37.9.

Figure 37.9 The List Field Names dialog box.

6. Highlight the **FULLNAME** field and press **Enter** or double click on the field. WordPerfect returns to the Parameter Entry dialog box.

7. Select **OK**. WordPerfect places the FIELD reference in you document.

Perform the following steps to place field references for Address and CityStateZip in your document.

1. Press **Enter** to move the cursor down one line.

2. Open the Tools menu, and select **Merge**, then **Define**.

3. Select **Field** in the Merge Codes (Form File) dialog box.

4. In the Parameter Entry dialog box, type in the field name you desire or use the **List Field Names** button to display the available fields. Your document should now contain three field name references:

```
FIELD(FULLNAME)
FIELD(ADDRESS)
FIELD(CITYSTATEZIP)
```

5. Press the **Enter** key twice and type the word **Dear** followed by a space.

6. Perform the previous steps to add a field name reference for *FirstName*:

```
FIELD(FULLNAME)
FIELD(ADDRESS)
FIELD(CITYSTATEZIP)
Dear FIELD(FIRSTNAME)
```

7. Type a comma, press **Enter** twice and type the remainder of the document text:

```
I am really glad you had a chance to come to the
party. Hope to see you at our party again next
year. Please call me if you have any questions
about our products.

Ted
```

8. Use the File menu **Save As** option to save your document to the file PARTYLTR.DOC. Your document is now ready to be merged.

Performing the Merge

To merge the entries in your data file into the template document:

1. Open the Tools menu, select **Merge**, and select **Run**. WordPerfect displays the Run Merge dialog box shown in Figure 37.10.

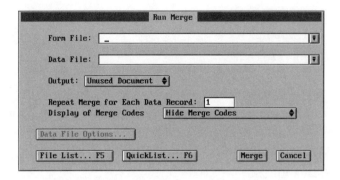

Figure 37.10 *The Run Merge dialog box.*

2. Select the **Output** option and choose **Printer**. As WordPerfect completes a merge, it prints the resulting letter.
3. Select **Merge**. WordPerfect prints the letter for each entry in your mailing list.

Creating a Different Letter

After you build your mailing list data file, you can use it in many different letters. Each time you want to create a new letter, just follow the steps presented in this section on creating the boilerplate document. Over time, the list of names you want to mail to will grow. By editing the mailing list file and inserting the proper End Field and End Record codes, you can quickly change your mailing list. Many businesses may develop several different mailing lists. For example, you might have one mailing list for customers in the United States and one for your international customers. When you perform your merge operation, you simply choose the mailing list you want to use.

Tracking Your Vehicle Use

If your business has one or more company cars whose use you want to track, or if you want to deduct the use of your car on your taxes, you may want to use the companion disk Vehicle Use Report document, shown in Figure 37.11.

Company Name
Company Slogan
9999 North Main Street
Anytown, USA 98765-4321
(702) 555-1212
(702) 555-1212 (Fax)

VEHICLE USE REPORT

Period Ending: _____
Vehicle ID: _____

Employee Name: _____
Employee Number: _____

Date	Description	Starting Mileage	Ending Mileage	Miles Driven	Mileage $0.22/mi	Gasoline and Oil	Parking and Tolls	Other	Total Cost
				0	0.00				0.00
				0	0.00				0.00
				0	0.00				0.00
				0	0.00				0.00
				0	0.00				0.00
				0	0.00				0.00
				0	0.00				0.00
				0	0.00				0.00
				0	0.00				0.00
				0	0.00				0.00
				0	0.00				0.00
				0	0.00				0.00
				0	0.00				0.00
				0	0.00				0.00

Total Cost — 0.00
Previous Balance (Credit)
Total Due (Overpaid) — 0.00

Employee Signature _____ Date _____

Approval Signature _____ Date _____

Figure 37.11 *The companion disk Vehicle Use Report document.*

To use the vehicle use report document:

1. Select **Open** from the File menu. Type in the filename **VEHICLE.DOC**.
2. Edit theform to customize it for your company.
3. Use the File menu **Save** option to save your changes.

When you need to record a vehicle's use, simply open the document and type in the corresponding information. Use your Arrow keys to move from one field to the next. After you record your entries, use the **Calculate All** option to total the expenses the vehicle has incurred. If you have several vehicles whose use you want to track, create a unique document for each.

Summary

If you send the same letter to many different people, you can simplify your work by taking advantage of WordPerfect's merge capabilities. To perform a merge operation, you create a data file that contains the names and addresses of the people to which you want to send the letter. Each entry in the file is called a *record*. Records are made up of fields, such as the person's name, address, and so on. After you define the file's records and fields, you create a template (or boilerplate) document that contains the letter you want to send. In the document, place references to specific field names. As WordPerfect performs a merge, it replaces each field name reference with the corresponding entry from your data file.

New Terms

- ◆ **Boilerplate document.** A document containing text and references to field names that WordPerfect replaces during a merge operation.
- ◆ **Field.** An entry in a record, such as a name or address line.
- ◆ **Merge.** The combining of two documents.
- ◆ **Merge data file.** A data file containing records and fields entries—such as a mailing list.

◆ **Record.** A complete entry in a merge data file. In the case of a mailing list, a record might contain a name, address, city, state, and zip code.

Chapter 38

Working with WordPerfect Codes

In this chapter you:

◆ Learn how WordPerfect uses special codes

◆ Display (reveal) the codes used in your document

◆ Edit the document codes

Understanding Formatting Codes

Throughout the chapters of this book you have used WordPerfect's document formatting capabilities to turn on bolding, to change margins, to justify text, and to change fonts. When you perform such operations, WordPerfect places hidden codes in your document. For example, the codes may tell WordPerfect where to begin bolding text and when to turn bolding off. Every time you change your document's formatting, WordPerfect adds or removes formatting codes. By default, WordPerfect does not display the codes on your screen, however, if you open the View menu and select **Reveal Codes**, you can display the document's codes, as in Figure 38.1.

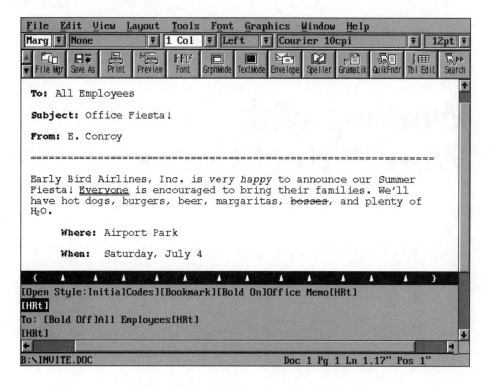

Figure 38.1 *Displaying document codes.*

When you direct WordPerfect to reveal its formatting codes, it divides your screen into two sections. The top section contains your document text. The lower section shows your document text and the formatting codes. As you can see, WordPerfect displays its formatting codes in left and right brackets

[Formatting Code]

Editing Formatting Codes

When you reveal the formatting codes, WordPerfect lets you highlight the codes using your Arrow keys or mouse. When you highlight a code, you can delete the code by pressing **Del** or **Backspace**. When you delete the formatting code, WordPerfect turns off the corresponding formatting in your document. To better understand format code editing, open the View menu and choose **Reveal Codes**. Next, type in the following sentence:

```
Text can be italic or bold.
```

Select the word *italic* and then open the Font menu and select **Italics**. Next, select the word *bold* and choose the **Bold** option. Your screen should look similar to Figure 38.2.

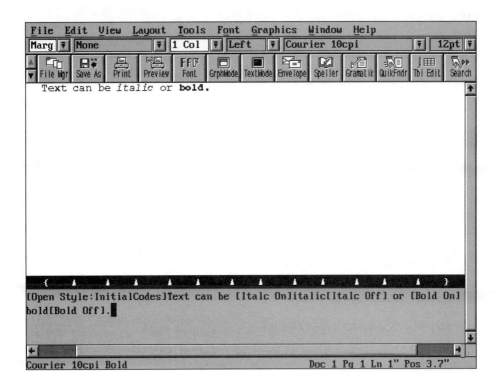

Figure 38.2 *Displaying formatting codes.*

Many WordPerfect formatting codes work in pairs. The first code turns a capability, such as italics on, and the second code turns the capability off. For example, the word *italic* is surrounded by two codes:

```
[Italc On]italic[Italc Off]
```

Other formatting options, however, only have one code that enables an option from that point in the document forward.

Using your Arrow keys, move the cursor from one character in the sentence to the next. Highlight the code [*Italc On*] and press **Del**. WordPerfect deletes the code, removing the italic attribute. When you delete one code from a pair of related codes, WordPerfect automatically deletes the second. When you delete the code [Italc On], WordPerfect automatically deletes [Italc Off]. By editing formatting codes this way, you can quickly turn different formatting on and off.

Codes You May Encounter

As you edit large documents, you may encounter many different formatting codes. To help you better understand the code's purpose, here is a listing of the formatting codes:

◆ **[-]** Hard hyphen character typed by user.

◆ **[- Hyphen]** Hyphen character.

◆ **[- Soft Hyphen]** Soft hyphen character.

◆ **[- Soft Hyphen EOL]** Soft hyphen character at the end of a line.

◆ **[Auto Hyphen EOL]** Automatic hyphen character at the end of a line.

◆ **[Back Tab]** Back tab character for a margin release.

◆ **[Bar Code]** POSTNET bar code indicator.

◆ **[Begin Gen Txt]** Beginning of generated text.

◆ **[Binding Width]** Specifies a binding offset amount.

◆ **[Block]** Indicates the start of a selected block of text.

◆ **[Block Pro Off]** End of a protected block.

◆ **[Block Pro On]** Start of a protected block.

◆ **[Bold Off]** Turns off bolding.

◆ **[Bold On]** Turns on bolding.

◆ **[Bookmark]** Indicates a document bookmark.

◆ **[Bot Mar]** Specifies the document's bottom margin.

◆ **[Box Num Dec]** The decrement value between successive boxes.

◆ **[Box Num Disp]** Controls the display of box numbers in the document.

◆ **[Box Num Inc]** The increment value between successive boxes.

◆ **[Box Num Meth]** Controls how box numbers are displayed in the document, letters, numbers, or roman numerals.

◆ **[Box Num Set]** Controls the character set used to display box numbers.

◆ **[Calc Col]** Specifies a math column calculation.

◆ **[Cancel Hyph]** Turns off hyphenation for a word.

◆ **[Cell]** Identifies a table cell.

◆ **[Change BOL Char]** Changes the beginning of line character.

◆ **[Change EOL Char]** Changes the end-of-line character.

◆ **[Chap Num Dec]** Specifies the decrement value between successive chapters.

◆ **[Chap Num Disp]** Controls the display of a chapter number.

◆ **[Chap Num Inc]** Specifies the increment value between successive chapters.

◆ **[Chap Num Meth]** Controls how chapter numbers are displayed in the document, letters, numbers, or roman numerals.

◆ **[Chap Num Set]** Specifies the character set used to display chapter numbers.

◆ **[Char Box]** Specifies a character box.

◆ **[Char Shade Change]** Changes the character background shading.

◆ **[Char Style Off]** Turns of a character style.

◆ **[Char Style On]** Turns on a character style.

◆ **[Cntr Cur Pg]** Centers the current page.

◆ **[Cntr on Cur Pos]** Centers text at the current position.

◆ **[Cntr on Mar]** Centers text on margins.

◆ **[Cntr on Mar (DOT)]** Centers text on margins using dot leader.

◆ **[Cntr Pgs]** Centers pages from top to bottom.

◆ **[CNTR TAB]** Hard centered tab stop.

◆ **[Cntr Tab]** Centered tab stop.

◆ **[CNTR TAB (DOT)]** Hard centered tab stop with dot leader.

◆ **[Cntr Tab (Dot)]** Centered tab stop with a dot leader.

◆ **[Col Border]** Specifies a column border.

◆ **[Col Def]** Specifies a column definition.

◆ **[Color]** Selects a text color.

◆ **[Comment]** Contains a document comment.

◆ **[Condl EOP]** Specifies a conditional end-of-page.

◆ **[Count Dec]** Specifies the decrement value between successive counters.

◆ **[Count Disp]** Controls how counters are displayed in a document.

◆ **[Count Inc]** Specifies the increment value between successive counters.

◆ **[Count Meth]** Specifies the counter display method.

◆ **[Count Set]** Specifies the character set used to display a counter.

◆ **[Date]** Inserts the current date/time.

◆ **[Date Fmt]** Specifies the format used to display the date/time.

◆ **[Dbl Und Off]** Turns off double underlining.

◆ **[Dbl Und On]** Turns on double underlining.

◆ **[Dbl-Sided Print]** Turns on double sided printing.

◆ **[DEC TAB]** Specifies a hard decimal tab.

◆ **[Dec Tab]** Decimal tab.

◆ **[DEC TAB (DOT)]** Specifies a hard decimal tab with a dot leader.

◆ **[Dec Tab (Dot)]** Specifies a decimal tab with a dot leader.

◆ **[Dec/Align Char]** Specifies the character upon which decimal tabs are aligned.

◆ **[Def Mark]** Specifies a definition marker.

◆ **[Delay]** Specifies codes you want to apply on pages after the current page.

- **[Delay Off]** Turns off delay code definitions.
- **[Delay On]** Turns on delay code definitions.
- **[Do Grand Tot]** Calculate a mathematical grand total.
- **[Do Subtot]** Calculate a mathematical sub-total.
- **[Do Total]** Calculate a mathematic total.
- **[Dorm HRt]** Specifies a dormant hard return.
- **[Dot Lead Char]** Specifies the character used as the dot in dot leaders.
- **[End Cntr/Align]** Ends center alignment.
- **[End Gen Text]** End a text generation field.
- **[Endnote]** Specifies an endnote.
- **[Endnote Min]** Minimum amount of an endnote that must be kept together.
- **[Endnote Num Dec]** Specifies the decrement value between successive endnotes.
- **[Endnote Num Disp]** Controls how endnotes are displayed.
- **[Endnote Num Inc]** Specifies the increment value between successive endnotes.
- **[Endnote Num Meth]** Specifies the method used to display endnotes.
- **[Endnote Num Set]** Specifies the character set used to display endnotes.
- **[Endnote Placement]** Restarts endnote numbering.
- **[Endnote Spacing]** Controls the spacing between successive endnotes.
- **[Ext Large Off]** Turns off the extra large font attribute.
- **[Ext Large On]** Turns on the extra large font attribute.
- **[Filename]** Specifies a filename.
- **[Fine Off]** Turns off the fine font attribute.
- **[Fine On]** Turns on the fine font attribute
- **[First Ln Ind]** Specifies the indent for the first line of a paragraph.
- **[Flsh Rgt]** Flushes text to the right.
- **[Flsh Rgt (DOT)]** Flushes text to the right with dot leading.
- **[Flt Cell Begin]** Begins a floating point cell.
- **[Flt Cell End]** Ends a floating point cell.

◆ **[Font]** Selects a font.

◆ **[Font Size]** Specifies the font size.

◆ **[Footer A]** Definition of footer A.

◆ **[Footer B]** Definition of footer B.

◆ **[Footer Sep]** Specifies the space between the text and a footer.

◆ **[Footnote]** Specifies a footnote.

◆ **[Footnote Cont Msg]** Specifies a continued footnote message such as "continued...".

◆ **[Footnote Min]** Specifies the minimum amount of a footnote that must be kept together.

◆ **[Footnote Num Dec]** Specifies the decrement value between successive footnotes.

◆ **[Footnote Num Disp]** Controls if footnotes are displayed.

◆ **[Footnote Num Each Pg]** Restarts footnote numbering on each page.

◆ **[Footnote Num Inc]** Specifies the increment value between successive footnotes.

◆ **[Footnote Num Meth]** Controls how footnotes are displayed.

◆ **[Footnote Num Set]** Specifies the character set used to display footnotes.

◆ **[Footnote Sep Ln]** Specifies the line style used to separate footnotes.

◆ **[Footnote Space]** Specifies the amount of space between footnotes.

◆ **[Footnote Txt Pos]** Specifies the footnote text positioning.

◆ **[Force]** Forces an even/odd page.

◆ **[Formatted Pg Num]** Specifies a formatted page number.

◆ **[Graph Line]** Specifies a graphics line.

◆ **[HAdv]** Specifies a horizontal advance.

◆ **[HCol]** Specifies a hard column break.

◆ **[HCol-SPg]** Specifies a hard column, soft page break.

◆ **[Header A]** Definition of header A.

◆ **[Header B]** Definition of header B.

◆ **[Header Sep]** Specifies the separation distance between the header and text.

◆ **[Hidden Off]** Turns off the hidden text attribute.

- **[Hidden On]** Turns on the hidden text attribute.

- **[Hidden Txt]** Specifies hidden body text.

- **[HPg]** Specifies a hard page break.

- **[HRow-HCol]** Specifies a hard table row hard column break.

- **[HRow-HCol-SPg]** Specifies a hard table row hard column break soft page break.

- **[HRow-Hpg]** Specifies a hard table row hard page break.

- **[HRt]** Specifies a hard return.

- **[HRt-SCol]** Specifies a hard return soft column break.

- **[HRt-SPg]** Specifies a hard return soft page break.

- **[HSpace]** Specifies a hard space.

- **[Hypertext Begin]** Begins a hypertext link.

- **[Hypertext End]** Ends a hypertext link.

- **[Hyph]** Specifies the state of hyphenation.

- **[Hyph SRt]** Hyphenation soft return.

- **[Index]** Index entry.

- **[Italc Off]** Turns off the italic font attribute.

- **[Italc On]** Turns on the italic font attribute.

- **[Just]** Specifies the justification.

- **[Just Lim]** Specifies the spacing limits that can be used to justify text.

- **[Kern]** Specifies the kerning.

- **[Labels Form]** Select the labels form.

- **[Lang]** Specifies the current language.

- **[Large Off]** Turns off the large font attribute.

- **[Large On]** Turns on the large font attribute.

- **[Leading Adj]** Specifies the leading adjustment.

- **[Lft HZone]** Specifies the left edge of the hyphenation zone.

- **[Lft Indent]** Specifies the indent amount from the left margin.

- **[Lft Mar]** Specifies the left-margin setting.

- **[Lft Mar Adj]** Specifies the left-margin adjustment.

◆ **[LFT TAB]** Hard left-aligned tab stop.

◆ **[Lft Tab]** Left-aligned tab stop.

◆ **[LFT TAB (DOT)]** Hard left-aligned tab stop with a dot leading.

◆ **[Lft Tab (DOT)]** Left aligned tab with a dot leading.

◆ **[Lft/Rgt Indent]** Left and right double indent.

◆ **[Link]** Specifies a spreadsheet link.

◆ **[Link End]** Specifies the end of a spreadsheet link.

◆ **[Ln Height]** Specifies the current line height.

◆ **[Ln Num]** Controls line numbering.

◆ **[Ln Num Meth]** Controls how line numbering is displayed.

◆ **[Ln Num Set]** Specifies the character set used to display line numbers.

◆ **[Macro Func]** Specifies a macro function.

◆ **[Math]** Specifies the current math state.

◆ **[Math Def]** Defines a math column.

◆ **[Math Neg]** Performs a mathematical negation.

◆ **[MRG:Command]** Contains a merge command.

◆ **[Mrk Txt List Begin]** Specifies the start of a marked text list.

◆ **[Mrk Txt List End]** Specifies the end of a marked text list.

◆ **[Mrk Txt Toc End]** Specifies the end of a marked table of contents entry.

◆ **[Open Style]** Specifies the document's open style.

◆ **[Outline]** Specifies a document outline.

◆ **[Outln Off]** Turns off the outline font attribute.

◆ **[Outln On]** Turns on the outline font attribute.

◆ **[Ovrstk]** Specifies an overstrike operation.

◆ **[Paper Sz/Typ]** Selects a paper size/type.

◆ **[Para Border]** Defines a paragraph border.

◆ **[Para Box]** Specifies a paragraph box.

◆ **[Para Num]** Specifies a paragraph number.

◆ **[Para Num Set]** Specifies the character set used to display paragraph numbers.

◆ **[Para Spacing]** Specifies the number of blank lines between blocked paragraphs.

◆ **[Para Style]** Specifies the paragraph style.

◆ **[Para Style End]** Turns off the paragraph style.

◆ **[Pause Ptr]** Pauses the printer.

◆ **[Pg Border]** Specifies the page border.

◆ **[Pg Box]** Specifies a page box.

◆ **[Pg Num Dec]** Specifies the decrement value between successive page numbers.

◆ **[Pg Num Disp]** Controls whether page numbers are displayed.

◆ **[Pg Num Fmt]** Specifies the format used to display page numbers.

◆ **[Pg Num Inc]** Specifies the increment value between successive page numbers.

◆ **[Pg Num Meth]** Controls how page numbers are displayed.

◆ **[Pg Num Pos]** Specifies where page numbers are displayed.

◆ **[Pg Num Set]** Specifies the character set used to display page numbers.

◆ **[Ptr Cmnd]** Specifies a printer command.

◆ **[Redln Off]** Turns off the redline font attribute.

◆ **[Redln On]** Turns on the redline font attribute.

◆ **[Ref Box]** Reference to a graphics box.

◆ **[Ref Chap]** Reference to a chapter number.

◆ **[Ref Count]** Reference to a counter.

◆ **[Ref Endnote]** Reference to an endnote.

◆ **[Ref Footnote]** Reference to a footnote.

◆ **[Ref Para]** Reference to a paragraph.

◆ **[Ref Pg]** Reference to a page.

◆ **[Ref Sec Pg]** Reference to a secondary page.

◆ **[Ref Vol]** Reference to a volume.

◆ **[Rgt IIZonc]** Spccifies the right edge of the hyphenation zone.

◆ **[Rgt Mar]** Specifies the right margin.

◆ **[Rgt Mar Adj]** Specifies the right margin adjustment.

- **[RGT TAB]** Hard right tab stop.
- **[Rgt Tab]** Right tab stop.
- **[RGT TAB (DOT)]** Hard right tab stop with a dot leader.
- **[Rgt Tab (Dot)]** Right tab stop with a dot leader.
- **[Row]** Specifies a table row.
- **[Row-SCol]** Table row soft column break.
- **[Row-SPg]** Table row soft page break.
- **[Sec Pg Num Dec]** Specifies the decrement value between successive secondary page numbers.
- **[Sec Pg Num Disp]** Controls the display of secondary page numbers.
- **[Sec Pg Num Inc]**Specifies the increment value between successive secondary page numbers.
- **[Sec Pg Num Meth]** Specifies how secondary page numbers are displayed.
- **[Sec Pg Num Set]** Specifies the character set used to display secondary page numbers.
- **[Off]** Turns off the shadow font attribute.
- **[On]** Turns on the shadow font attribute.
- **[Sm Cap Off]** Turns off the small caps font attribute.
- **[Sm Cap On]** Turns on the small caps font attribute.
- **[Small Off]** Turns off the small font attribute.
- **[Small On]** Turns on the small font attribute.
- **[Sound]** Specifies a sound clip.
- **[Speller/Grammatik]** Specifies the Spell Check/Grammatik state.
- **[SRt]** Soft return.
- **[SRt-SCol]** Soft return soft column break.
- **[SRt-SPg]** Soft return soft page break.
- **[StkOut Off]** Turns off the strikeout font attribute.
- **[StkOff On]** Turns on the strikeout font attribute.
- **[Subdivided Pg]** Specifies a subdivided page.
- **[Subdoc]** Specifies a subdocument in the master document.

◆ **[Subdoc Begin]** Specifies the beginning of a subdocument.

◆ **[Subdoc End]** Specifies the end of a subdocument.

◆ **[Subscpt Off]** Turns off the subscript font attribute.

◆ **[Subscpt On]** Turns on the subscript font attribute.

◆ **[Subtot Entry]** Specifies a mathematical subtotal.

◆ **[Suppress]** Suppresses a header, footer,...

◆ **[Suprscpt Off]** Turns off the superscript font attribute.

◆ **[Suprscpt On]** Turns on the superscript font attribute.

◆ **[Tab Set]** Specifies the tab set.

◆ **[Target]** Specifies the target of a cross reference.

◆ **[Tbl Dec Tab]** Specifies a table decimal tab stop.

◆ **[Tbl Def]** Specifies a table definition.

◆ **[Tbl Off]** Turns a table off.

◆ **[Tbl Off-SCol]** Specifies a table off soft column break.

◆ **[Tbl Off-Spg]** Specifies a table off soft page break.

◆ **[Tbl Tab]** Specifies a table tab.

◆ **[THCol]** Specifies a temporary hard column break.

◆ **[THCol-SPg]** Specifies a temporary hard column soft page break.

◆ **[Third Party]** Specifies a non-WordPerfect code.

◆ **[Thousands Char]** Specifies the character used to separate thousands digits (comma).

◆ **[THPg]** Temporary page break.

◆ **[THRt]** Temporary hard return.

◆ **[THRt-SCol]** Temporary hard return soft column break.

◆ **[THRt-SPg]** Temporary hard return soft page break.

◆ **[ToA]** Specifies a table of authorities entry.

◆ **[Top Mar]** Specifies the top margin.

◆ **[Total Entry]** Specifies a mathematical total.

◆ **[TSRt]** Temporary soft return.

◆ **[TSRt-SCol]** Temporary soft return soft column break.

◆ **[TSRt-SPg]** Temporary soft return soft page break.

- **[Und Off]** Turns off the underline font attribute.
- **[Und On]** Turns on the underline font attribute.
- **[Undrln Space]** Underline space characters.
- **[Undrln Tab]** Underlines tab characters.
- **[Unknown]** Unknown code.
- **[VAdv]** Specifies a vertical cursor advance.
- **[Very Large Off]** Turns off the very large font attribute.
- **[Very Large On]** Turns on the very large font attribute.
- **[Vol Num Dec]** Specifies the decrement value between successive volumes.
- **[Vol Num Disp]** Controls how volume numbers are displayed.
- **[Vol Num Inc]** Specifies the increment value between successive value.
- **[Vol Num Metho]** Specifies how volume numbers are displayed.
- **[Vol Num Set]** Specifies the character set used to display volume numbers.
- **[Watermark A]** Defines watermark A.
- **[Watermark B]** Defines watermark B.
- **[Wid/Orph]** Specifies the state of widow and orphan control.
- **[Wrd/Ltr Spacing]** Specifies word and letter spacing.

Automating Your Telephone Book

If you find that you are currently adding names and numbers to your Rolodex, you may want to take advantage of the Telephone Book document provided on this book's companion disk. Shown in Figure 38.3, the document lets you record names, address, telephone and fax numbers, as well as notes about the entry.

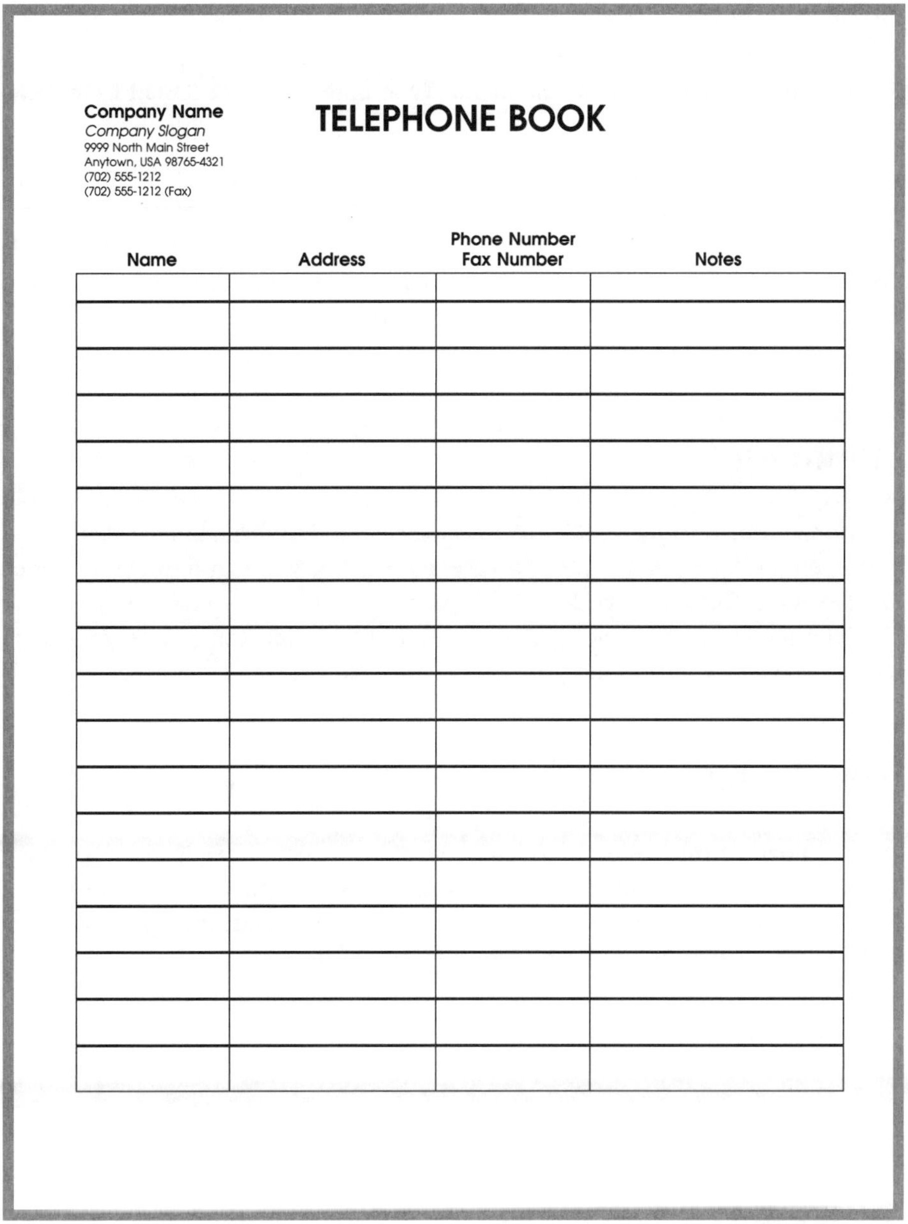

Company Name
Company Slogan
9999 North Main Street
Anytown, USA 98765-4321
(702) 555-1212
(702) 555-1212 (Fax)

TELEPHONE BOOK

Name	Address	Phone Number Fax Number	Notes

Figure 38.3 *The companion disk Telephone Book document.*

To use the telephone book document:

1. Select **Open** from the File menu. Type in the filename **TELEPHON.DOC**.
2. Edit the form to customize it for your company.
3. Use the File menu **Save** option to save your changes.

The telephone book document is actually a WordPerfect table (see Chapter 31). To move from one entry to the next, press your Arrow keys. When you fill all of the entries in the phone book, use the techniques discussed in Chapter 31 to add more table entries.

Summary

To format your document, WordPerfect places hidden formatting codes in it. If you open the View menu and select **Reveal Codes**, you can direct WordPerfect to display its formatting codes. With the formatting codes displayed, you can highlight the codes using your Arrow keys and then delete them. As your documents become more complex, you will edit formatting codes on a regular basis.

New Terms

◆ **Formatting code.** A hidden code WordPerfect places in your document to control formatting. For example, to display a word in italics, WordPerfect groups the word between two formatting codes, one that turns italics on, and one that turns italics off:

```
[Italc On]Word[Italc Off].
```

Chapter 39

Placing Sound Clips in Your Documents

In this chapter you:

- ◆ Place a sound clip in your document
- ◆ Play back the sound clip
- ◆ Edit sound clip descriptions and delete sound clips
- ◆ Record your own sound clips

Getting Started with Sound

The 1990s is the multimedia era–using the combination of text, graphics, sound, and video to present information in a meaningful way. As such, many users are adding sound boards to their computers that let them play back voice messages, different sounds ranging from gun shots to barking dogs, and even music. For those users whose computers have a sound board, WordPerfect 6.0 brings multimedia into the word processing environment. By placing sound clips in your document, another user who is editing the document file can play back the sound clip, hearing the corresponding sounds. If you are sending a memo to another user, the sound clip might contain the date and time of a meeting, or more likely, your true feelings about a matter. If you work in the marketing department, the sound clip might contain a new jingle or sounds for which you are soliciting user opinions. For the person who is reading your document to hear a sound clip, they must have the document and their computer must contain a sound card.

Placing a Sound Clip in Your Document

To help you get started, the WordPerfect installation places a few sound clip files in the directory \WP60\GRAPHICS. To place one of these sound clip files into your document:

1. Open the File menu and choose **New**.
2. Type in the following text:

```
Dear Tom,
I picked out the music for the party. Tell me what
you think.
Jeff
```

3. Place the cursor on the line that follows the name *Jeff.*
4. Open the Tools menu, select **Sound Clip**. WordPerfect cascades the menu, as shown in Figure 39.1.

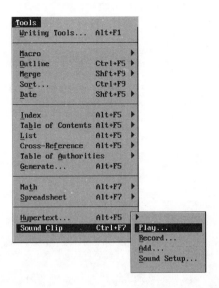

Figure 39.1 *Cascading the Sound Clip menu.*

Verifying Your Sound Board Selection

The WordPerfect installation lets you select the sound board installed in your computer. To make sure that sound card is correct, open the Tools menu, select **Sound Clip,** then **Sound Setup**. WordPerfect displays the Sound Setup dialog box, as shown in Figure 39.2.

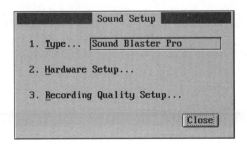

Figure 39.2 *The Sound Setup dialog box.*

If the Type field does not contain your sound board name, type **T** or click on the **Type** option. WordPerfect displays the list of available sound boards.

Selecting the Sound Clip

To add a sound clip to your document:

1. Open the Tools menu, select **Sound Clip**, and choose **Add**. WordPerfect displays the Add Sound Clip to Document dialog box shown in Figure 39.3.

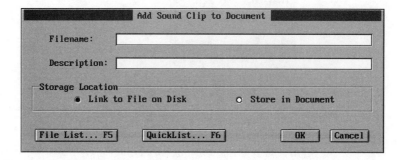

Figure 39.3 *The Add Sound Clip to Document dialog box.*

2. Type in the filename **\WP60\GRAPHICS\FANFARE1.MID**.
3. Press **Enter**.
4. Select **OK**.
5. WordPerfect places the sound clip in the document shown in Figure 39.4.

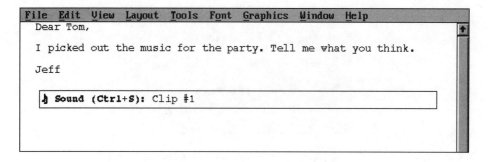

Figure 39.4 *Placing a sound clip in a document.*

Playing a Sound Clip

To play back a sound clip:

1. Open the Tools menu, and select **Sound Clip**, then **Play**. WordPerfect displays the Sound Clips in Document dialog box shown in Figure 39.5.

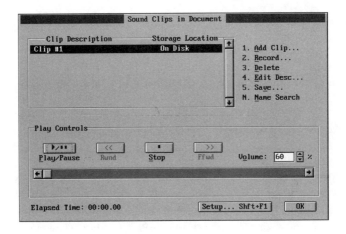

Figure 39.5 *The Sound Clips in Document dialog box.*

2. Highlight the sound clip in the Clip Description field.
3. Type **P** or click on the **Play/Pause** button. WordPerfect starts the sound playback.

Understanding the Play Controls

If you examine the lower half of the Sound Clips in Document dialog box, you will find a set of buttons that resemble those you would find on a tape recorder. To select one of these buttons, type the underlined letter or click on the button. As the sound plays, WordPerfect displays the sound's elapsed time.

Where to Store the Sound Clip

When you place a sound clip in your document, the Add Sound Clip to Document dialog box lets you store the sound clip in your document file or you can leave the sound clip on your disk.

If you plan to give the document file to another user, store the sound clip in the document file. When you leave the sound clip on disk, WordPerfect must locate the sound clip file in order to playback the sound. If you share a network directory with other users, you may leave the sound clip file on disk in the directory to reduce your document size. In most cases, however, you will want to place the sound file in your document file.

Deleting a Sound Clip

Just as there are times when you edit and delete document text, the same may be true for sound clips. To remove a sound clip from your document, select the sound clip using a block operation and press **Del** or **Backspace**.

Working With Multiple Sound Clips

Depending on your document's contents, there may be times when you will place multiple sound clips in your document. By default, WordPerfect names the sound clips using successive numbers, such as Clip 1, Clip 2, and so on. To play a specific sound clip, you simply highlight the corresponding name in the Sound Clips in Document dialog box and select **Play/Pause**. However, as shown in Figure 39.6, as the number of sound clips in your document increases, selecting the correct sound clip may be difficult.

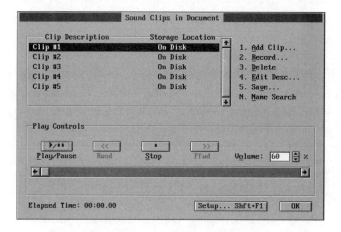

Figure 39.6 *Multiple sound clips in a document.*

To avoid such confusion, you can assign meaningful names to each sound clip as you add them, or using **Edit Desc** in the Sound Clips in Document dialog box.

By assigning meaningful names to sound clips, you make it much easier to select the correct sound clip. Figure 39.7, for example, illustrates the use of meaningful sound clip names within a document.

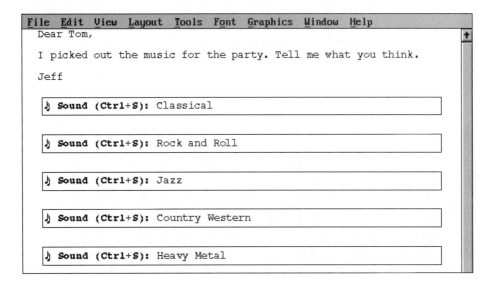

Figure 39.7 Using meaningful sound clip names.

Recording Your Own Sound Clips

If your sound board supports a microphone, you can use it to record your own sound clips. To record a sound clip into your document, open the Tools menu, and select **Sound Clip** then **Record**. WordPerfect displays the Record Sound Clip dialog box. Turn on your microphone. Type **R** or click on the **Rec** button. WordPerfect starts recording. When you are done recording, type **S** or click on **Stop**. Type **I** or click on the **Insert** button to place the sound clip into your file.

Tracking Your Monthly Budget

If you have trouble remembering which bills you need to pay each month and when, you may want to use the companion disk Monthly Budget Checklist. Shown in Figure 39.8, the form lets you record when a specific bill is due, the bill's amount, the address to where the bill is sent, and even comments.

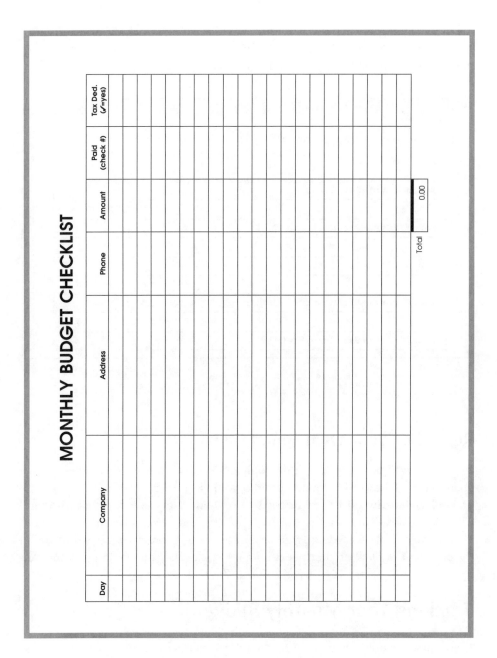

Figure 39.8 *The companion disk Monthly Budget Checklist.*

To use the Monthly Budget Checklist:

1. Select **Open** from the File menu and type in the filename **MONTHLY.DOC**.
2. Edit the form to customize it for your company.
3. Use the File menu **Save As** option to store the document on your hard disk as BUDGET.DOC.

The next time you pay your bills, open the document and fill in the corresponding information. As you type, use your Arrow keys to move from one field to another.

Summary

Multimedia is the use of text, graphics, sound and video to present information in the most meaningful way. If your PC has a sound board, WordPerfect lets you insert sound clips into the document that another user can later playback. If your sound board supports a microphone, you can even record your own sound clips.

New Terms

◆   **Multimedia**. The combination of text, graphics, sound, and video to present information.

◆   **Sound clips**. A recording that can be inserted into a WordPerfect document.

Chapter 40

Building a Table of Contents or Index

In this chapter you:

◆ Create a table of contents for a document

◆ Create an index of key document terms

◆ Understand WordPerfect lists and tables of authorities

◆ Understand master documents

Creating a Table of Contents

If you are working on a large report, you may want to include in your document a table of contents that describes the document's key sections. WordPerfect makes it very easy to create a table of contents. To begin, select **New** from the File menu and type in the following text:

```
Chapter 1 My Life Story

This is the abridged reader's digest version of my
life story-at least my life to this point.

The Early Years

I was born in Seattle, Washington. In grade school I
learned to shoot a basketball.

The Middle Years

By the time I moved to Phoenix for high school, I
could shoot the basketball really well.

The College Years

Basketball got me to college, which introduced me to
computers. 11 years of college later—I don't shoot
the basketball quite as well, but I really understand
computers.
```

In Chapter 26 you used text similar to this when you learned how to apply WordPerfect styles. To better understand table of contents entries, place each section of text on its own page. Place the cursor in front of the text *The Early Years* and press **Ctrl-Enter**. WordPerfect places a hard page break in your document. Using this same technique, place a hard page break before the text *The Middle Years* and *The College Years*. Your document looks like Figure 40.1.

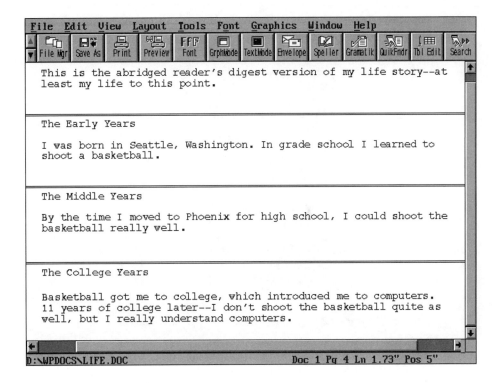

Figure 40.1 *Creating a multipage document.*

Entries in a table of contents are similar to styles in that you may have a major level entry, such as the chapter name and then lesser entries as shown here:

```
Chapter 1 My Life Story 1
   The Early Years 2
   The Middle Years 3
   The College Years 4
Chapter 2 Writing a WordPerfect Book 5
   Getting Started 6
```

In this case, select the text *Chapter 1 My Life Story* by performing a block operation.

1. Open the Tools menu and choose **Table of Contents**. WordPerfect cascades the menu shown in Figure 40.2.

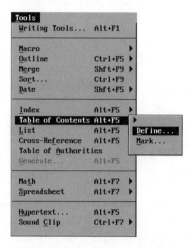

Figure 40.2 *The cascading Table of Contents menu.*

2. Select the **Mark** option. WordPerfect displays the Mark Table of Contents dialog box shown in Figure 40.3.

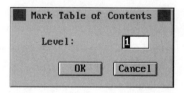

Figure 40.3 *The Mark Table of Contents dialog box.*

3. In the level field, type the value **1** (this is a major entry) and press **Enter**. Selecting an entry for the table of contents is that easy.

4. Select the text *The Early Years* and choose **Mark**.

5. This time, when WordPerfect displays the Mark Table of Contents dialog box, type in the value **2** (a lesser entry). Assign the level 2 for the text *The Middle Years* and *The College Years*.

Your table of contents entries are now complete and you are ready to generate the table.

Generating the Table of Contents

The first step in generating the table of contents is to determine where in your document you want WordPerfect to place it. In this case:

1. Move the cursor to the start of your document and press **Ctrl-Enter** to insert a hard page break.

2. Open the Tools menu, select **Table of Contents**, and choose **Define**. WordPerfect displays the Define Table of Contents dialog box shown in Figure 40.4.

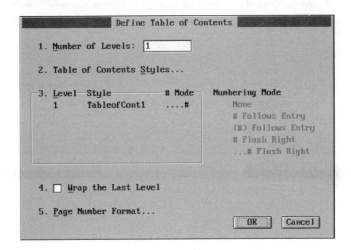

Figure 40.4 *The Define Table of Contents dialog box.*

3. The Define Table of Contents dialog box lets you control how many levels of the table of contents WordPerfect includes and the format used to display each level.

4. For now, select the **Number of Levels** option and type **2**. Select **OK**.

5. Use the Tools menu **Generate** option. WordPerfect displays the Generate dialog box shown in Figure 40.5.

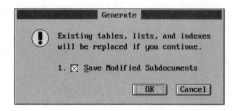

Figure 40.5 The Generate dialog box.

6. Select **OK**. WordPerfect builds your table of contents, placing it at the start of your document, as in Figure 40.6.

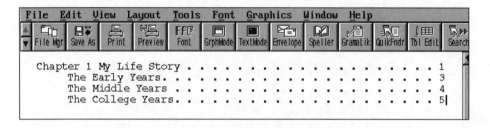

Figure 40.6 Generating a table of contents.

Building an Index

Building an index of key terms WordPerfect is similar to building a Table of Contents. To start mark each word that you want in the index. Next, place the cursor at the location where you want the index to appear, and define and generate the index. To better understand this process:

1. Select the word *Seattle*.

2. Open the Tools menu and choose **Index**.

3. When WordPerfect cascades the menu, choose **Mark**.

4. Repeat this process, marking the words *Phoenix* and *computers*.

5. Move your cursor to the end of your document and press **Ctrl-Enter** to insert a hard page break.

6. Open the Tools menu, select **Index,** and choose **Define**.

7. The Define Index dialog box is displayed. In this dialog box you can specify which entries you want WordPerfect to display and the entry format. Choose **OK**.

8. Open the Tools menu and choose **Generate**. WordPerfect creates an index, as in Figure 40.7.

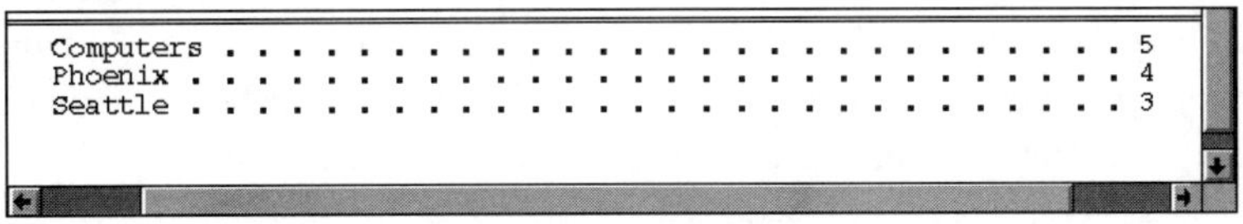

```
Computers . . . . . . . . . . . . . . . . . . . . . . . . 5
Phoenix . . . . . . . . . . . . . . . . . . . . . . . . . 4
Seattle . . . . . . . . . . . . . . . . . . . . . . . . . 3
```

Figure 40.7 *Creating an index.*

Other Tables and Lists

In addition to creating a table of contents, there may be times when you need to include such items as a List of Figures or a List of Tables and their corresponding page numbers. Select the text you desire, such as a figure or table caption and use the Tools menu **List** option to mark the text, assigning it to a specific list. After you have marked all of the entries, position the cursor at the location at which you want WordPerfect to place the list. Next, select the **List** option and choose **Define**. WordPerfect displays the Define List dialog box. Highlight the list you want and choose **Select**. Next, open the Tools menu and choose **Generate**. WordPerfect displays the list items and their corresponding page numbers. Using these same steps, you can create a table of authorities, which is often used in legal documents.

Understanding Cross References

As you create a long document, you may want to refer to a previous topic. For example, you might include the following sentence:

```
As it turned out, the speaker was Joe Davis (See
page 4).
```

As you type a large document, you may not know on which page a cross reference will appear. Many people print their document and then go back and correct the cross references. Luckily, WordPerfect simplifies this process. To better understand, open the File menu and choose **New**. Next, type the following text:

```
Joe Davis is our company President.
```

Select the name *Joe Davis* using a block operation. Open the Tools menu and choose **Cross-Reference**. WordPerfect cascades the menu. Choose **Target** (the name will later be the target of a cross reference). WordPerfect displays the Mark Cross-Reference Target dialog box shown in Figure 40.8.

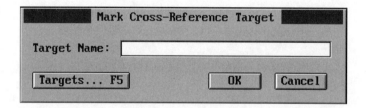

Figure 40.8 *The Mark Cross-Reference Target dialog box.*

Enter the name **Joe Davis** and select **OK**. Next, position the cursor at the end of the line and press **Ctrl-Enter** to generate a hard page break. Type in the following text:

```
I enjoyed our luncheon. It turned out the speaker was
Joe Davis (see page
```

Next, to refer back to the previous reference, open the Tools menu, and select **Cross-Reference**. When WordPerfect cascades the menu, choose **Reference**. WordPerfect displays the Mark Cross-Reference dialog box, shown in Figure 40.9.

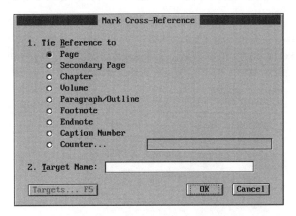

Figure 40.9 *The Mark Cross-Reference dialog box.*

In this case, select the **Page** option to tie the reference to the page number at which Joe Davis is described. In the Target Name field, type the desired name (it's already here in this case). To view available cross reference targets, press **F5** or click on the **Targets** button. Select **OK**. WordPerfect displays a question mark in your document to indicate the cross reference. Type a right parenthesis to complete the reference followed, by a period.

Next, open the Tools menu and choose **Generate**. WordPerfect replaces the question mark with the correct page number. If change your document so the name Joe Davis moves to a different page, you can update all of your cross references by selecting **Generate** from the Tools menu.

Understanding Master Documents

When you are building a large document, such as a book, you will probably place each chapter in its own document file. However, you need a way to tell WordPerfect about each chapter so that your index, cross reference, and table of contents entries contain the correct book page numbers. To help you build large documents, WordPerfect lets you create a master document (the book), in which you define all of the subdocuments (the chapters). After you define the master document, you can generate your table of contents, index, and cross references and WordPerfect assigns the correct book pages. To create a master document, open the File menu and select **Master Document**. WordPerfect cascades the menu shown in Figure 40.10.

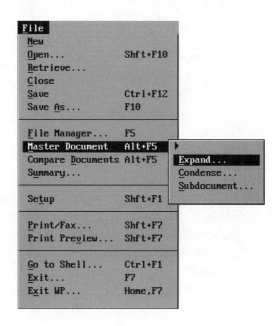

Figure 40.10 *The cascading Master Document menu.*

Select the **Subdocument** option. WordPerfect displays a dialog box asking for a document filename. In the case of the book, type **CHAPTER1.DOC**. Repeat this process for each book chapter. Assuming your book contains eight chapters, your master document will look similar to Figure 40.11.

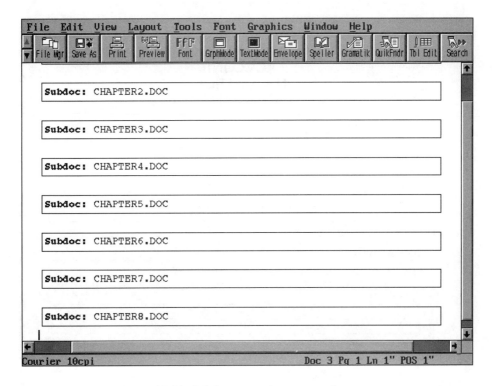

Figure 40.11 Subdocuments in a master document.

Using the File menu Master Document option, you can expand a subdocument to edit it's text, or you can condense an open subdocument back into the named box format. If you expand the subdocuments and print the master, WordPerfect prints all of the corresponding subdocuments. By letting you build large documents, WordPerfect makes its very easy to manage your projects.

Tracking Customer Information

If you work with customers, you may want to use the companion disk Account Information Checklist to record specifics about your customer. As shown in Figure 40.12, the form lets you track information ranging from the account's name and address to specifics about their children and pets.

Company Name
Company Slogan
9999 North Main Street
Anytown, USA 98765-4321
(702) 555-1212
(702) 555-1212 (Fax)

ACCOUNT INFORMATION CHECKLIST

PROFESSIONAL INFORMATION

Contact Name:	Account Name:
Phone Number:	Address:
Title/Position:	
Since (How Long):	Type of Business:
Responsible For:	Supervisor's Name:
Previous Position/Title:	Position/Title:
With:	Phone Number:

PERSONAL INFORMATION

Home Phone:	Date of Birth (age):		
Spouse/Family Member Name	Relationship	Date of Birth (age)	Sex

Pets (Names and Types):
Likes/Dislikes:

CONTACT LOG

Date/Time	Type - Location - Subjects Discussed

SUSPENSE LIST

Due Date	Date Done	Description (Recall, Send information, Contact References)

Figure 40.12 *The companion disk Account Information Checklist.*

To use the Account Information Checklist:

1. Select **Open** from the File menu and type in the filename **ACCOUNT.DOC**.
2. Edit the form to customize it for your company.
3. Use the File menu **Save** option to save your changes.

When you want to record information about an account, open the document file, type in the account information (using the Arrow keys to move from field to another) and then save the document to a file on disk whose name corresponds to the account.

New Terms

◆ **Cross reference target.** Text in your document to which you refer back.

◆ **Master document.** A WordPerfect document that is made of several other document files, as chapters making up a book.

◆ **Subdocument.** A WordPerfect document file that is used to build a larger master document.

Chapter 41

Using the Equation Editor

In this chapter you:

◆ Use WordPerfect's equation editor to create mathematical expressions

◆ Understand the equation editor's built in commands

Getting Started with the Equation Editor

Most offices today can't get away from producing reports that contain some type of arithmetic operations. For example, if you are creating a budget report, you may want to show how you calculated your company's revenues. Likewise, if you are basing decisions on calculated statistics, you may want to show the equation you used to determine your result. To help you place complex equations in your documents, WordPerfect provides an equation editor. Using the equation editor, you can easily create complex equations similar to the one shown in Figure 41.1.

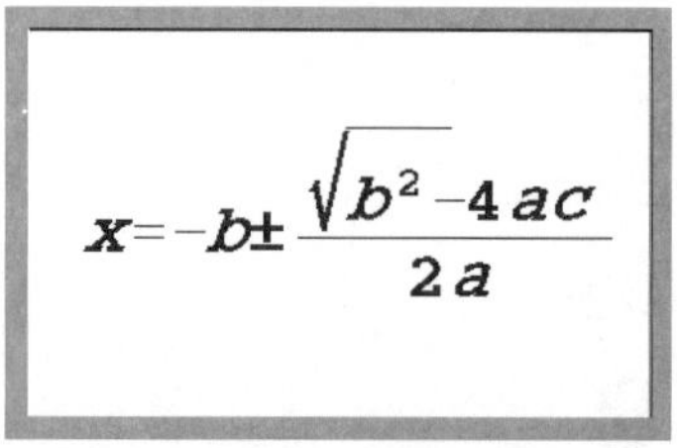

$$x = -b \pm \frac{\sqrt{b^2 - 4ac}}{2a}$$

Figure 41.1 *Placing a complex equation in your document.*

To create a complex equation, open the Graphics menu and choose **Graphics Boxes**. WordPerfect cascades the menu shown in Figure 41.2.

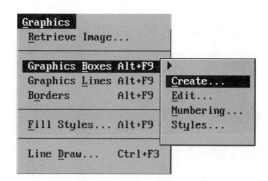

Figure 41.2 *Cascading the Graphics Boxes menu.*

Select **Create**. WordPerfect displays the Create Graphics Box dialog box shown in Figure 41.3.

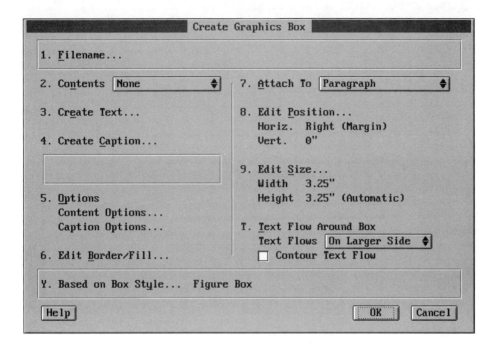

Figure 41.3 *The Create Graphics Box dialog box.*

Type **2** or click on the **Contents** option. WordPerfect displays a list of items you can place in the box.

Select **Equation**. Next, type **3** or click on the **Create Equation** option. WordPerfect displays its Equation editor shown in Figure 41.4.

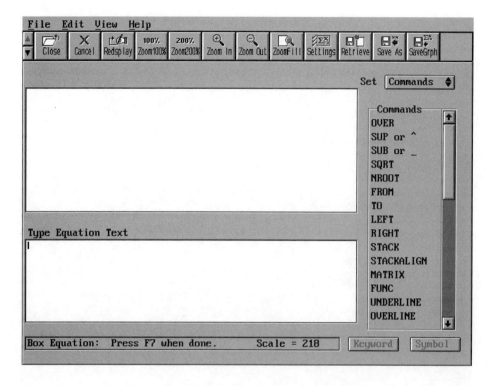

Figure 41.4 *The equation editor.*

The equation editor dialog box has two large windows. As you create your equation, WordPerfect displays in the top window how the equation will appear in your document. Type the equation in the lower window. Note the list of commands that appear along the right edge of the dialog box. These commands specify symbols or layout options. For example, the SQRT command directs WordPerfect to place the square root symbol (√)in your document. Likewise, the command OVER directs WordPerfect to display the preceding expression over the expression that follows. For example, 1 OVER 4 would create a fraction ¼.

In addition to these commands, WordPerfect provides various symbols, arrows, Greek letters, function names, and set symbols you can place in your document.

Creating a Simple Expression

Assume that you want to use the equation editor to create the following equation:

$$x = y^2 + \sqrt{11}$$

To begin, select the **Equation** editor. Next, click on the equation text box or press **Tab** until WordPerfect highlights the box. Type in the following text:

$$x = y$$

Next, from the Commands list, select **SUP OR** ^. Type **2**. If you are using a mouse, click on the **Redisplay** button. WordPerfect displays your equation as shown in Figure 41.5.

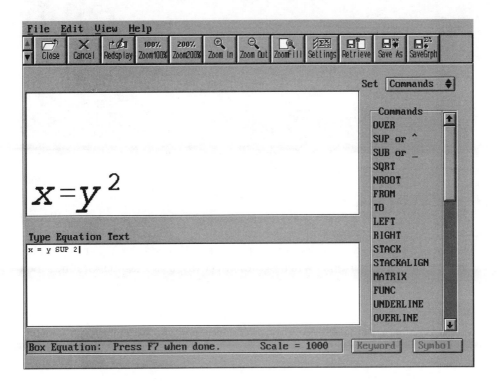

Figure 41.5 *Displaying an equation in the equation editor.*

Next, type a plus (**+**) and select the Commands list **Sqrt** option. Complex the equation by typing 11. Click your mouse on the **Redisplay** button. WordPerfect displays your equation as shown in Figure 41.6.

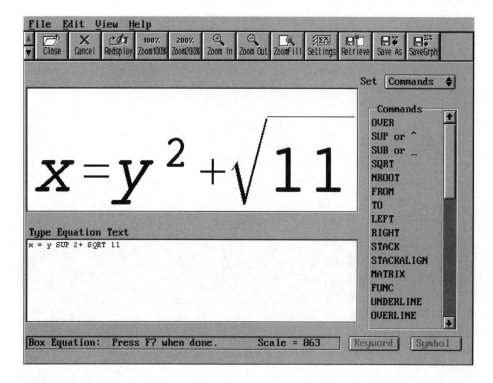

Figure 41.6 *Completing the equation.*

Click on the **Close** button or select the File menu **Close** option. WordPerfect returns to the Create Graphics Box dialog box. Select **OK**. WordPerfect displays the equation in your document. If you need to edit the equation, double click on the equation box. When WordPerfect displays the Edit Graphics Box dialog box, select the **Edit Equation** option. WordPerfect returns to the equation editor.

Customizing the Equation Editor

When you create an equation using the equation editor, you can control the font, size, and so on. In the equation editor, select the File menu **Settings** option. WordPerfect displays the Equation Settings dialog box, shown in Figure 41.7.

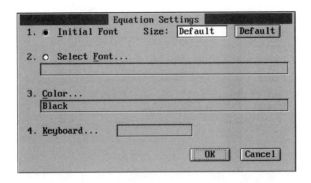

Figure 41.7 *The Equation Settings dialog box.*

In this dialog box you can control the font, size, and color. The **Keyboard** option lets you select the keyboard template similar to that discussed in Chapter 6.

Understanding the Equation Editor's Commands

The equation editor provides several different commands you can insert in your documents:

◆ **OVER** displays the previous expression over the expression that follows creating a fraction.

◆ **SUP** or ^ Superscripts the expression that follows .

◆ **SUB** or _ Subscripts the expression that follows.

◆ **SQRT** displays the square root symbol.

◆ **NROOT** displays the root symbol, using the preceding expression as the root.

◆ **FROM** displays the expression that follows as the lower limit of an integral.

◆ **TO** displays the expression that follows as the upper limit of an integral.

◆ **LEFT** specifies the character that follows as a left delimiter.

◆ **RIGHT** specifies the character that follows as a right delimiter.

◆ **STACK** stacks two expressions grouped by { } and separated by a pound sign # on top of each other.

◆ **STACKALIGN** stack aligns two expressions grouped by { } and separated by a pound sign # on top of each other.

◆ **MAXTRIX** displays expressions grouped by { } and separated by a pound sign # in a table form.

◆ **FUNC** is a user-defined function name.

◆ **UNDERLINE** underlines the expression that follows.

◆ **OVERLINE** overlines the expression that follows.

◆ { } Grouping symbols.

◆ **HORZ** moves horizontally n spaces.

◆ **VERT** moves vertically n lines.

◆ ~ places a normal space between two expressions.

◆ ` places a thin space between two expressions.

◆ **BINOM** creates a binomial using the two expressions that follow.

◆ **&** separates matrix columns.

◆ **#** separates matrix rows.

◆ **MATFORM** selects matrix column format.

◆ **ALIGNL** left aligns the expression that follows.

◆ **ALIGNR** right aligns the expression that follows.

◆ **ALIGNC** center aligns the expression that follows.

◆ **PHANTOM** reserves a place holder for the expression that follows.

◆ **.** specifies no delimiter (used with LEFT RIGHT).

- ◆ \ defines a literal symbol such as \~ or \&.
- ◆ **BOLD** displays the expression that follows as bold.
- ◆ **ITAL** displays the expression that follows as italic.
- ◆ **OVERSM** creates a small fraction placing preceding expression on top of the expression that follows.
- ◆ **BINOMSM** creates a small binomial using the two expressions that follow.
- ◆ **LINESPACE** specifies the vertical line spacing.
- ◆ **LONGDIV** displays the long division symbol.
- ◆ **LONGDIVS** displays a square long division symbol.
- ◆ **SCALESYM** scales the symbol by the specified factor.

Creating a Purchase Order

If you order supplies or other products from different companies that require a purchase order, you may want to use the companion disk Purchase Order form. As shown in Figure 41.8, the form lets you specify shipping instructions, terms, items purchased, their quantity and cost, as well as tax.

Company Name
Company Slogan
9999 North Main Street
Anytown, USA 98765-4321
(702) 555-1212
(702) 555-1212 (Fax)

PURCHASE ORDER

Purchased from: **Ship to:**

P. O. Number	Purchase Date	Delivery Date	Order Taken By	Terms	FOB	Ship Via

Item	Quan	Units	Description	Price	Total
					0.00
					0.00
					0.00
					0.00
					0.00
					0.00
					0.00
					0.00
					0.00
					0.00
					0.00
					0.00
					0.00
					0.00
					0.00
					0.00
					0.00
					0.00
					0.00
					0.00
					0.00

				Sub-Total	0.00
				Sales Tax (7%)	0.00
				Shipping & Handling	
				Total Order	0.00

_____   _____
Authorized Buyer   Date

Figure 41.8 *The companion disk Purchase Order form.*

To use the form:

1. Select **Open from** the File menu. Type in the filename **PURCHASE.DOC**.
2. Edit the form to customize it for your company.
3. Use the File menu **Save** option to saveyour changes.

Next, you may want to edit the document, placing your company name, slogan, address, and phone numbers in the upper-left corner. Also, you may need to update the Sales Tax amount shown. Save your changes to the document file. When you later need to write a purchase order, open the document and type in the corresponding fields. Use your Arrow keys to move from one field to the next. Use the File menu **Print/Fax** option to print the document. Using the File menu **Save As** option, save the document to a file that meaningfully describes the order.

Summary

To help you place complex equations in your documents, WordPerfect provides an equation editor. To place an equation in your document, position the cursor at the location at which you want the equation. Next, open the Graphics menu, choose **Graphics Boxes** and select **Create**. When WordPerfect displays the Edit Graphics Boxes dialog box, select the **Contents** option and choose **Equation**. Next, select the **Edit Equation** option. WordPerfect displays its equation editor.

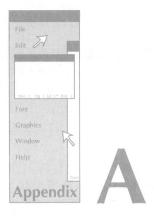

Installing WordPerfect 6.0

If you have not yet installed WordPerfect 6.0 on your disk, use the DIR command to determine the amount of available space on your disk:

```
C:\> DIR <ENTER>
```

At the end of the directory listing, DIR displays a line that tells you the number of bytes free. To install WordPerfect 6.0, you need 14.5 Mb of free disk space. If you are currently using WordPerfect 5.1, the installation of WordPerfect 6.0 will not affect your files. The installation creates new directories for version 6.0.

Performing the Installation

Place the disk labeled Install 1 in drive A or B. Select the drive as the current drive. If you are using drive A, you use the following command to select drive A as the current drive:

```
C:\> A:  <ENTER>
A:\>
```

Next, type the **INSTALL** command and press **Enter**.

```
A:\> INSTALL  <ENTER>
```

WordPerfect displays a screen that contains three colored boxes. If the colors appear on your screen type **Y**. If the boxes are not colored, type **N**. WordPerfect displays the screen shown in Figure A.1, asking you to specify the type of installation you want to perform.

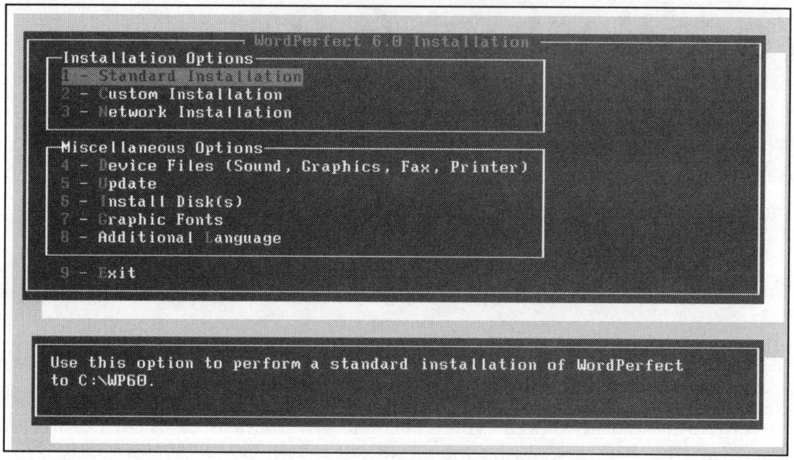

Figure A.1 *The prompt for the installation type.*

Using your Arrow keys, highlight the **Standard Installation** option and press **Enter**. WordPerfect displays a screen asking you to approve the location of the installation files and the location to which WordPerfect will be installed. Type **N** to leave the directories unchanged. WordPerfect displays a screen showing you the amount of disk space available on your disk and that the installation requires 14.5 Mb. Type **Y** to continue the installation. WordPerfect then displays the screen shown in Figure A.2 asking how you would like WordPerfect to prompt you before replacing a file on your disk.

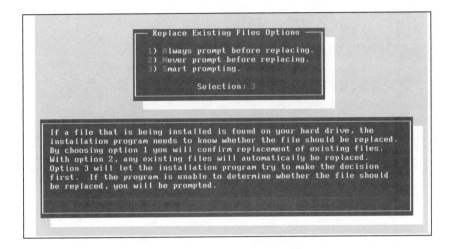

Figure A.2 *The file replacement prompt.*

Type **3** to select WordPerfect's Smart prompting option. WordPerfect then displays a dialog asking you if it can add the WordPerfect program directory to your path in AUTOEXEC.BAT. Type **Y**. WordPerfect displays a screen asking you if you want to install additional video drivers. Type **N**. WordPerfect then asks you if you want to install printer drivers. Select **Yes**. WordPerfect displays the screen shown in Figure A.3, in which you can select your printer type.

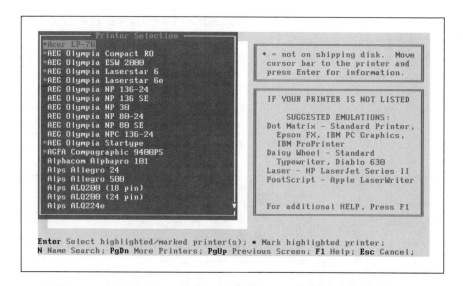

Figure A.3 *The printer selection screen.*

Using your Arrow keys, highlight your printer type and press **Enter**. WordPerfect displays a small box asking you if you want to select the highlighted printer. Type **Y**. WordPerfect briefly reads the installation disk and then asks you if you want to install another printer. Unless you have more than one printer attached to your system, type **N**. The installation then begins reading the installation disk. As the installation finishes one disk, WordPerfect displays a box directing you to insert a specific disk. Place the disk in the drive and press **Enter**.

After several disks, WordPerfect asks you if you want to install fax files. If your computer has a fax modem and you want to use it from in WordPerfect, type **Y**. If you type **Y**, WordPerfect displays a screen asking you to specify your modem type. Type the number that corresponds to your modem type and press **Enter**. WordPerfect then asks you if you want it to include any sound drivers. If your PC has a sound board, you can place and play back sound clips from in your documents. If you have a sound board, type **Y**. WordPerfect displays a dialog box asking you to specify your sound board type. Using your Arrow keys, highlight your sound board type and press **Enter**. WordPerfect asks you to verify your selection. Type **Y**. WordPerfect asks you if you want to install additional sound board drivers. Type **N**.

Insert the disks as needed. WordPerfect then displays a screen asking you to type in your registration number. Type in the number and press **Enter**. When the installation completes, press the **Ctrl-Alt-Del** keyboard combination to reboot your system. Then, turn to Chapter 1 and get started!

Appendix B

WordPerfect Keystrokes

WordPerfect defines many different keyboard combinations. This appendix presents the function of each.

Cursor Positioning

Home, Home, Home, Up Arrow Moves the cursor to the start of the document, before codes.

Home, Home, Up Arrow Moves the cursor to the start of the document, after codes.

Home, Home, Down Arrow Moves the cursor to the end of the document.

Home, Home, Home, Left Arrow Moves the cursor to the beginning of the line, before codes.

477

Home, Home, Left Arrow	Moves the cursor to the beginning of the line, after codes.
Home, Home, Right Arrow	Moves the cursor to the end of the line.
Home, Home, Down Arrow	Moves the cursor to the end of the document.
Home, Up Arrow	Moves the cursor to top of the screen.
Home, Down Arrow	Moves the cursor to the bottom of the screen.
Left Arrow	Moves the cursor to the previous character.
Right Arrow	Moves the cursor to the next character.
Ctrl-Left Arrow	Moves the cursor to the previous word.
Ctrl-Right Arrow	Moves the cursor to the next word.
Down Arrow	Moves the cursor down one line.
Up Arrow	Moves the cursor up one line.
PgDn	Moves the cursor down one page.
PgUp	Moves the cursor up one page.
Ctrl-Home	Moves the cursor to another document window.
Tab (in a dialog box)	Move to the next control.
Shift-Tab (in dialog box)	Move to the previous control.
Tab (in outline)	Insert next level.
Shift-Tab (in outline)	Move to the previous level.

Insert Operations

Enter	Hard return.
Ctrl-Enter	Hard page break.
Spacebar	Space.
Home-Spacebar	Hard space.
Home -	Hard hyphen.
Ctrl-Shift -	Soft hyphen.
Home-Enter	Hyphen with a soft return.

Tab	Tab.
Shift-Tab	Margin release.
Ctrl-Ins	Copy and paste selected text.
Ctrl-Del	Cut and paste selected text.

Delete Operations

Del	Current character.
Backspace	Previous character.
Ctrl-PgDn	Remainder of page.
Ctrl-End	Remainder of line.
Ctrl-Backspace	Current word.
Ins	Toggles typeover.

Ctrl Key Shortcuts

Ctrl-A	Compose.
Ctrl-C	Copy.
Ctrl-F	Find QuickMark.
Ctrl-I	Italics.
Ctrl-N	Normal font.
Ctrl-O	Outline edit.
Ctrl-P	Insert formatted page number.
Ctrl-Q	Set QuickMark.
Ctrl-R	Repeat.
Ctrl-S	Play sound clip.
Ctrl-T	Toggle text or paragraph number.
Ctrl-V	Paste.
Ctrl-W	WP characters.
Ctrl-X	Cut selected text.
Ctrl-Y	Cycle through windows.
Ctrl-Z	Undo.

Function Key Definitions

F1	Selects Help.
F2	Search.
F3	Switch to.
F4	Indent left.
F5	File Manager.
F6	Bold.
F7	Exit.
F8	Underline.
F9	End field.
F10	Save As.
F11	Reveal codes.
F12	Block.
Shift-F1	Setup.
Shift-F2	Search backward.
Shift-F3	Switch.
Shift-F4	Double indent.
Shift-F5	Date.
Shift-F6	Center.
Shift-F7	Print/Fax.
Shift-F8	Format.
Shift-F9	Merge codes.
Shift-F10	Open/Retrieve.
Shift-F11	WP characters.
Shift-F12	Bookmark.
Alt-F1	Writing tools.
Alt-F2	Replace.
Alt-F3	Reveal codes.
Alt-F4	Block.
Alt-F5	Mark.

Alt-F6	Flush right.
Alt-F7	Columns/Tables.
Alt-F8	Style.
Alt-F9	Graphics.
Alt-F10	Play macro.
Alt-F11	Table edit.
Alt-F12	Envelope.
Ctrl-F1	Shell.
Ctrl-F2	Speller.
Ctrl-F3	Screen.
Ctrl-F4	Move.
Ctrl-F5	Outline.
Ctrl-F6	Decimal tab.
Ctrl-F7	Notes.
Ctrl-F8	Font.
Ctrl-F9	Merge/Sort.
Ctrl-F10	Record macro.
Ctrl-F11	Tab set.
Ctrl-F12	Save.

Index

Graphics Mode Screen Type/Colors dialog box, 71-72

H

[HAdv] (formatting code), 426
hanging indents, 242
hard fonts, 95-96
hard hyphens, 243-244
hard page breaks, 238
hard returns, 236-237
[HCol] (formatting code), 426
[HCol-SPg] (formatting code), 426
Header A dialog box, 229-231
[Header A] (formatting code), 426
[Header B] (formatting code), 426
Header/Footer/Watermark dialog box, 229
Header/Footer/Watermark option (Layout menu), 229
[Header Sep] (formatting code), 426
header(s), 228-233. *See also* footers
   controlling spacing around, 232
   creating, 229-231
   displaying, 231
   editing, 233
   odd and even pages, different headers on, 231
   searching for text in, 137
   suppressing, 266
   turning off, 233
headwords, 161
Help, 192-200
   coaches with, 198-199
   How Do I questions, answers to, 197-198
   index, using online, 193-197
   online Help, 192-197
   technical support, displaying information for, 199
Help menu, 192
[Hidden Off]/[Hidden On] (formatting

codes), 426-427
[Hidden Txt] (formatting code), 427
History dialog box, 162-163
Home-key, 39
home position (cursor), 22
horizontal scroll bar, 17-18
HORZ command (Equation Editor), 466
How Do I option (Help menu), 197-198
[HPg] (formatting code), 427
[HRow-HCol] (formatting code), 427
[HRow-HCol-SPg] (formatting code), 427
[HRow-Hpg] (formatting code), 427
[HRt] (formatting code), 427
[HRt-SCol] (formatting code), 427
[HRt-SPg] (formatting code), 427
[HSpace] (formatting code), 427
[Hypertext Begin]/[Hypertext End] (formatting codes), 427
[Hyph] (formatting code), 427
[Hyph SRt] (formatting code), 427
hyphenation, 242-244
   customizing, 74
hyphenation zones, 244

I

iconic symbols, 253
icons, 15
Image Editor, 354-355
importing files, 293-294
incremental sizing of windows, 186
indents, hanging, 242
INDEPEND.DOC, 390-396
[Index] (formatting code), 427
Index (online Help), 193-197
Index option
   Help menu, 194-195
   Tools menu, 450
indexes
   creating, 450
   file, 215-217

[LFT TAB] (formatting code), 428
[Lft Tab] (formatting code), 428
Line Draw dialog box, 363-364
Line Draw option (Graphics menu), 363
Line Format dialog box, 239-240
line numbering, 240-241
Line option (Layout menu), 239
line spacing, 239-240
Line Styles dialog box, 370-371
line wrapping, automatic, 24-25, 236-237
lines (graphic). *See also* borders
    boxes, creating, 367-369
    creating, 369-371
    customizing, in tables, 342-344
    drawing, 362-364
line(s) (text)
    adding, with Enter-key, 23-25
    deleting, 39-40
    moving up or down one, 38
    numbering of, 240-241
    spacing of, 239-240
LINESPACE command (Equation Editor), 467
[Link]/[Link End] (formatting codes), 428
List Field Names dialog box, 412
List option (Tools menu), 451
lists, bulleted, 250-255
    Bullet Coach, 254
    creating, 250-253
    WordPerfect characters as bullets, using, 253-254
[Ln Height] (formatting code), 428
[Ln Num] (formatting code), 428
[Ln Num Meth] (formatting code), 428
[Ln Num Set] (formatting code), 428
location of files
    backup files, 86
    customizing, 77-78
Location of Files dialog box, 77-78
Long Distance Telephone Call Log,

creating, 314-316
Long Edge option (double-sided printing), 265
LONGDIV command (Equation Editor), 467
LONGDIVS command (Equation Editor), 467
Look option
    File Manager, 204
    Help, 195-196
Look Up Word dialog box, 64-65
LPT1 port, 49, 50

M

Macro Button List dialog box, 322
[Macro Func] (formatting code), 428
Macro option (Tools menu), 318
macros, 318-328, 330
    button bar, assigning to, 320-322
    creating customized, 327-328
    defined, 318
    predefined, 322-328
        display of available fonts, 325
        list of, 323
        Memo macro, 325-327
        on-screen calculator, 324
        viewing commands used to create, 327-328
    recording, 318-320
MACROS button bar, 225
mail merges, 404-414, 416-417
    boilerplate document, creating, 409-414
    merge file, creating, 404-409
    performing merge, 413-414
MANTRV.DOC, 119
Margin Format dialog box, 241-242
margins, controlling, 241-242
Margins option (Layout menu), 241
Mark Cross-Reference dialog box, 452-453

POSTNET bar codes, 301, 303
power loss, recovering from, 85-86
predefined key combinations, 4-5
predefined macros, 322-328
   display of available fonts, 325
   list of, 323
   Memo macro, 325-327
   on-screen calculator, 324
   viewing commands used to create, 327-328
previewing documents, 50-52
Print/Fax dialog box, 46
Print/Fax option (File menu), 46
Print Multiple Pages dialog box, 54, 206-207
Print Preview option (File menu), 50-52
printer, installing, 473-474
Printer Filename dialog box, 48
printing, 46-57
   block of text, 125
   canceling print jobs, 56
   color printer palette, selecting, 78
   control of printout, 53-57
   document summary, 112-113
   double-sided, 265
   envelopes, 265
   with File Manager, 206-207
   labels, 263-264
   macro to speed up, 320
   multiple printers, 49
   number of copies, selecting, 53
   pages to print, selecting, 53-54
   previewing document, 50-52
   print quality, selecting, 54-55
   rush jobs, 56
   selecting printer, 46-49
   suspending print jobs temporarily, 57
   trouble-shooting printer, 49-50
Prompt for Hyphenation option, 74
[Ptr Cmnd] (formatting code), 429
pull-down menus. *See* menus
Purchase Order form, creating, 467-469

PURCHASE.DOC, 469

Q

QuickFinder File Indexer, 215-217
QuickList dialog box, 213
QuickLists, 212-213, 215

R

readability statistics, 172-173
recently used files, opening, 36-37
Record Macro dialog box, 319
recording
   macros, 318-320
   sound clips, 441
records, 405, 407-408
Redisplay button (Equation Editor), 463-464
redlining, 277-278
[Redln Off]/[Redln On] (formatting codes), 429
[Ref Box] (formatting code), 429
[Ref Chap] (formatting code), 429
[Ref Count] (formatting code), 429
[Ref Endnote] (formatting code), 429
[Ref Footnote] (formatting code), 429
[Ref Para] (formatting code), 429
[Ref Pg] (formatting code), 429
[Ref Sec Pg] (formatting code), 429
[Ref Vol] (formatting code), 429
relative font size settings, 95, 99
relative tab stops, 378-379
removing. *See* deleting
renaming files, 205-206
renumbering footnotes, 311-312
replacing text, 139-142
   formatting codes, 141-142
   number of replacements, restriction on, 141
   single word or phrase, 139-141
   with thesaurus, 163-164

[Sec Pg Num Disp] (formatting code), 430

[Sec Pg Num Inc] (formatting code), 430

[Sec Pg Num Meth] (formatting code), 430

[Sec Pg Num Set] (formatting code), 430

secondary page numbers, assigning, 261

Select Box to Edit dialog box, 367-368

Select Button Bar dialog box, 322-323

Select Data File For Field Names dialog box, 411-412

Select option (Edit menu), 129-130

Select Printer dialog box, 46-47

Select Summary Fields dialog box, 113

selected text, display of, 123-124

sentence, selecting, 129-130

serial mouse, 70

Set Footnote Number dialog box, 311-312

Set Page Number dialog box, 260-261

Setup Delimited Text Options dialog box, 76

Setup Mouse Type dialog box, 14

Setup option (File menu), 13-14, 70

shading
   borders, 366-367
   columns, 399-400
   pages, 268-269
   tables, 342-344

Shift-key
   combinations, 4-5
   with function keys, 480
   typing uppercase letters using, 23

Short Edge option (double-sided printing), 265

shortcut keys, 11-12, 479

size, paper, 262-263

Size/Position options (Font menu), 95

sizing windows, 184-186

incremental sizing, 186

minimizing/maximizing, 185-186

[Sm Cap Off]/[Sm Cap On] (formatting codes), 430

[Small Off]/[Small On] (formatting codes), 430

soft fonts, 95-96

soft hyphens, 244

soft page breaks, 238

soft returns, 236-237

sorting directory list (with File Manager), 207-208

Sound Clip option (Tools menu), 436

sound clips, 436-441, 443
   deleting, 440
   multiple, 440-441
   play controls for, 439
   playing back, 439
   recording, 441
   selecting, 438
   sound board selection, verifying, 437
   storing, 439-440

sound drivers, installing, 474

[Sound] (formatting code), 430

Sound Setup dialog box, 437

spacing
   above and below graphics lines, 371
   around headers and footers, 232
   between columns and rows, 398
   of lines, 239-240
   of paragraphs, 242
   between words, full justification and, 242-243

Specific Codes dialog box, 138-139

Specify File Manager List dialog box, 202-203

speed
   cursor, changing, 74
   mouse, changing, 71

spell checking, 60-67
   misused words, 66-67

Installing the Companion Disk Forms

The companion disk that accompanies this book contains twenty ready-to-use forms you can immediately put to use in WordPerfect. The pages that follow provide illustrations of each form. After you have successfully installed WordPerfect 6.0 (Appendix A of this book tells you how), you can install the forms on to your hard disk. The forms require 560 Kb of disk space.

The WordPerfect 6.0 installation creates the directory WPDOCS on your hard disk, in which it stores the document files that you create. Using the CHDIR command, select WPDOCS as the current dirrectory. Assuming that you installed WordPerfect 6.0 on drive C, issue the following command:

```
C:\>CD\WPDOCS <ENTER>
C:WPDOCS>
```

Your system prompt should change to C:\WPDOCS as shown. Next, place this book's companion disk in drive A or B. Depending on the drive in which you placed the disk, issue either the command:

```
C:\WPDOCS>A:WPFORMS <ENTER>
```

or

```
C:\WPDOCS>B:WPFORMS <ENTER>
```

The WPFORMS command uncompresses the files (they were compressed to fit on the floppy) placing them into the WPDOCS directory on your hard disk.

As you read through the book's chapters, different chapters discuss the steps you must perform to use a specific form. If WordPerfect displays an error message stating that it cannot find a document file, specify a complete path name to the document file—such as C:\WPDOCS\FAX-LOG.DOC or C:\WPDOCS\ACCOUNT.DOC.